MW00813373

"If one is seeking a contemporary John the Baptist, then Michael Budde may be the one sought: crying out in the wilderness, making plain judgments we'd rather obscure. Herein are hard realities and honest appraisals of distressing failures. Yet he does not despair, and points us toward truths which all of us in the American empire desperately need. May God bless the reading of this book, and the reception of its words."

—LEE C. CAMP, Professor of Theology and Ethics at Lipscomb University

"We tend to think of colonialism as something that happened in the past, something we have left behind. But Budde finds it lurking in all our forms of white supremacy, triumphalism, America First-ism, patriotism, war preparations, and citizenship. After looking all around and through these structures of power, he stands to the side and asks quietly, 'Where in all this is Jesus?' The Catholic church's attitude he sums up in addresses to American nations of the Southern Hemisphere—Pope John Paul asking how these nations can ever be grateful enough for the gift of the faith that the church brought them, Pope Francis asking how we can ever apologize enough for what the church did to them. Francis too is just asking, 'Where is Jesus in all this?'"

—GARRY WILLS, author of *What Jesus Meant*

"The reader must be warned, *Foolishness to Gentiles* is a terrific, but not easy, book. In his usual eloquent, informed, and witty style, Michael Budde offers a penetrating diagnosis of what is wrong with much of present-day cultural Christianity. Like St. Paul, Michael simply wants Christians to take the Gospel seriously, and thus to not conform to patterns of the world but have their minds renewed so as to seek what is good, pleasing, and true (Rom 12:2). *Foolishness to Gentiles* offers ways of how to begin that difficult journey."

—EMMANUEL KATONGOLE, Professor of Theology and of Peace Studies at University of Notre Dame

FOOLISHNESS TO GENTILES

THEOPOLITICAL VISIONS

SERIES EDITORS:

Thomas Heilke
D. Stephen Long
and Debra Murphy

Theopolitical Visions seeks to open up new vistas on public life, hosting fresh conversations between theology and political theory. This series assembles writers who wish to revive theopolitical imagination for the sake of our common good.

Theopolitical Visions hopes to re-source modern imaginations with those ancient traditions in which political theorists were often also theologians. Whether it was Jeremiah's prophetic vision of exiles "seeking the peace of the city," Plato's illuminations on piety and the civic virtues in the Republic, St. Paul's call to "a common life worthy of the Gospel," St. Augustine's beatific vision of the City of God, or the gothic heights of medieval political theology, much of Western thought has found it necessary to think theologically about politics, and to think politically about theology. This series is founded in the hope that the renewal of such mutual illumination might make a genuine contribution to the peace of our cities.

FORTHCOMING VOLUMES:

James Reimer
Toward an Anabaptist Political Theology: Law, Order, and Civil Society

David Deane
The Matter of the Spirit: How Soteriology Shapes the Moral Life

FOOLISHNESS to GENTILES

Essays on Empire, Nationalism, and Discipleship

MICHAEL L. BUDDE
Foreword by D. Stephen Long

CASCADE *Books* • Eugene, Oregon

FOOLISHNESS TO GENTILES
Essays on Empire, Nationalism, and Discipleship

Theopolitical Visions 26

Cascade Books
An Imprint of Wipf and Stock Publishers
199 W. 8th Ave., Suite 3
Eugene, OR 97401

www.wipfandstock.com

PAPERBACK ISBN: 978-1-7252-6430-4
HARDCOVER ISBN: 978-1-7252-6431-1
EBOOK ISBN: 978-1-7252-6432-8

Cataloguing-in-Publication data:

Names: Budde, Michael L., author. | Long, D. Stephen, 1960–, foreword.

Title: Foolishness to gentiles : essays on empire, nationalism, and discipleship / Michael L. Budde ; foreword by D. Stephen Long.

Description: Eugene, OR : Cascade Books, 2022 | Series: Theopolitical Visions 26 | Includes bibliographical references and index.

Identifiers: ISBN 978-1-7252-6430-4 (paperback) | ISBN 978-1-7252-6431-1 (hardcover) | ISBN 978-1-7252-6432-8 (ebook)

Subjects: LCSH: Church and the world. | Christianity and politics—United States. | Church and social problems. | Christian sociology. | National characteristics—Religious aspects—Christianity. | National characteristics, American. | Church and state—United States.

Classification: BR115.P7 B826 2022 (print) | BR115.P7 B826 (ebook)

Chapter 1 was delivered as a plenary lecture on discipleship and politics on July 12, 2019, at the Ekklesia Project's annual gathering in Techny, IL.

Chapter 2 was prepared for the Pan-African Catholic Conference in Enugu, Nigeria, in December 2019; a version of it appeared in *Faith in Action, Vol. III: Reimagining the Mission of the Church in Education, Politics, and Servant Leadership in Africa*, edited by Stan Chu Ilo, et al. (Abuja, Nigeria: Paulines Africa, 2020). Used with permission.

Chapter 3 was presented on May 4, 2019, at the 2019 World Catholicism Week Conference, "Put Away Your Sword: Gospel Nonviolence in a Violent World,"

sponsored by the Center for World Catholicism and Intercultural Theology (CW-CIT) at DePaul University in Chicago.
Some of the material in chapter 4 appears in *Advancing Nonviolence and Just Peace in the Church and the World: Biblical, Theological, Ethical, Pastoral, and Strategic Dimensions of Nonviolence*, edited by Rose Marie Berger, et al. (Brussels: Pax Christi International, 2020). Used with permission.

Chapter 5 was delivered on April 12, 2015, as a lecture on political economy and ecology at the 2015 World Catholicism Week Conference, "Fragile Earth: Ecology and the Church," sponsored by the Center for World Catholicism and Intercultural Theology (CWCIT) at DePaul University in Chicago.

Chapter 6 was published in Portuguese in *Fé, Justiça, e Paz: O Testemunho de Dorothy Day*, edited by Maria Clara Lucchetti Bingemer and Paulo Fernando Carneiro de Andrade (Rio de Janeiro: PUC-Rio and Paulinas, 2016). Used with permission.

A shorter version of chapter 7 appeared as "Real Presences and False Gods: The Eucharist as Discernment and Formation," *Modern Theology* 30:2 (2014) 282–99. Used with permission.

Chapter 8 appeared as "Giving Witness, Receiving Testimony," in *Witnessing: Prophesy, Politics, and Wisdom*, edited by Peter Casarella and Maria Clara Bingemer (Maryknoll, NY: Orbis, 2014). Used with permission.

Chapter 9 appeared as "Happy Carnage: Sacrifice and Popular Entertainment," *Concilium* 2013:4 (2013) 59–67. Used with permission.

A shorter version of chapter 10 appeared as "Political Theology and the Church," *Landas: Journal of Loyola School of Theology* 26:2 (2012) 17–40. Used with permission.

Chapter 11 appeared in French as "Dieu, bénis l'Amérique—Ou autrement," *En Question* 95 (December 2010). Used with permission.

Chapter 12 was a lecture delivered on May 1, 2019, for "The Twentieth Anniversary of *Ecclesia in America*: A North-South Dialogue on Church Reform, Global Politics, and Local Engagement," sponsored by the Office of Latin American–North American Church Concerns and the Kellogg Institute for International Studies at the University of Notre Dame.

Contents

Foreword

D. Stephen Long

Michael Budde is my friend. He is a dear friend, but he is not an easy friend to have. He knows too much, and what he knows is often disturbing. He is like the butcher who knows what goes into sausage. Unlike the butcher who mercifully keeps that information from us for fear that knowing the conditions for its possibility might keep us from frequenting his establishment, Budde directs our gaze to those conditions again and again until we, in fact, see clearly the cultural productions that are otherwise hidden from view. He will not give us the luxury of looking away. Let me provide an example. I was having lunch with Mike, something we frequently did when I lived in the Chicago area, and I was going on, in a way perhaps only a Protestant or Catholic convert could, about how grateful I was for John Paul II's papacy. I was not only a fan of his encyclical *Veritatis Splendor*, but I also thought his frequent rallies that drew massive crowds had energized the papacy and the Catholic Church. Mike reminded me that those rallies were not spontaneous uprisings of the faithful but manufactured events sponsored in part by the corporation Famous Artists Merchandising, who was also the image shaper for the Rolling Stones, Paul McCartney, Paul Simon, and the Toronto Blue Jays. In fact, as he wrote in *The (Magic) Kingdom of God*:

> Like Disney and Time-Warner, the Catholic Church is establishing formal licensing arrangements to generate income for Church activities. Product tie-ins, joint promotions, licensing arrangements—though not yet large compared with commercial firms—are becoming more frequent and widely pursed by Catholic leaders.[1]

1. Budde, *The (Magic) Kingdom of God*, 105.

As if making us look at the selling of the papacy through Famous Artists Merchandising was not already bad enough, he then reminds us that the partnership "ended unhappily." The US bishops had to sue Famous Artists Merchandising for "unpaid royalties." Famous Artists Merchandising counter-sued. They claimed that they had lost money because they should have had exclusive rights to the papal insignia, but it was being used too liberally by Catholic laity who had not paid for its use. I would rather not know this. I would rather look at the beauty of the outdoor Mass, the large number of gathered youth, the beautiful music, John Paul II's powerful sermons. Budde will not give you the solace of looking at the product without attending to its production.

I would rather not know "that a Catholic military chaplain" blessed "the atomic bomb that destroyed the largest concentration of Catholics in Japan, including seven orders of nuns"—something Budde reminds us in his *Borders of Baptism*.[2] I would rather not know how Protestants and Catholics sold out to the funeral industry, how and why Christians killed each other in Rwanda, how consistently we place national loyalties above baptism, but Budde will not let us be. He refuses any easy gaze; he demands that we look at the cultural production even of our religious vision. To see behind the finished product and look directly upon the means of its production is to make one's self and others vulnerable to forces that confuse, disorient, and potentially destroy. The end result could be cynicism and despair. Yet he directs our gaze to what is ugly, not in order to make us cynics, but to make us love what is in its ugliness, so that it might become what it is called to be. He knows that we cannot have the latter without the former.

I am not alone in this interpretation of Budde's work. In fact, on the inside cover of *Christianity Incorporated,* you will find one of the best blurbs I have ever read, and one that captures Budde's work well. The philosopher Albert Borgmann wrote these words: "This is not a pleasant book. It is bitter and bracing like the wormwood tea my grandmother used to make—something I remember with gratitude and affection. And so I will remember this book." Budde has now added to his disturbing and disrupting works this important collection of essays, *Foolishness to Gentiles.* It begins with an analysis of the US as an empire that refuses to identify itself as such. He reminds us, once again, of what we would like to forget.

2. Budde, *Borders of Baptism*, 10.

US citizens lack memory. We do not want to remember that the empire was built on "land from the indigenous" and "labor from the Africans." This forgetfulness contributes to the empire's serious decline, for which we see daily evidence. Most of what remains, he suggests, is "its military hammer and not much else." Coupled with its dogmatic commitment to economic growth, the US generates a way of life that is a way of death, an ever-expanding cycle of death incorporating more and more people and taking the environment with it. I was in the audience when Budde delivered this first chapter as a lecture. It was met with a rather stunned silence. After all, he tells us that it is already too late to halt the devastation to the climate and the inevitable dislocation of people it has caused and will cause. Then our mutual friend, the Baptist minister and theologian Kyle Childress, punctured the silence with an exclamation: "Well, thank you for that rosy picture." Rev. Childress knows what he was saying; he was not only being humorous. We should be grateful, because these are not days for sentimental nostalgia or a misplaced optimism. Things are as bad as Budde shows. Of course, as Terry Eagleton reminds us, hope is not optimism and, in fact, the latter can be deadly for the former. Budde's realistic look at the world-as-it-is can only make us attend more intentionally in witness and action to the world as it should be, the world disclosed in the revelation of Christ.

For this reason, I think it important that Budde begins this collection of essays with the three chapters that he does. They take us deep into what seem to be intractable problems: the unrelenting consequences of settler colonialism; climate and ecological collapse; the ineptitude of the US's two political parties to make significant responses; the poor biblical lesson that the Son of Uncle Sam is nothing but Samson redux willing to tear the whole system down by his might; the slaughter of whole populations past and present. Budde presents an un-triumphalistic Catholicism (and Christianity) that refuses to look away from racism past and present, a sober and oddly refreshing reminder in an era when a certain kind of triumphalistic Catholicism and evangelicalism have found each other and taken over the corridors of power, all the while proclaiming more vociferously their loss of religious freedom through a politics of grievance. It is almost too much to take. I'd prefer to turn away, but each page of *Foolishness to Gentiles* says, "Look!"

I also remind my friend that I have done what I could. I've been a bicycle commuter for the past thirty years; my investments are socially conscious; I've worked in restorative justice at the local level; I don't own or use guns; I attend the BLM protests and put the signs out in my front yard. Without diminishing small acts, he reminds me that they are not righting the sinking ship—and I know he's right. It is still the case, as he reminds us in chapter 2 of this work, that

> Catholic immigrants from marginalized groups could and did improve their condition by embracing the racist tenets of the American system—they could "move up" by becoming "white" as seen by the state and society, by affirming and incarnating the anti-blackness that sustained the entire edifice.

And that system proves itself seemingly always more powerful than even the outpouring of protests. What does Budde expect of us? Does he want to leave us in despair?

Of course not. He is a Christian and thus knows that despair is a sin against the Holy Spirit. His vision is apocalyptic in the best sense of that term. Apocalyptic is not a celebration of the catastrophic, somehow glorifying in destruction. It is an unveiling that refuses to look away from human suffering, because it refuses to look away from the cross and God's odd victory upon it. Budde takes us "deeper into eschatology" so that we will not misplace our hope, as if once we get the billionaire populists exposed and defeated by the neoliberal progressives, everything will return to normal. He calls us to live into the eschaton, even now, and take joy in the hope it brings. In fact, the eschatological interlude of this work has to come in the middle, his chapter 4, because that is where it comes in history. The end comes in the middle. The eschaton is not an ever-disappearing horizon; it is the present possibility of a way of living in keeping with God's good creation available now in the "interim community" that is the Church on its pilgrimage to the fullness of God's reign. The interlude is more than an interlude; it fills this work with joy and sustains even its darkest corners with hope. In his *Confessions,* St. Augustine wrote, "For love of your love, I will retrace my wicked ways."[3] Budde has done something like that, not for a troubled conscience, but for a troubled people. The interlude points backward and forward, transforming the bitter wormwood of some chapters into Eucharistic wine.

So we can move forward, looking without defensiveness at the errors of "development," sustainable and otherwise, at a frightening future without blinking. As he tells us here in chapter 5,

3. Augustine, *Confessions* 2.1.

> We know that the future will be even more militarized than is the present and that ecological problems—movements of people, crises of flood and drought, wars to control necessities and assets, and more—will figure centrally in much of this. We also know that the development machine has and will continue to respond to all of this even as it presents itself as the only way out—the "new name for peace," as Paul VI described it.

But don't learn to speak peace falsely when war and crisis after crisis are already making their effects present. Instead, learn to look to those places that we have not yet looked for wisdom, such as the Christian anarchism of Dorothy Day and others.

Readers should not misunderstand Michael Budde's work. As I already mentioned, he is by no means a Catholic triumphalist. Neither is he a Christian triumphalist. Attending the Eucharist and waiting on the Reign of God do not solve our considerable problems. Christian anarchism does not fight the battle (so to speak) alone. It can find allies with non-Christian anarchists, libertarian socialists, distributists, Anglican socialists, and others. Notice how often Budde points us to sources of wisdom wherever they are found. When I first came upon his work in political science, before we became friends, I was taken by his constant references to world systems theory. I tracked down every book I could find by Immanuel Wallerstein in an effort to discern reasons for global inequality. This is what Budde does to you; he points to people, movements, and sources of wisdom, generosity, and hopefulness that you would not otherwise know. His friends become your friends; his influences your influences. Notice how often *Foolishness to Gentiles* is riddled with the term "solidarity." *Riddled* is the correct term because impatient readers—either those looking for one more source in which Christianity somehow has all the answers or those for whom it has none—will miss the generosity that this work contains. Look to Jesus, yes. Look to the Church, yes. Look to Dorothy Day, yes. But don't forget Chomsky, the Berrigans, Ruskin, and all those nameless persons who were and are the true victims of the Church's and society's great failures. Budde's work is often a riddle for other reasons. He does not impose his pacifism or anarchism on those who would refuse it. He listens to his opponents and reads them as charitably as possible. He shows them their own arguments and then invites them to live into the best of their convictions with surprising twists such as this: "I have a proposal. If one is serious about conducting armed interventions in ways that respect the Christian convictions described herein,

I see that you have no other choice than to bring back religious military orders—explicitly Christian armies." Who would have seen that coming?

There is so much more I could say about this important work. If you are reading this foreword, then you have already been taken in by Michael Budde's wisdom, wit, and generosity. He is my friend because he knows how to laugh well. We have worked together through the Ekklesia Project and other ventures for nearly three decades. He is the most Anabaptist Catholic that I have ever met. We once visited Rome together for a theology conference and were standing outside St. Peter's. I was taken in by the beauty and grandeur, and he could tell it. "Don't forget," he, the Catholic, reminded me, the Protestant, "It was built by indulgences—a monument to the Church's failure to be the Church." I once asked him why he remained a Roman Catholic. He said that, growing up a white Catholic in the Chicago area, he found the Catholicism of his youth so bland, so empty, so uninspiring that he knew that there had to be something more to it than what he received. He decided to stick around and search for it. I'm glad he did. *Foolishness to Gentiles* is one of the many fruits of his unrelenting search for what is true, good, and faithful, and how we might strengthen it.

D. Stephen Long
Southern Methodist University

Introduction

Michael L. Budde

Every time I start writing this introduction, the world gets strange, and I have to start over. A worldwide epidemic, another wave of authoritarians come to power, environmental collapses on a daily basis, and back-and-forth upheavals over state violence and racial hierarchy. And then there's Donald Trump.

Most of the essays in this book were written before white Christians, Protestant and Catholic, carried Donald Trump into office. Those that were written during his first term were not written in response to provocations of the day—no one could keep up with the daily outrages that emerged from his fevered mind and vengeful spirit. More than just an unwillingness to write in response to a Twitter feed, I have refused to separate Trump—the avatar of the moment—from the context that gave birth to him, one hundreds of years in the making. Trump is not the exception to the norm in American life; he is American character unchained and unfiltered. Neither decorum, nor prudence, nor decency, nor complexity, nor the long game—Trump is America, because Trump wants it all, he wants it now, he wants it forever. In many ways, he is the most American of American leaders.

Christians have known his type before, but being aware of this requires a type of memory formed by ecclesial communities who know they are different from the cultures they inhabit. Knowing that the Church has seen Trump, and worse, in the past presupposes a deep formation in the stories, symbols, songs, and saints (and sinners) who have tried to live the gospel in different times and places. But in the United States and elsewhere, that type of intensive formation is a thing of the past, because most people are more deeply formed by other identities and roles.

They think of themselves as many things, but one of the most pernicious among these identities is that of "citizen."

Citizens see themselves as tied to a particular political body, to which they give loyalty, obedience, and service. In return, citizens expect varying levels of protection and service. These are some of the textbook descriptions of citizenship—true as they go but inadequate, because they are incomplete (in much of the modern world, for example, citizenship is also racialized and gendered at its roots). Citizenship is about so much more than what most of us believe. At its deeper registers, citizenship is about love.

Love of country. Love of homeland. Love of heritage. Love of one's way of life. Love of community. Love of being part of something greater than oneself. Love of a shared purpose and mission. Love of the historic importance of one's people. Love of stories and symbols, landmarks and benchmarks. Love of a legacy of suffering overcome, injustice vanquished, sacrifice vindicated. Love of valor and victory.

I know about the Christian tradition that sees citizenship as part of the "natural loves," as Aquinas describes them, which give shape and contour to human life. To love one's country is natural and good, in this view; it is only its excesses and derangements that are to be resisted. Grace builds upon nature; the gospel calls for the purification and not the elimination of natural loves. The embodied love of the particular is preferable to the abstract, gnostic love of a world community that does not exist in the real world. I understand all of this. I also think most of this is unhelpful to Christians.

Modern citizenship, and modern nation-states, are not "natural." They are the products of power plays and indoctrination, slaughter and conquest, coincidence and coercion. To equate citizenship with a natural reality that Christians are obliged to love is a mistake of historic importance. The body of Christ—which is the real, deeper-than-"natural" ("super-natural," perhaps?) home of disciples of Jesus—is a worldwide community that is anything but abstract and gnostic; it is a product of love and mutuality rather than coercion and historical accident (or of coercion and history overcome and claimed as one's own). To be a Christian in this sense means that, while citizenship might be imposed or accepted as a practical necessity (like submitting to a driving test if you want to operate a motor vehicle while staying out of jail), it should not be an object of love. Christians are not to "love their chains," in Rousseau's words;

they should recognize them as chains and obstacles to living the fullness of their calling.

I have argued for this view of the Church and Christian discipleship in other places and times. I have urged fellow Christians to see themselves as pledged first and foremost to the Prince of Peace rather than to the countries of their birth. I have tried to make them see how attempts to affirm both, and to argue that being a good Christian requires being a good citizen, ultimately undermine and liquidate the gospel. I think this is true for the Church in all parts of the world, but it is especially true for the church that finds itself enmeshed in the daily life and territory of empires. It is especially true for Christianity as it has existed in the United States; as the American empire seems determined to bring down the entire world with its death throes, it will take down the American church with it.

It seems that a large part of my work is in showing anyone who cares to look what comes from loving one's country and its economic ideology—in my case, the United States and capitalism—and making those a primary object of loyalty and allegiance. In these modest interventions, I offer a picture of what you get, or where you end up, when you make something other than being a Christian in community with other disciples the determinative answer to the question, "Who or whose are you?" These pictures of the present, as well as excursions into the past and future, try to illustrate the distortions to the gospel when other convictions dominate Christian thought and action in everything from economics to international politics, war and popular culture, racism and empire.

Making good imperial citizens out of Christians requires institutions and ideologies of power to overcome many built-in obstacles that inhere in the Christian tradition and Scriptures. Many of those obstacles, alas, have been removed by Christians themselves in pursuit of power and security in pursuit of a Christian view of the world—such is the lamentable legacy of "Christendom," the idea of a Christian culture with the power to steer the ship of state and society toward preferred states of virtue.

Yet for all its compromises and moral outrages, Christianity remains a tradition that retains the capacity to subvert itself and its own pretentions. Its origins in a Jew executed as a political enemy of the state, a movement that dared to claim that God came first and foremost for the weak and worthless, a roster of persons famous and unnamed killed by the forces of order and stability around the world—the rough edges of

Christianity remain persistently resistant to being smoothed over permanently, whether by force or by self-surrender.

To me, the most indigestible part of Jesus' mission and message, the part that is most embarrassing and inconvenient—the biggest obstacle to its final and permanent domestication and bastardization—is one that the critics and nominal supporters of Christianity find objectionable. It is the simple insistence, as recorded in the Gospels and the life of the early church, that Christians aren't to kill people. They shouldn't kill people even in a good cause, even to do good or prevent evil. More than two-thousand years after Jesus disarmed Peter, we're still confronted with the incarnation of the Creator who forbids His followers from killing people. It remains, in my view, one of the things that is "foolishness to Gentiles" (1 Cor 1:23)—one of the absurd or objectionable things that flows from following Christ crucified and raised from the dead. Hence, the title for this book.

It is this thing—the refusal of Christians to legitimate killing—that must be overcome if Christians are to be fully incorporated into the lesser loves and allegiances of the world. Empires and states, nations and races, classes and movements and ideologies—all of them presuppose the right and the rightness of using lethal force when necessary to accomplish collective aims. Call it order or security or freedom or liberation or justice or peace or equality—the goals of most of the principalities and powers of our time presuppose the right to force compliance, or punish opposition, up to the point of killing. Lawbreakers must and should be punished (as Stephen Carter notes, even a humble local ordinance is backed ultimately by the lethal coercive power of the state).[1] Threats to the community, or to the vulnerable, or to property, or to human rights—in the end, all of these must be put down with whatever means necessary. The ultimate necessary means is the indispensable one in the eyes of the world—namely, the killing of those who cannot be dissuaded any other way. And the world demands that Christians endorse this arrangement—for the common good, for security, for the victimized, for prosperity. The worldly wise describe this as a tragic reality. But sometimes it is necessary to make one person die for the sake of the whole.[2]

I hate writing about why Christians shouldn't kill people. It is the part of my professional and ecclesial life that I most dread these days, but

1. Carter, "Laws Come with Deadly Consequences."

2. See John 11:50 and the political philosopher named Caiaphas.

one that is almost unavoidable inasmuch as I am convinced that followers of Jesus should not be killers, no matter how just the cause.

What I hate most about writing about Christianity's opposition to killing is that it seems so pointless and absurd. No matter how well argued the case, how proficient the argument on scriptural and theological grounds, the entire enterprise seems like an exercise in futility. For those persons who take Jesus at His word, that Christians are to love and not kill their enemies, writing to convince about the non-lethal nature of Christianity seems redundant to the extreme. Even to persons outside the Christian tradition, the message is hard to miss. As Gandhi once reputedly said in an impossible-to-source quote, "Everybody in the world knows Jesus is nonviolent except for the Christians." Just having to invoke this worn-out Gandhi quote seems obligatory and impotent. Even though the earliest Christians understood that being a killer and being a Christian were mutually exclusive (a conviction carried forward by smaller groups through the subsequent centuries), most Christians want their Jesus to approve of the killing they want to do. They want a weaponized Jesus, or at least one who raises no objection to the necessity of the lethal force they want to employ.

Perhaps the preferred posture of Jesus in relation to violence, what we want, is something like a mafia leader who never bloodies his own hands and is never seen to employ violence in the pursuit of objectives. We could follow a leader like this, one who empowers, countenances, supports, sanctifies, overlooks—whatever is necessary to provide justification or silence, with varying degrees of reluctance or affirmation. It's a fallen world, and sometimes the choices forced upon us are tragic; sometimes one has to compromise principles to achieve a legitimate end. Not everyone is called to lead a life of moral purity—such laments come easily from clergy and ethicists, leaders of states, and leaders of gangs. If your Jesus is standing in the way of that, your Jesus has to go, or be replaced, or rewritten. Taking a cord of rope to scatter livestock from the Temple becomes justification for nuclear weapons; upending the tables of loan sharks gives a blank check to police states and death squads.

Or we go over Jesus' head to His Father—the God of the Old Testament, for whom killing is less of a problem, or so it seems to us who seek approval for what we want to do. Here is a God who knows what the world is like—this is the world God made or allowed us to make—and this God is free with the smiting, the crushing, the slaughtering, and the ordinary day-to-day killing required to protect life and livestock.

The God of wrath, the vengeful Yahweh, the scourge of the Canaanites and the Amalekites and whoever else gets in the way—this is a God we understand, who understands our predicament. Don't bother us with biblical interpretations that trouble the waters or show that Jesus' way of discipleship requires changes in how we read the Old Testament (we're happy to have Jesus free us from dietary laws, but don't let Him mess with our swords and spears). The Yahweh we want, the Jesus we want, is a muscular, masculine, no-nonsense kind of boss—a Jesus who won't let us kill is an effeminate, timid sort, unable to protect womenfolk and children, property and prosperity. A Yahweh no longer reliable to bless our righteous killing is an emasculated god unworthy of our attention, much less our devotion. A god that won't let you kill when you need to is a useless god—nobody else in the world has such an inferior deity, so why should we Christians? Don't we deserve the best—or at least a god that facilitates our functions?

This is the demand of most persons in the Church—and most of the non-Christian world takes this majority at its word that Christians can and sometimes should be killers. There is no amount of argumentation, no measure of eloquence, no depth of scholarship, that will disabuse most Christians of this sort of Christ. We want Him, we have Him, and we will not let go of Him. We do not want to see anything contrary to the Christ of violence, and we are prepared to take drastic steps—including killing—to protect our right to a Savior armed and at our beck and call, or at least one willing to bless us in whatever roles require us to kill. We like this picture of Christ, and for us to give Him up, you will have to pry Him loose from our cold, dead hands.

Ours is a civilized age, of course. Not all of us dwell on justified killing in a face-to-face or hand-to-hand situation, although the romance of such continues to captivate the imaginations of people around the world—defending the innocent, protecting one's family, vanquishing the spree-killer shooting up a school. Some of us may drink more deeply than others from this well of heroic killing; for the most part, scenarios like this don't usually require that we trot out the name of Jesus in defense of what we want to do. A garden-variety western movie hero suffices to legitimate the lone hero with a gun; one saves Yahweh and Jesus for the bigger jobs.

Far more extensive in reach and scope, in depth and breadth, is the killing done by and for and through nations and states as institutions. We have many names for it—security, justice, protection of property and person and procedure. We have many names for it because killing is so versatile. It constructs and maintains order; it underwrites rulemaking, distinguishes between friends and foes, creates and sustains hierarchies and systems of domination and processes of liberation, and so much more. If God Almighty were to come and tell us directly—again—that Christians shouldn't kill people, then we would have to crucify Him again, and again, until He gets the message. Return to sender. Try to get it right next time.

The human insistence on violence as a nonnegotiable is understandable on many levels. Much of its appeal flows from the unshakable conviction that violence works so well for so many things. It is not foolproof, but it is almost universally applicable, like a multipurpose tool that can be used for almost any job with at least some degree of utility. A Jesus who won't let us kill is worse than useless; He is an obstacle to peace and good order. Far from being a quaint oddity or object of curiosity, such an incarnation of divinity would be menacing and poisonous to peace, justice, and freedom; again, better that such a person die than harm the nation (see John 18:14 NRSV). This sort of Jesus is an equal-opportunity indigestible. Capitalists and anti-capitalists, white supremacists and advocates for equality, heteropatriarchs and activists for equality, globalists and localists—almost everyone wants the power of violence to advance the true, the good, and the beautiful. In part, this is because violence makes possible much of what is advantageous to human life: a degree of predictability, certain common goods (under certain circumstances), some manner of collective action, procedures that deflect some sorts of violence from some groups of people, and more. To refuse the package deal—pursue the good or the right, with lethal means as an irremovable part of the tool kit—is to refuse to be part of human community as conventionally understood. It is to be subhuman or a beast, in Aristotle's terms (or a god, but such is inadmissible in our context).[3]

Again, it must be said: against this powerful conventional wisdom, the usual Bible verses are largely impotent; against the relentless demand to act "responsibly" on terms the world dictates, concern for personal and communal holiness seems selfish and heartless; against the ceaseless cries of pain and agony in the world, one sets aside the "imitation of Christ" in favor of a Jesus who would abandon His own teaching to save

3. Aristotle, *Politics* 1.1253.

the oppressed.[4] A Jesus who will not allow His followers to kill in person, or at least via the machinery of government, is not a Jesus to honor; such a Jesus is an enemy to good order and justice, an obstacle to peace and stability, a force for irrationality and chaos. Anyone persuaded to follow such a Jesus is a fool or a pampered poodle, a parasite who depends upon the sacrifices of others—on both ends of the gun—for the good things in life.

You can see why I hold so little enthusiasm for trying to write yet again about why Christians shouldn't kill people, and about what follows from the conviction that they shouldn't kill people. What was once the shared conviction among Christians in the early centuries of the Church—that being a Christian and taking up the sword were incompatible ways of inhabiting the world—was crushed on all sides as Christianity moved through history. East and West, North and South, rich and poor—the Prince of Peace died the death of a thousand cuts, of qualifications and exceptions and hard cases and outrages that cried out to heaven. This Jesus would not do, would have to be set aside or sequestered, supplemented by a Jesus more in tune with how the world really works and what the world needs now—not love, sweet love, as the song goes, but law and order, justice and stability. The Jesus who would direct His followers to suffer rather than to kill, to accept a martyr's death rather than save themselves or their loved ones—this Jesus deserves no friends and no respect. Anyone stupid enough to hitch a wagon to this sort of incarnation of God deserves nothing but contempt and condemnation.

The appeal of a different kind of savior (one at peace with killing when necessary) to states and empires, corporations and property holders, is obvious enough. The appeal of this sort of Christ on the side of history's victims, for causes of justice and mercy, is apparent to anyone who isn't heartless or a nihilist. Neither the rulers of states nor the advocates for the oppressed describe themselves as advocating for a savior who kills, to be sure; still, the outcome in theological and ethical terms is similar, regardless of how they describe their actions or motivations.

More disturbing, though, is how much we Christians want our Christ to be armed and ready, or at least to deputize us into the ranks of the earthly sheriffs and centurions. In fact, the latter may be preferable: keep our Christ peaceful and loving (at least on the outside) so that we

4. Such is a popular reading of the meaning of Shūsaku Endō's *Silence*; it is also the interpretation proffered by the imperial interrogator to his Jesuit prisoner. This is not, however, my interpretation of Endō's novel.

as followers can feel righteous in using the gun and the flamethrower and the militia against the evildoers of the world. If Christ is just as big an enforcer as we know we are, our consciences might be troubled by the degree to which we have manipulated our image of God to suit our common sense and right reason. Better that we keep Christ's hands clean while we take on the dirty work of the world; even this is proof of our selfless devotion, sacrificing our moral consistency (or "purity," as worldly people say with a sneer) for the greater good. Christ becomes the Czar who doesn't know all the atrocities conducted in His name by the devoted functionaries that make sure the empire keeps running even as the noble reputation of the emperor is not besmirched by bloodstained robes.

The Christian tradition has built a mighty fortress designed to protect the world from the Jesus who turned His back on killing, a fortress from which a lethal Christianity may survey the earth and empower the prosecutors and jailers, soldiers and mercenaries, occupiers and exploiters. The thin blue line, the forces of freedom, the last best hope, the revolution of the oppressed, the indispensable nation, the city on a hill, the civilized world—so many lines to draw and territories to protect from so many human weaknesses and conflicts. Without the ability to make and enforce rules at the point of a sword, where would we be? Perhaps another question: With them, where are we? With them, where go the promises of God for a new heaven and a new earth?

So, we construct earthworks to hold at bay the Christ who would abjure violence. We erect natural laws and right reason. We divorce actions from intentions (which allows us to kill as long as we do so with love—thank you, Augustine). We partition our private lives and our public roles (Luther allows us to renounce violence in our private life, but requires us to take it up—even becoming the town executioner, if necessary—in our public life). We cushion our actions with casuistry of various types, with double effects and unintended consequences stretched beyond recognition in order to maximize the range and reach of the violence we need and the violence we want.

We hold onto our Christ of the sword because we fear the alternative. We are afraid—deathly afraid, ironically—that if Jesus meant what He said about loving enemies and putting away the sword, we would have to do likewise. We fear the depth of our unbelief would be exposed and our faithlessness be on display for the whole world to see. The world might see that we really don't believe that God became human in the person of Jesus of Nazareth, that this marked the beginning of a new age in the history of the world, that God could and did raise a human being from the dead after three days, and that love—not hate or indifference—holds the universe together. We fear being shown for who and what we are, all the churches and choirs and chants to the contrary. Holding tight to Christianity at peace with violence allows us to pretend that we still believe in something beyond or better than this sad world without having that belief impinge on much of importance. So, we herald a Savior who chose death rather than prolonging life via violence, and in so doing, shouted to the world that death is not the last word. But curiously, we herald such by continuing to act as though killing to prolong life is beyond reproach and, in so doing, confess that we do, in fact, believe that death is the ultimate and final reality to be avoided or forced on others, so that we and ours can grasp at every additional breath and moment of life. It is literally unimaginable that we might choose to die rather than to live by bloody means, and we would prosecute someone who would allow his or her family to die rather than protect them via apostasy or lethal force. No wonder we have made the early church martyrs—who did exactly that—into exotics or superhumans, or (as in some contemporary scholarship) fictional characters meant to inspire faith but not imitation.

How much better to shove Jesus back into the mold of Old Testament violence—this is a god we understand, after all. We want that smiting and vanquishing, crushing heads against rocks and destroying men, women, children, livestock, and crops as needed. Never mind that we have a long history of reading the warrior God of the Old Testament in ways that distort violence and conquest, and that we consistently misperceive ourselves as the righteous heirs of Yahweh's might rather than as those deserving of destruction.[5] We can't put the gun directly back into Jesus' hands, however—hard to square that with being a good shepherd or some other frothy, frilly picture of comforting divinity. But we can reinscribe Him into a genealogy of justified violence in the service of all the things God loves: children and freedom and prosperity and security and all the other blessings of creation. We want Jesus to preach about sparrows and lilies of the field, but we want Him to allow us access to Yahweh's arsenal in pursuit of righteousness. In this, we show our captivity to the old age, our preference for the theological fleshpots of Egypt over the dangerous exodus toward the new Jerusalem. Saddest of all, we think we are moving forward rather than staying stuck in the past.

5. See Boyd, *Crucifixion of the Warrior God.*

About the Book

This book is not an attempt to convince people that Jesus would prefer His followers not to use lethal force, even for a good cause. Instead, in many of the chapters that follow, I aim to give Christians a taste of what they're buying when they affirm the legitimacy of even a little bit of lethal force, even in the most reasonable of cases. They want a Christ that allows them to kill, so I'm giving them that, especially when they think they're affirming something else.

It is a series of explorations and reflections on how the world looks to those Christians who are already persuaded that Christians shouldn't be killers—how things look in the realms of church and politics, economics and culture, and more. In so doing, I also hope to illustrate to those still pledging allegiance to a Christianity at peace with lethality where those convictions can lead them—and how perverse such points of arrival actually are. These essays share several common themes but take them in different directions; they were prepared for different audiences with diverse concerns, and I make no claim that they constitute a seamless narrative from start to finish.

There is no overarching scheme or theme that dictates the order in which this book presents these essays for your consideration. Each one has a brief introduction that situates its time and intention. A few of the more recent pieces are at the beginning of the book, which reflects the intuition that many readers engage more readily with contemporary issues and references. One brief essay—which I'm calling an "interlude," for lack of a better way to think of it—appears not quite halfway through the book, and perhaps it should have come at the beginning. It makes explicit what perceptive readers have long noted about my approach—namely, that it privileges eschatology as a framework and category for thinking Christian-ly. I wasn't sure that, were it put first, many people would get through a discussion on eschatology to get to more topical or recognizable matters. If nothing else, putting it near the center of the book illustrates how eschatology is a fulcrum for what and how I see.

Most of these chapters assume the importance of the Church as a transnational community. Many of them were written in response to invitations from Christians or Christian institutions in the so-called global South, where the majority of the world's Christians now live. I know better than to tell my brothers and sisters what to do or how to live the gospel in their varied contexts, and in situations where violence and injustice present themselves in ways different than in the United States. What I have to say is sent out in the name of dialogue, not dictation; people will do with it what seems best to them.

Whether these essays add up to an integrated whole is not mine to decide, and I'm not sure that such is a necessity at this point. They might better be seen as invitations to look at the world through lenses ground to conform, however imperfectly, with the idea that being a disciple of Jesus should change how we see our world and our places in it. There are continuities and linkages across the chapters, and maybe some repetition.

Most of these chapters arose from the work of the Center for World Catholicism and Intercultural Theology (CWCIT), a research institute at DePaul University in Chicago, in which I serve with gratitude among good and generous faculty and staff, and colleagues from around the world. I am grateful to each and every one of its members, past and present. Thank you to William Cavanaugh, Stan Chu Ilo, Karen Kraft, Marlon Aguilar, Graciela Saucedo, Elijah Gray, Francis Salinel, Peter Casarella, Anna Galon, and anyone whom I've forgotten to mention. I owe a large debt and much gratitude to Graciela Saucedo, Elijah Gray, and Karen Kraft for helping prepare the manuscript for publication.

CHAPTER 1

Uncle Sam and His Son: The Church and the End of the American Empire

A plenary lecture on discipleship and politics delivered on July 12, 2019, to the Ekklesia Project's annual gathering. The Ekklesia Project is a group of Christian pastors, scholars, and lay people interested in what it means to aspire to Christian discipleship in contemporary times. While its membership is predominantly drawn from the United States and Canada, it crosses many denominational and confessional barriers. It sees itself as a "school for subversive friendships" and creates a variety of publishing ventures, congregational formation programs, and fellowship among people who wouldn't otherwise know one another. To learn more about the work of the Ekklesia Project, visit www.ekklesiaproject.org.

Introduction

Whatever their other virtues may have been, the people who set up the settler colony eventually known as the United States seemed to have had a stunning tendency to miss the point, to misplace themselves in the grand narratives of Scripture. Such has shown itself at various times and under varied circumstances:

- enthralled with the Exodus account, but seeing themselves as the enslaved Israelites rather than the enslaving Egyptians;
- enchanted with a promised land of milk and honey, they derive inspiration from the example of Joshua—the poster child for ethnic cleansing and slaughter of the defenseless;
- excited by their self-proclaimed generosity to the world, they see themselves as the Good Samaritan selflessly helping the victimized instead of as the robbers who assault the defenseless along the road.

I will return to this scriptural astigmatism later, for it continues into our time and place.

My objective today, in our time together, is to offer you what I see and hear and remember about being church on the cusp of American imperial decline. You don't need someone standing up here to tell you that the ground is shaking under our feet, or that the immediate future may well be one that threads together the hitherto unimaginable with the all-too-familiar. If nothing else, I hope to provide a very crude map of the likely terrain before us—when I say crude, you should think more of pencil scratchings on the back of an envelope than the turn-by-turn directions of Google Maps. I make no claims that what I have to say will be "useful" or "relevant" to any of the immediate concerns that people bring to this conversation or our time together this week. I will try not to make this a waste of your time.

Let me state my conclusions in advance, then tell you what action I think follows from them. First, I believe that the context for politics worldwide, and within the United States in particular, is in the early stages of a profound shift that overall promises to be significantly more violent, more oppressive, and more aggressive. This is in addition to the past and present levels of violence and public/private marginalization deriving from the activity of a powerful form of racialized capitalism that has defined the context of American politics for the past five centuries, and which has been the constant companion of African Americans, indigenous peoples, and other groups far from the privileges of white wealth and power.

Second, two important factors are driving the emergence of this more violent and aggressive political context. The first is the steady but uneven erosion of political, economic, and cultural power worldwide enjoyed by the United States—sometimes this is referred to as the dynamics of an "empire in decline." The second factor is collapse of limitless economic growth as a plausible assumption and practicable policy goal in the politics of capitalist democracies. The constellation of crises collected under the term "climate change" exposes for all to see what had always been unacknowledged except among experts: unlimited economic expansion, which is a constitutive feature of capitalism and the political regimes associated with it, is impossible in a bounded and limited biosphere. The politics of growth has been at the center of political ideology and practice throughout the modern period; with that no longer an option, politics will inevitably shift to an increasingly apparent zero-sum conflict (and in many respects has already begun to do so); the promise of growth forestalled the reality of politics as redistributive, and redistributive politics are the most vicious sort.

Third, it is important that the Church find a way not to go down with the American imperial ship. Unless at least some sectors of the Church manage to distance themselves in a public and visible way from allegiance to the United States, the Church in its entirety will be seen by present and later generations as having blessed and endorsed—or at least stood by quietly—while even more horrific things are perpetrated by the imperial power that Christians helped to build, sustain, and bless. The Ekklesia Project has named empire as a rival to the ultimate allegiance that for Christians belongs only to God; some of us have maintained that the transnational body of Christ should be more fundamental to our notion of belonging and community than the nation state. We need to push out into deeper waters, the waters that our enemies may well call treason.

The Church is on the cusp of another potentially world-class scandal against the gospel, perhaps on the level of the Crusades, the Inquisition, and more; we need to find a way to speak a word of truth for the sake of the Church today and tomorrow, and for the world should it ever return from madness with a willingness to listen. Were the Church to be seen as complicit and supportive of the coming rages, on top of everything else we will be erecting still more obstacles to faith, similar to how the scandals of earlier Christians made it impossible for millions to take seriously the prospect that God is love and Jesus is the Prince of Peace. If we are derelict, better that we don a millstone and be flung into the sea (Mark 9:42; Matt 18:6; Luke 17:2).

I'd like to spend a few minutes talking about what kind of empire America is, and what it means to say this sort of empire is in decline.

1. *America the Anti-Empire*

I proceed on the assumption that making the case for describing the United States as an imperial project is less difficult among members of the Ekklesia Project than in front of other audiences. The Declaration and Invitation that emerged from the founding gathering of the Ekklesia Project twenty years ago named empire as among the claimants on allegiances that the Church is meant to refuse and resist in the name of being the called community of disciples whose allegiance is to the Kingdom of God initiated by Jesus and consummated by God through the Holy Spirit.[1]

I want to take a few moments to explain what I mean by the American sort of empire—its origins, enduring structures and processes, and adaptions across time and circumstance. And while "decline" of empire is often a difficult matter to conceptualize—most empires do not collapse in a discrete historical moment, *à la* the Russian Empire in 1917—it may be worthwhile to offer a few thoughts on what such does and does not mean.

Across the mainstream of American politics—Democratic and Republican, liberal and conservative, North and South—describing the United States as an empire has been a longstanding historical taboo, violated only by unreconstructed leftists far from the public square of cultural life. The Founders associated empire with the corrupt regimes of old Europe, unlike their republic of free citizens. Dispossessing Mexico of one-third of its territory after the war of 1846 provided the United States with "annexed" territories that, unlike colonies to be exploited, were welcomed and integrated into the Union as the states of Colorado, California, Arizona, New Mexico, Utah, and Nevada. Mainstream historians often described the United States as an "accidental" imperial power when it absentmindedly acquired Cuba, Puerto Rico, the Philippines, and other territories in the course of the Spanish-American War—and it granted independence, or sort-of independence, to almost all of them in good time (notwithstanding killing more than two-hundred thousand Filipinos who rebelled against American rule after 1898).

This sort of framework continued through the twentieth century. The Europeans held colonies around the world, but Woodrow Wilson championed the self-determination of nations at Versailles. During the Cold War, the Soviet Union was the Evil Empire, having kept as "captive

1. For full details, see the "Declaration and Invitation" page of their website at http://www.ekklesiaproject.org/about-us/who-we-are/declaration-and-invitation.

nations" those countries it occupied during the Second World War; in contrast, the United States rebuilt, rehabilitated, and released those areas it occupied during the war (save for some particularly interesting parcels like Okinawa and the Marshall Islands)—no captive nations held by the United States. As a country born in revolution against imperial Britain, the United States has typically seen itself as genetically incapable of being a colonial power, given that imperial powers are those whose prosperity and security required the subordination, exploitation, or domination of other countries and peoples.

We have the neoconservative intellectuals that ran wild during the years of George Bush the second to thank for breaking the recent popular embargo on the description of the US as an imperial power. The collapse of the Soviet Union and the unrivaled power of the United States allowed a moment of candor in such circles, albeit with a redefinition of the meaning of empire. What had previously been a term with substantial negative baggage—a powerful state using and abusing weaker ones for its own advantage, to the detriment of the weaker—became a badge of honor. People like Max Boot, Niall Ferguson, and Paul Johnson, among others, refurbished the notion of empire, returning to an earlier defense of it that stressed the civilizing responsibilities of the powerful, the advantages enjoyed by weak countries as they are mentored by powerful ones, and the benefits of prosperity, peace, and progress made possible by the leadership of empire of the American sort. This sort of paternalistic don't-call-it-empire sort of imperialism, portions of which showed up in American debates about the Philippines in the early 1900s, still made many members of the American establishment nervous and uneasy with the term—think Donald Rumsfeld and Colin Powell here, for example. One advantage of this glimmer of honesty, at least according to Tariq Ali, is that "American imperialism has always been the imperialism that has been frightened of speaking its name. Now it's beginning to do so. In a way, it's better. We now know where to kneel."[2]

Part of what the Church needs, for its own sake and for the world it serves, is to re-tell this story of America. Given the role of Christianity in the conquest of the Americas and the establishment of the so-called New World, the Church has important contributions to make in re-telling the story of American empire in the interest of truth and confessing of sins. What has been obscured, minimized, rationalized, and bastardized needs

2. Barsamian, "Tariq Ali Interview."

to be abandoned and replaced. In the replacement version, keep whatever "truth" you find in the official versions, but make some structural ties to the lies. For the American Experiment, like all imperial projects, has been built on lies—lies and blood, lies and conquest, lies and extermination, lies and enslavement, lies and racism, lies and exploitation, lies and manipulation. These lies made America possible, and the Church helped to fashion these lies. Strategic forgetting, whitewashing, and projection allowed for the American story to be one of a chosen people, the pinnacle of social evolution—the lie of what's known as American exceptionalism—to be joined to the story of America as a country of uncommon virtue: never the aggressor, never the invader—instead, the victimized, the reluctant defenders of freedom and prosperity against all comers.[3] Never the one to start a fight, but always the one to finish it; carrying out a mission to the nations, with the blessings of the Church in nearly all of its manifestations—Catholic and Protestant, evangelical and Pentecostal, eventually (albeit in a more complex fashion) black, Latino, Asian, and more. Those eras that howl to heaven as outrages against human dignity and life become uncharacteristic missteps, errors, or lamentable features of the era; the presumed elimination of these outrages becomes yet another opportunity to trumpet the virtue of America. What other country admits its mistakes, reforms itself, and continues moving toward its eschatological destiny by being more free, more inclusive, more fully a beacon of light and opportunity for all in a world still marked by tyranny and darkness? Truly a country and people of exceptional goodness.

While the official story trumpets the newness of the American experiment—the *novo ordo seclorum*, the "new order of the ages," as it says on the official seal of the United States—from the beginning it unfolded unaware of how typical was the story it told itself and the world. As Edward Said noted in 1978,

> Every single empire in its official discourse has said that it is not like all the others, that its circumstances are special, that it has a mission to enlighten, civilize, bring order and democracy, and that it uses force only as a last resort. And, sadder still, there always is a chorus of willing intellectuals to say calming words about benign or altruistic empires, as if one shouldn't trust the

3. These twin concepts are explored in the new book by Roberto Sirvent and Danny Haiphong, *American Exceptionalism and American Innocence*.

Settler colonialism

> evidence of one's eyes watching the destruction and the misery and death brought by the latest mission civilizatrice.[4]

The study of empire and colonialism is very much a comparative enterprise: trying to discern commonalities and distinctive features, what things admit of substantial variability and what things seem more tightly limited by structures and systems. The United States is among those often studied as an example of settler colonialism, a very specific subset of colonialism over the centuries. Whereas many of the colonial enterprises of the past five hundred years have been of a fairly remote type—the colonizer sends some soldiers and clerks to another country in order to extract wealth and resources, but doesn't make much of an effort to transform or wipe out the country it's invaded (think of the Europeans in much of Africa and Asia)—settler colonialism is a very different thing.

In settler colonialism, the invaders come to stay—in large numbers. They come to set up a world of their own, sometimes a version of what they left behind and sometimes a vision of something new to create; and in doing so, they very much transform the places to which they move. "Transform" here is a euphemism—the goal is the acquisition of land upon which to build the new colony or country, clearing out all evidence of the land's previous inhabitants, and usually eradicating the indigenous population so that over time the settlers themselves become the "real" owners and indigenous peoples of the land. Compared to other forms of colonialism, settler colonialism is of necessity substantially more violent, often genocidal (or practicing what today we call ethnic cleansing), and ideologically aggressive in proclaiming its expropriations as legitimate and even praiseworthy, a superior people putting to better and more efficient uses the land hitherto wasted on inferior or wasteful groups of the uncivilized. The United States is studied as a settler colony, along with places like Australia, South Africa, Canada, New Zealand, and Israel, among others. The American settler project was successful on a massive scale—dispossessing the indigenous inhabitants of 1.5 billion acres of land since 1776 while killing off 95 percent of their number.

Viewed through the lenses of settler colonial studies, so much of what can be seen as isolated aspects of American history start to make more sense and tell a more adequate picture than the lie that America has told itself and the world. Stealing the lands of indigenous people was a necessary but not sufficient condition for the prosperity of what was

4. Said, "Orientalism Once More," 4.

to become America—so much land was stolen that more than settler labor was necessary. It soon proved impractical to try to enslave the indigenous peoples—they had friends and family on the outside, including from other tribes, who would help them resist or escape, and they knew the terrain once they escaped. African slaves proved to be a much better solution to the lack of labor—persons kidnapped from different parts of Africa, speaking different languages and sometimes being historic enemies of one another, were unable to unite against American slave masters; even for those who managed to escape, they found themselves thousands of miles from home, in unfamiliar territory, surrounded by hostile slaveowners and indigenous communities who were not averse to owning slaves themselves under certain circumstances.

Land from the indigenous, labor from the Africans—the formula worked, and worked too well in many respects. By 1700, the number of enslaved Africans in the Americas had exploded, outnumbering whites twenty to one in some parts of the Caribbean, and constituting a majority in the Carolinas by 1708.[5] As Gerald Horne notes in a recent study, the slave aristocracy found themselves in a dilemma of their own making: slavery had become so lucrative and profitable that every entrepreneur wanted slaves, more all the time; in the process, however, the number of slaves had increased so much as to make slave revolts more frequent and threatening.[6] Even with the settlers and slavers well-armed, the threat of slave revolts kept them well aware of the demographic implications of their greed. And if you want to know about the origins of American obsession with guns, the roots of the Second Amendment, and the real history of policing, here's the era to study: you get militias formed to put down slave revolts, to kill indigenous peoples, and to catch escaped slaves. White people were required to own guns in many of the colonies, and white men could be fined if they didn't bring their gun to church since that was often a time slaves chose to stage a revolt or escape.[7]

The settlers themselves were too few in number to put down slave revolts and kill those indigenous people who objected to having their land stolen. While some poor Europeans came to the new settler colony as indentured servants or prisoners, initially they were unreliable allies in the settlers' quest to take, hold, and work land; as a disenfranchised and

5. See Horne, *The Counter-Revolution of 1776*, 39; see also Goodman, "Counter-Revolution of 1776."

6. Horne, *The Counter-Revolution of 1776*, 195.

7. See Dunbar-Ortiz, *Loaded*.

exploited class themselves, European indentured servants might make common cause with the slaves in rebellions against the slave owning elite—which happened in the first recorded slave revolt in the United States, in Gloucester County, Virginia, in 1663. All the while, the dynamic was more land taken by illegal speculators like George Washington, more indigenous peoples slaughtered by private-sector killers like Andrew Jackson, resulting in more land in need of labor, more slaves brought in to provide that labor, and more instability as the number of slaves rose throughout the seventeenth and eighteenth centuries.

Enter two innovations: first, the large-scale recruitment of new immigrants from across Europe, enticed by cheap or free land (courtesy of indigenous extermination and removal) that they would work and occupy on behalf of the pre- and post-independence America. Second, the creation, or at least the further development, of "whiteness" as a category of stratification. While wealthy landowners monopolized political power, as reflected in the property-owning restrictions on political participation in colonial and later the United States Constitution, the underclasses of Europe were amalgamated into a new category called "white"—a cross-class status that provided them some benefits not available to indigenous and African peoples while diluting and redirecting these poor Europeans' animosity away from the upper classes.

As settler colonial studies has coalesced into a distinctive research tradition over the past twenty-five years, Australian scholar Patrick Wolfe expressed what became one of the foundational assumptions of the field: that settler colonialism is a structure, not an event. In other words, the dynamics of settler colonialism are not matters of the dead and settled past, matters of antiquity that do not continue into contemporary times. There is no "post-colonial" period for settler colonies. There's an old joke about an indigenous person being told that the US is now a postcolonial country, to which she responded, "You mean they've left?"

On the contrary, as Wolfe and others note, the settler dynamics of the United States continue into the present and shape the story of America as an empire. Rather than being a late arrival in American history—with the Mexican War in 1846 or the Spanish War in 1898—America has been imperial from the outset: its first colonies were themselves the fruits of conquest over indigenous peoples, the move into the American Midwest was an imperial conquest, the settling of the Louisiana territories was a matter of conquest, the American West, Hawaii—the whole thing has been an imperial exercise from start to finish. Conquer more land, eradicate or shrink the indigenous population, bring in more settlers—call them "pioneers," or homesteaders, or ranchers, or cowboys, if you're in a nostalgic mood—and the process has never stopped. Open and close the immigration spigot as you need, send labor recruiters across Europe when there are new lands to hold and defend against indigenous resistance; when the Civil War looks to have dried up the supply of cheap labor available from former Africans, then you open the gates to Asia, sending recruiters to China with false promises of work and land only to insert them into the ironclad racial hierarchy of America. Settler colonies past and present seem to have a hard time with limits—they resist the ending of frontiers, seek out new areas in which to spread their culture and unsettle-then-resettle areas they already control, as needed. The logic of settler colonialism continues apace, as we'll see, in moves to secure new lands, resources, bioregions, and territories for the powerful at the expense of the uncivilized.

Making the case that the American empire is now in a period of irreversible decline is a substantially easier matter, at least in terms of finding support for the trend across a variety of disciples and ideological dispositions. At the popular level, of course, there's an undeniable schizophrenia about the matter—the two dominant political parties regularly accuse one another of having undermined the nation's power and influence even as they try to outdo one another in singing hosannas to the unmatched power and glory of America (think Trump's "Make America great again," and Hilary Clinton's "America was always great"). Had we more time, we could go into some interesting features of this decline—everything from the collapse of the Bretton Woods system of capitalist economic rules following World War II and the erosion of the three pillars of power that many political economists see as constitutive of a hegemonic power (unmatched strength in the areas of production, commerce, and finance), to the rise of other actors unencumbered by the fixed costs of being the incumbent hegemonic actor (as an example, here we might discuss China's ambitious Belt-and-Road initiative, which is plowing billions of dollars of infrastructure investment into 152 countries around the world, as well as its attempt to construct an alternative system of global finance outside the orbit of the IMF and World Bank).

Instead, I want to mention one feature of imperial decline that has special significance for our conversation today. In 1987, historian Paul Kennedy published a comparative study called *The Rise and Fall of the Great Powers*, a study of how powerful states achieve and lose dominance.[8] One of his conclusions is that the most powerful states sustained a virtuous circle of economic power and military power—economic power making possible the creation of a dominant military, and a dominant military making possible the acquisition of economic power. That's how it happens on the way up. At some point, however, the costs of maintaining what has been achieved become an impossible burden to sustain. In the case of the United States, for example, having constructed and underwritten the world economy since 1944, with a military budget as large as the next seven nations combined even as late as this year,[9] military spending and subsidies that ensure the functioning of the world economy become a drag. New economic powers emerge, unburdened by the heavy fixed costs of keeping the whole thing afloat (much of the postwar prosperity of Japan, Korea, Taiwan, and Hong Kong, for example, came about because of the US being willing to run substantial balance-of-trade deficits as a way to subsidize the market-centered rebuilding of these countries). Kennedy called this "imperial overstretch,"[10] while the Marxist Immanuel Wallerstein referred to it as the cost of hegemony.[11]

With its economic power diminished and comparative advantage eroding steadily, the United States no longer has nearly unmatched influence in any area of world political economy—not in production, nor in finance, nor in innovation, nor in rulemaking. Where its power remains unmatched to date is in the area of military force. And as Paul Kennedy and others note, empires in decline use whatever tools remain at their disposal to hold on to their power as long as they can—in this case, that means moving conflicts from areas of declining influence—in economic or diplomatic realms, for example—into areas where the US is still likely to prevail: transforming things into military conflicts when all else fails. It's the international version of "when all you have is a hammer, the whole world looks like a nail." The United States has its military hammer and not much else, at least in comparative terms; if you want to know why it still supports more than 750 military bases overseas, with soldiers in at least 150 countries, you might start here.

I think Kennedy and others are right about this: the already-pronounced tendency of American policymakers to translate problems of

8. Kennedy, *The Rise and Fall*.

9. See, for example, "US Defense Spending Compared to Other Countries."

10. See Kennedy, *The Rise and Fall*.

11. See Wallerstein, "The Three Instances of Hegemony."

almost any type into military matters is going to increase in the years ahead. From development to disaster relief to ideological competition to domestic unrest to migration to whatever else you think of—you scratch the surface and you will find the United States military involved. All the other tools in the toolbox may be corroding, but the American empire still has its hammer.

2. *Into the Fire: Climate and Ecological Collapse*

Among the sentient beings for whom human-generated climate change is real, and for whom the magnitude of the changes now underway is apparent, people have sorted themselves into four general schools of response. Roughly speaking, one can see:

1. The Mitigators: those for whom the key is to adopt policy and behavioral changes in order to arrest and reverse the changes now underway—lower carbon emissions, move to alternative fuel sources, and so forth.

2. The Adaptors: those who recognize that the changes underway cannot be stopped or slowed to an appreciable degree; what can be done is to prepare in advance for what is to come—build seawalls around important coastal cities, make plans for securing sources of water/food/resources once existing ones become depleted or unavailable, etc.

3. The Optimists: those for whom new technologies exist and are in development sufficient to avert the worst of what's to come while preserving most of the benefits of existing economic, political, and lifestyle arrangements. For some of the optimists, global climate crises represent a near-limitless opportunity for profitable investment and business activity—building the new infrastructure, providing ambitious programs in geo-engineering, benefiting from new process, product, and technology innovations.

4. The "We're F***ed" Group: those for whom the cumulative and interactive effects of ecological degradation are already too far gone to reverse, the effects of which are and will be so great as to overwhelm efforts at adaptation. The interactive and intensifying effects of feedback loops, the prospect of irrevocable "tipping points" regarding key natural cycles, and the cascading nature of climate collapse all

> combine to lead many persons to conclude that it's too late to stop the train, there is nothing that will have much effect in cushioning the blows, and the casualties will be catastrophic—even if all industrial activity were to stop today.

We don't have a lot of time together, so I will cut to the chase and leave the defense to another time. I am among those who are convinced that the primary and secondary biophysical systems that sustain much of the regularities of our natural world have become irreversibly changed in ways that bring with them degrees of death, chaos, and suffering with no parallels in human history. No amount of carbon capture, no amount of green energy, no set of policies like a Green New Deal, no treaties or programs can undo what has already been done. The unraveling of the biosphere has already begun; its effects will only broaden and deepen in the next few decades, and there is nothing we can do about it. Let me repeat: this is going to happen no matter what we do.

It seems that many of the best climate models, including those from the IPCC (Intergovernmental Panel on Climate Change)—the United Nations agency that summarizes the best and most current research on climate change broadly construed—have significantly underestimated the immediacy and range of the threat. Even with a modest rise in sea level of six meters (more than eighteen feet), which is far below most reputable estimates, we will see cities housing 375 million people underwater.[12] Twenty-five years from now, the US will lose three-hundred thousand homes to ocean incursion; by 2100, more than a trillion dollars will be lost just in the United States.[13] And if you don't know about feedback loops, you soon will: a warming planet leads to melting Antarctic and Arctic ice, which means less sunlight reflected back into space (something called the Albedo effect); melting Arctic ice exposes and melts permafrost, which contains 1.7 trillion tons of carbon, much of it released as methane, which is thirty-four times as powerful a greenhouse gas as CO_2; a hotter planet kills plant life in many zones and causes a loss of forests, which reduces the ability of plants to absorb carbon; warmer weather means drier forests, meaning more and bigger forest fires, which release more carbon; a warmer planet means more water vapor in the atmosphere, which traps more heat; warmer oceans absorb less heat and contain less oxygen, which means death to phytoplankton, which wipes

12. Wallace-Wells, *The Uninhabitable Earth*, 61.

13. Riederer, "The Other Kind of Climate Denialism."

out fish species that feed on them while also reducing the oceans' ability to absorb carbon, which heats the planet further.[14] And this is just one small slice of the world of feedback loops and relationships—beyond this simple little snippet, things start to get complicated.

Most people have at least heard that climate change is related in part to a measure of carbon in the atmosphere—how many parts per million, with the more PPM, the hotter things are going to get. A dozen years ago, Bill McKibben named his climate-change advocacy group 350.org (now 350 Action) as a symbol of the level of atmospheric world carbon dares not exceed; we're now over 400 parts per million, and the rate of increase is accelerating, forget moving in the opposite direction. You may also hear about degrees of temperature rise (usually in the Celsius scale): what happens at one degree of temperature rise, what at two or four or six degrees. Many climate scientists and advocates have warned for years that things become really awful with any temperature rise above two-and-a-half degrees. The Paris Accords of 2015, if fully implemented, would result in a 3.2 degrees Celsius rise in temperatures (5.8 degrees Fahrenheit), which represents "three times as much warming as the planet has seen since the beginning of industrialization, bringing the unthinkable collapse of the planet's ice sheets not just into realm of possibility but into the present."[15] None of the rich country signatories to the Paris Accord are on target to meet its objectives.

The psychology of all of this matters, inasmuch as the numbers are abstract, bloodless, and sound so small to those of us who aren't scientists. As one of the better accounts of the literature reports:

> At two degrees, the ice sheets will begin their collapse, four hundred million more people will suffer from water scarcity, major cities in the equatorial band of the planet will become unlivable, and even in the northern latitudes, heat waves will kill thousands each summer. There would be thirty-two times as many extreme heat waves in India, and each would last five times as long, exposing ninety-three times more people. This is our best-case scenario. At three degrees, southern Europe would be in permanent drought, and the average drought in Central America would last nineteen months longer and in the Caribbean twenty-one months longer. In northern Africa, the figure is sixty months longer—five years. The areas burned each year

14. Derived from Wallace-Wells, *The Uninhabitable Earth*, 21–23.
15. Wallace-Wells, *The Uninhabitable Earth*, 11.

> by wildfires would double in the Mediterranean and sextuple, or more, in the United States. At four degrees, there would be eight million more cases of dengue fever each year in Latin America alone and close to annual global food crises. There could be 9 percent more heat-related deaths. Damages from river flooding would grow thirtyfold in Bangladesh, twentyfold in India, and as much as sixtyfold in the United Kingdom. In certain places, six climate-driven natural disasters could strike simultaneously, and, globally, damages could pass $600 trillion—more than twice the wealth as exists in the world today. Conflict and war could double.
>
> Even if we pull the planet up short of two degrees by 2100, we will be left with an atmosphere that contains 500 parts per million of carbon—perhaps more. The last time that was the case, sixteen million years ago, the planet was not two degrees warmer; it was somewhere between five and eight, giving the planet about 130 feet of sea-level rise, enough to draw a new American coastline as far west as I-95.[16]

Whew. No wonder so many people want to deny what's coming or avoid human responsibility for it. And no wonder that there's something of a rigid policing of thought should anyone suggest that it's too late to avert the worst of ecological crises—such has been denounced as an attempt to undermine the motivation of movements of resistance and reform that work on these issues, or as helping continue the rule of the elites that have plundered the ecosystem in the name of white supremacy and global capital. I'm also aware that some people see an acknowledgment of my position as an expression of white male privilege, presumably because people like me can sit back and enjoy life while everything continues to corrode. Just to be clear: I'm not telling anyone to give up, or to abandon whatever they think is worth doing. I could well be wrong, since I'm wrong on so much else in my life, in which case we want to avoid a self-fulfilling prophesy of bringing about a doom that might have been avoided. And second, even if I'm right, much of what is being done or proposed is good in itself, as a way to honor and respect the goodness of creation and show love to neighbors near and far. But I won't be a peddler in false hopes or false optimism. Not gonna happen.

16. Wallace-Wells, *The Uninhabitable Earth*, 12–13.

3. *Politics as if the Biosphere Mattered*

I'm at the mercy of researchers when it comes to much of the science of climate change and related matters, but it happens that I've been something of a student of the political consequences of ecological change for some time. My doctoral studies began in this area some thirty-five years ago, exploring the political economy of growth and contraction, and I studied with some of the pioneers who worked on issues of politics and scarcity in both domestic and international politics. Returning to these issues over the past few years has been something of a homecoming, and no less depressing this time around than it was the first time.

Again, we have no time, so we'll have to go with the highly abbreviated version; the case is stronger than I can probably manage to convey in this slice of time, but I'll just focus on one feature that I think is of greatest import to today's topics. One of the most important features of the modern era—of capitalism and liberalism broadly construed—is one that has been hidden in plain sight for centuries. I am referring to the idea of economic growth—more goods, more services, more stuff—as absolutely central to the stability of liberal democracy and its associated goods, including civil liberties, human rights, constitutionalism, and the rule of law. Regardless of regime type, states around the world derive much of their ideological legitimacy from their ability to deliver what the US Constitution calls "the general welfare"—prosperity and the materially comfortable life. If the reality of prosperity is not yet in hand, the promise of it in the form of future growth must be cultivated, pursued, and championed—growth is the glue that holds modern societies together.

Economic growth, at least in principle, allows for those at the bottom to gain something without taking from the wealthy at the top—it represents "enlarging the size of the pie" rather than arguing over why the few get all the big slices while the many get the crumbs. The promise of economic growth allows for the preaching of patience and political compromise to the have-nots: you may be doing poorly today, but you may do better tomorrow if we're able to generate more goods and services for everyone.

As sociologist Alan Wolfe observed nearly forty years ago, the commitment to growth is the universally shared assumption of American politics—indeed, of the politics of capitalist democracy anywhere in the world. It is the unquestionable end shared by Democrats and Republicans alike—they may disagree on what policies best advance the goal (more taxes on the rich or fewer taxes on them; less regulation or more; a higher or lower minimum wage), but the objective cuts across all that divides them. Grow the economy at all costs.[17]

In this, they draw inspiration from neoclassical economists, for whom growth is a possibility without ultimate limits—one may encounter scarcities of one resource or another (oil, iron, etc.), but such may always be overcome via substitution, innovation, or policy choices. The conquest of the Americas itself is a testimony to the assumption that the natural world itself is an inexhaustible source of growth—to John Locke, the pristine world of the Americas made it possible for laborers to take as much from nature as they like while leaving behind "enough and as good" for everyone else.[18]

What makes the politics of growth so crucial to politics is what it purports to avoid—namely, the politics of redistribution. In a redistributive politics, for one sector or actor to gain, another must lose—for the poor to improve their lot, the rich have to lose something. Redistributive politics is the bloodiest of all politics—the rich defend their privileges with whatever violence is necessary, the poor turn to violence out of desperation. It is a zero-sum world in which law shows its true colors as an instrument of domination, in which human rights and civil liberties are either instruments of domination or pieces of ideological window dressing, and in which Hobbes' Leviathan is not a peacekeeper but a partisan, killing whomever is necessary to protect established property and privilege. The political theorist C. B. MacPherson noted a generation ago that rights of political participation were only extended to those without property in Britain once elites were sure that the impoverished majority could not use politics to redistribute property;[19] the same reasoning is baked into the numerous hindrances to effective political action in the US Constitution, nearly all of which were designed to put redistribution out of reach of the majority. Settler colonialism itself is a political structure and ideology built on expansion without limits—take more land, displace more people, extend one's system—and this expansionism is not deterred by the "closing of the frontier." There are always other places that can be appropriated, other regions that would benefit from the management of

17. Wolfe, *America's Impasse.*

18. Locke, *Second Treatise on Government*, sec. 27.

19 See MacPherson, *The Life and Times of Liberal Democracy.*

a superior culture, other zones that need the kind of protection only the most powerful can provide.

Limitless growth has always been a lie, an illusion, seen as such by anyone who wasn't an economist or a politician. The biophysical impossibility of limitless growth in a limited biosphere was recognized centuries ago, even as those voices were shouted down—long before the terms "climate change" or "global warming" became part of the public discourse.

Economists like Nicholas Georgescu-Roegen and Herman Daly (the latter before he went to work at the World Bank and started collaborating with John Cobb) pointed to the impossibility of endless growth in a world in which the laws of thermodynamics—especially the second one, the law of entropy—held sway. Take away the lie of unlimited expansion and you take away the agreed-upon fiction that made a minimum of social peace possible, that hid the inequalities inherent in capitalism under the promise of more for the poor if only they wait for the results of the next policy innovation, the next technological breakthrough, the next gravy train just around the corner. Hidden, I should say, only from those at the bottom—most of the more perceptive overlords never lost sight that capitalism is always—always—redistributive, whatever the rhetoric of an ever-expanding pie might suggest.[20]

What we call climate change has stripped away the lie of unlimited growth—the lubricant of modernity—for anyone who is paying attention. Think about the basic throughput models you had to look at in high school or college: raw materials like resources and labor are on the input side as what goes into the economic process, and stuff—goods and services—comes out on the output side. In truth, the real limits are mostly not, and have never been, on the input side; the real hard limit has always been on the output side, specifically the absorptive capacities of the ecosystem. This hard limit wasn't called global warming when I started working on these things a lifetime ago—the catch-all term we used was "heat," referring to the degraded and unusable byproducts of all transformative processes that invariably accumulate in the closed system called planet earth—closed because we have and need an atmosphere. As you remember from your high school physics class, matter and energy can neither be created nor destroyed, only transformed. This is why all human activity, especially the type we call work or production, never makes anything "new" or *ex nihilo*—we rearrange or recombine or change what

20. Georgescu-Roegen, *The Entropy Law and the Economic Process*; Daly, *Steady State Economics.*

already exists, but we don't end up with more matter or energy than we start with. In fact, we end up with less-usable forms of each inasmuch as all transformative activity generates waste (in the form of heat, if nothing else). Such is the relentless operation of the entropy law. The absorptive capacity of the biosystem has a limit that one can use up gradually or quickly. For almost all of human history, it was used gradually, resulting in untold numbers of generations engaged in subsistence activities with a slow throughput rate. In the past few decades, but especially in the past forty years, it has been used up rapidly, extending the lifespans and quality of life for a minority of people but at the expense of the majority in this generation and for whatever generations follow us.

The decline of the American empire, the empire that Christians helped to build and sustain, coincides with the return of zero-sum politics. It will not be advertised as such, for ideological and strategic reasons, but the politics of redistribution are guaranteed to make politics more violent, more deadly, more uncompromising—between states and within states, among communities and across boundaries. As the losers in the capitalist game push for a more adequate share, they are already meeting with fewer carrots and more sticks, fewer concessions and more aggressions, if you will. While much of conventional politics looks the same on the surface—elections, protests, elite posturing, and the like—the context is shifting and will continue to shift as constraints accumulate and buying off discontent becomes less attractive as a strategy for elites.

Let me give you a few examples of how zero-sum politics is already underway as a result of climate collapse; to me, these are not exceptions to the coming rule but merely the first fruits of the coming dispensation. And just for fun, I will take these from outside the overheated realm of American domestic politics, where the visage of Trump overshadows everything.

1. Hard on the heels of the world economic collapse of 2007, major corporations and national governments set out on a buying spree around the world, most fully in Africa. The object of their desire? Land, land, land—especially for food crops. What the economic collapse did was to remind the wealthy that having money does you no good during an economic collapse if others refuse to sell to you or have nothing to sell—the massive shortages of grain, corn, and the like that followed on the heels of the collapse looked like a harbinger of the future. So you see, sovereign wealth funds (massive piles of

investment funds controlled by sovereign governments) from Saudi Arabia, South Korea, China, and elsewhere buying up millions of acres of land throughout sub-Saharan Africa—kicking the Africans off their land, with the connivance of the national governments in place, perhaps hiring a few of them back as badly paid laborers. The others are now targeted as trespassers, poachers, and threats to national security for daring to interfere with the deals struck by wealthy buyers and national governments.[21] There is no promise of shared prosperity, no fiction about the increased productivity of the soil being a rising tide for all boats—at least not in the sense that anyone believes it.

2. Speaking of poachers, one of the least reported stories of the past twenty years has been the rise of so-called Green Armies—military forces developed and deployed around the world to "protect" pristine environments and ecologically sensitive regions. The boom in ecotourism, in which rich people travel around the world to look at big wildlife and little flowers, has brought badly needed foreign currency to certain poor countries worldwide. Protecting the tourist areas for eco-safaris, eco-snorkeling, and eco-birdwatching has meant the deployment of armed soldiers with the authority to shoot to kill to keep the parks and conservation areas suitably populated with what outsiders want to see. And protect against whom? Poachers, of course—while the few media stories that emerge focus on armed gangs that target high-value items like rhino horns and elephant ivory, the real enemies to be excluded and kept at bay are the thousands upon thousands of people who were evicted from their ancestral lands in the first place in the process of creating conservation areas (something similar happened in the United States in the creation of the national park system—somebody should tell Ken Burns about that aspect of "America's Best Idea," the name he gave his documentary series on the American National Parks). With no other way to survive (not everyone is lucky enough to work as a porter or dishwasher for the tourists), displaced persons are forced to return to foraging and hunting on the lands that were once theirs—except now, their subsistence has been criminalized as a threat against commerce, against the ecosystem, and against the health of the planet. Some of the most famous and successful conservation

21. See, for example, Liberti, *Land Grabbing*; see also Pearce, *The Land Grabbers.*

charities are deeply implicated in this modern-day version of primitive accumulation and large-scale displacement—there's big money to be raised with pictures of exotic African animals, no matter how many non-exotic African men and women have to die as a result.[22] You can expect many and more diverse ways in which states will use military violence to advance ecological objectives—secure water sources, commandeer arable land, threaten weaker states to absorb the costs of ecological adjustment, and much more.

From both of these, it's a small step toward a more fully militarized ideology of climate adaptation and environmental protection. Let's look for a moment at the movement of people worldwide: more than 13 million people were forcibly displaced in 2018, adding to the 57 million already adrift in the world. Most of these seventy million people land in the laps of their mostly very poor neighbors, even as the Europeans and the United States squeal in panic when a small fraction—a very small fraction—of them dare to seek refuge in these safer, prosperous countries. Among US military leaders, plans for armed interventions are already in place, with budgets and resources deployed in order to forestall large-scale refugee movements toward the United States. Such will never be presented as such to outsiders like the American public, but instead as expressions of the benevolent humanitarianism codified in the so-called Responsibility to Protect (R2P) doctrine (I think it should be renamed "Resources to Protect" in many cases, but that's another matter). As I said, you can also expect more moves to put what remains of sensitive ecosystem areas worldwide under military (excuse me, "conservation") control, given the need to manage such regions more efficiently than the primitive and backward peoples who now inhabit them. Such is precisely the liberal view of property, with its claim that to leave land relatively undisturbed was wasteful and inefficient, which justified and impelled the extermination of the indigenous peoples in North America. Indigenous peoples' apparent disinterest in European-style agriculture and individualized land tenure was itself proof that they were too backward and lazy to keep all the land that more civilized peoples could exploit

22. Some of the best work in this area comes from Bram Büscher, professor and chair of the Sociology of Development and Change Group at Wagenining University in the Netherlands; he also holds academic appointments at the University of South Africa and Stellenbosch University. On this topic, see Büscher and Fletcher, "Under Pressure"; Büscher, "From Biopower to Ontopower?"; Büscher and Ramutsindela, "Green Violence"; and Duffy, "The Militarization of Anti-Poaching."

more effectively. And lest you think such may amount only to minor skirmishes in the years ahead, keep in mind that—contrary to the self-fulfilling myth that "all the Indians are dead"—indigenous peoples still control approximately one-quarter of the earth's landmass, two-thirds of which is "essentially natural," according to a recent report in the journal *Nature Sustainability*.[23] Too much land of value remains under the *de jure* or *de facto* control of peoples who have shown insufficient enthusiasm to exploit those lands for capitalist benefit—clearly a luxury one can no longer afford in a zero-sum political world. The irony, of course, is that the lands under indigenous control are in substantially better shape ecologically than those "rationally" managed by white rationalists.

Even a cursory look at American domestic politics these days gives evidence of techniques of repression usually confined to America's colonies being brought to bear against people at home when people at home stand in the way of accumulation under conditions of hard constraints and diminished possibilities for co-optation. Strategies and tactics previously concentrated on overseas adventures and in the "internal colonies"—a term used by radical activists in the United States to refer to African-American communities and indigenous populations—are now here or en route for the rest of the population, even as they become more blatantly visited upon non-white communities. If you want to know how security people think about internal unrest caused by ecological or climate crises, just take a moment and think about one popular scenario, namely, the collapse of the private and public insurance regime worldwide. The business and military communities worldwide are well aware of the precarity of the insurance industry, given the likelihood of events similar to Hurricane Katrina, Hurricane Sandy, Hurricane Maria, and more—all in the same year in the same place, year after year. Imagine the politics of America or Europe when the disasters start piling up if state rebuilding efforts are scaled back or abandoned, if governments are unable or unwilling to go beyond bankruptcy time and again.

There's a book you might like, sort of, dealing with some of this, by a historian named Nick Estes. Entitled *Our Past Is the Future*,[24] it explores how indigenous peoples at the Standing Rock reservation in North Dakota worked to block an oil pipeline that threatened the reservation's water sources. These "water protectors" were met with new and frightening

23. See "Indigenous peoples control one quarter of world's land surface."

24. Estes, *Our Past Is the Future*.

sorts of repression as they sought to stave off the combined power of multinational energy conglomerates, the United States government, the combined resources of state, county, and municipal law enforcement and business communities, even private mercenaries hired by local police departments. According to Estes, what was brought to bear against them—the violence, the surveillance, the agent provocateurs, the economic blackmail, the use of the judiciary—all of this is your future, white America, if you dare to get out of line as the empire pursues its agenda in a time of economic and climate-driven scarcity. It's a return to all the things and more that the US government did to the Black Panther Party in the 1960s and 70s, when the federal government decided it should be eradicated and its leaders executed or imprisoned for life. This time, though, it won't be limited to groups that white America could ignore or be happy to see destroyed. You can see the same things happening in Canada, where the smiling face of Justin Trudeau is pulling out all the stops to shove through whatever the Alberta tar sands companies want. When faced with delays caused by opposition from the Province of British Columbia and several First Nations groups, he simply nationalized a pipeline project, handing 4.5 billion (CDN) to the Kinder Morgan corporation and overruling the authority of provincial and indigenous bodies.

The indigenous resurgence represented by Standing Rock is being treated by American leaders as akin to another Indian uprising to be put down with the full weight of the law lest other indigenous peoples and any misguided non-Indians think about doing the same. To date, seven states have upgraded laws against criminal trespass and unlawful protest—which used to be misdemeanors—to felonies with long prison terms, prohibitive fines, and much more. Louisiana led the way in making it a felony to protest near things like pipelines, which are now considered "critical infrastructure." For good liberals, no more ritualized civil disobedience from now on, where you get your arrest, get out the same day, and feel good about yourself at relatively low cost. Pipeline protesters in Louisiana can now get five years in prison and a hefty fine. Not to be outdone by its neighbor and fellow oil-and-gas fiefdom, the state of Texas mandates up to *ten* years in prison for such protests now—and as a sweetener, Texas has eliminated liability for drivers who plow into protesters blocking roadways as long as they were exercising "due care." And not to be outdone by Texas, the Trump administration has introduced a law that calls for *twenty* years in prison for such protests, along with fines of $250,000 for individuals and $500,000 for organizations. For those of you who see protecting the environment as a serious matter rather than as a bit of self-promotion (our friend Kyle Childress represents the former when he put himself and his congregation in the cross-hairs of the authorities by aiding and abetting Keystone XL protests a few years ago), you'll be in prison for a long time, treated like a terrorist and others who dare threaten the "critical infrastructure" of American capitalism.

If the general public is unprepared for life in a time without the promise of growth to smooth off the edges of capitalism and empire, more practical minded people are way ahead of the game. Private security and mercenary companies are seeing their prospects rise as elites seek to protect themselves, their enclaves, and their investments from climate refugees, victims of drought or famine, and whatever else comes to pass. The *New York Times* had a lovely little story about the new and improved Pinkerton Agency—once limited to killing industrial workers on the orders of coal and steel companies and local law enforcement agencies—retooling and retraining for life as hired guns working during natural disasters, civil unrest, and other sure-to-increase opportunities for profitable enterprise.[25] And while human rights groups look with horror at the ethnic cleansing underway in western China, where the regime has put more than a million Uighur Muslims in concentration and "re-education" camps as part of an effort to repopulate the region with ethnic Han Chinese more loyal to the regime (more settler colonialism), state security agencies in the United States and elsewhere look on with interest to see how China's sophisticated systems of surveillance (facial recognition, blanket coverage of public spaces, and an amazing exercise in big-data integration called the "social credit" system) might be applied to the benefit of American interests. Without the promise of limitless growth, politics becomes constrained, and losers must be dealt with preemptively before they figure out that the game is rigged, and was always rigged, at least against some people.

4. The Church after American Empire: Some Thoughts

At another gathering of the Ekklesia Project many years ago, one of our wiser members, Barry Harvey from Texas, said this or something close to it: "I know two things for certain: There will come a day when America no longer exists, and the Church will still be here." He reminded us of

25. Shannon, "Climate Chaos is Coming."

Jesus' promise to Peter in Matthew 16:18 that "the gates of hell shall not prevail against it" (KJV), which should give us some sort of comfort even as we look into a time of uncertainty.

The Church will still be here, but it's yet to be determined what sort of church we will be; whether on balance we will be a sign of the love of God for all creation and all people, or a scandal to the gospel (I say "on balance" because the Church is always both, because we are people still on the way of discipleship, still stumbling toward the promised Kingdom of God). As we think together on what is required of us as the Church in this already-begun period of imperial desperation and ecological upheaval, here are a few things that I think might be useful as we think about the demands on the Church today and tomorrow.

I am aware that engaging something as big and abstract as "American Empire" is something of an absurdity—it verges on the immaterial and irrelevant to almost everyone. Still, it has power, and much of that power comes from the stories it tells—of itself, of us, and of God.

Whatever else we may be, all of us in the Ekklesia Project are storytellers—in worship, in prose, in teaching, in the arts, in proclamation via word and deed. And we live stories—of fear and failure, of a Messiah who said it was better to die than to kill, of an outlandish Kingdom of God that has already made its arrival known. We can and should cut the American Empire down to size by telling a more truthful story about it, and by offering the world a different and better story about church and empire than what's been crafted thus far. In this way, we make the American Empire material and tangible, showing its victims as the flesh-and-blood people they are. We make the American empire tangible and incarnate, ironically, by telling and living a better set of stories. This is what I hope we will decide to do together.

One of our most valuable ventures over the past twenty years has been the Congregational Formation Initiative (CFI). Through it, we have seen what God can do when Christians start to unlearn one set of stories and learn to tell one of discipleship so substantive that they become capable of wrestling with the likes of the Sermon on the Mount. Perhaps our experiences in CFI might facilitate a new sort of engagement in which we unlearn some of the explicit stories of empire while learning to sing the Lord's song in a foreign land (Ps 137).

To our scholars and publishing partners, our social-media communicators: perhaps we should develop a coordinated series of materials that aim to subvert the story America tells of itself, while opening up space for new stories and analyses, with new voices and conversation partners. In doing so, we should draw upon persons outside our ranks from whom we have much to learn. There might be value in crafting a major, cohesive project—multiyear, multiplatform, multivolume—that is forthright, uncompromising, and unambiguous.

I have no illusions that such would be "effective" or make a "difference" or constitute an adequate "praxis" in the eyes of many, but since we came together twenty years ago, the Ekklesia Project has always kept score in a different way. Our hope remains as it has always been—do what we can together in hopes that God can do something with it. In this case, we should think of what we do as a modest offering to believers that come after us. Whatever comes to pass in the years ahead, as the American empire rages and thrashes in ways old and new, it would be important that some people tried not to be an embarrassment to the Christians who followed them. It would matter that some tried to act as if death was not the end of the story, that life is gained by losing it, and that the Resurrection might actually be true.

5. *Time for Some Questions*

To help us decide whether this is worth doing, I'd like to conduct a short exercise, something of a fictional question-and-answer session with unnamed Christians who might be offended by what I have said so far. Unlike the usual question-and-answer session, I want to be the one who asks the questions.

But first, a brief aside that helps set the stage: At some point, people like me will be accused of neglecting proper Christian theology regarding the legitimacy of "natural loves," with love of country as a legitimate expression of this. To this, I plead guilty. There is nothing natural about modern nations or states or countries or peoples—they are constructed bodies, forged over time by proximity and violence, deliberate inclusions and exclusions, propaganda and fear, manipulated loves and desires, and much more. Show me a modern nation, show me citizenship, and I will show you a set of roles constructed by violence and manipulation.

Do I hate America? I don't think I "hate" America, but I recognize it as my enemy. As a Christian, I am told to love my enemies, not hate them. But I am under no illusion that the America I encounter and that has encountered countless victims during its run is my enemy and should be seen as an enemy of a Christianity that aspires to be worthy of the calling given it by Christ. For those Christians who are outraged that I see America as an enemy, for my brother and sister Christians who profess their love for America, I have some questions:

- Is there anything that the United States could ever do that would be too much for you? At what point might you say "that's enough"?
- If you haven't yet reached that point, does that mean that you're okay with the horrific things done by the American empire up to this point? That you've been able to live with genocide and centuries of slavery and anti-black supremacy, unimaginable wealth squeezed from poor people at home and abroad, wars and conquests and overthrows and murders known and unknown—what about your understanding of following Jesus makes these things something other than a deal breaker?
- If you point instead to all the good that America has done—its practices of freedom, its religious liberty, its welcoming of immigrants and refugees, its ability to generate wealth and prosperity on hitherto unimaginable levels—are you saying that the price paid to achieve these was worth it, a price paid with the blood of Indians and slaves and workers and women and people on the wrong end of American policies abroad? How do you square this sort of consequentialism, of cost-benefit analysis, with the Christian call to protect the most vulnerable and marginalized, even if oppressing them is an efficient way to improve the lot of the majority? What separates this sort of thinking from that of Madeline Albright, Clinton's Secretary of State, for whom the deaths of half a million Iraqi children, killed by US sanctions in the 1990s, was "worth it" in achieving American policy goals? What separates this sort of thinking from the reasonable calculus that asserts that "it is better for you to have one man die for the people than to have the whole nation destroyed"—this from the political theologian known as Caiaphas (John 11:50, NRSV)?

If these questions above aren't helpful, let's try another approach. What if I tell you that on balance the American empire hasn't just been a "normal" nation, but in fact might better be seen as a monster, a monstrous presence in the world for untold millions of people? What if I told you that Christians shouldn't pledge loyalty or love or allegiance to a monster, even or especially one of Christian origin?

If that seems outrageous and hateful, please indulge me with a few more questions:

- If you say that there are larger monsters in the world, and that the American Empire with all its faults is "the indispensable nation" in standing against these even worse monsters, why is your argument any different from the logic of a protection racket, in which one pays one group of killers to protect against another group of killers? Does the Mafia, or the Cali drug cartel, or El Chapo in Mexico, have a legitimate ministry of Christian love and responsibility in our fallen world? Is there a threshold of persons killed by one's own monster as part of its everyday operations that qualifies or disqualifies for a Christian blessing?
- If you point out that distancing ourselves from the American empire, even if it is monstrous in whole or in part, abandons poor and vulnerable people around the world to the tender mercies of all the other empires and monsters, why do you presume that our fellow Christians (and even non-Christians of good will) are not already contending against their own monsters even as we are called to contend against our own? Why should we not instead consider how to help them resist those monsters in a spirit of ecclesial solidarity across borders even as we contend with the American monster?
- If you contend that all of this asks too much of people who are already victimized by monstrous practices of violence, exploitation, dehumanization, and abandonment, why, I commend you for raising a very good question indeed. Why not have those among Christians in America who have lived at the top of the pile take extra risks, stick their necks out farther in a spirit of penitential solidarity, in all of this? Why not ask the white church to lead the way—not in its usual fashion of dominating and dictating to persons of color or otherwise marginalized in our world, but as those whose divestment from the empire it helped to build might provide some modest example for others to follow, especially given that such a divestment will be treated as treason by persons in the Church and in society?
- For those who might inquire where in this is the Christian sense of gratitude for the country that has generated unprecedented wealth and prosperity, lifting millions out of abject poverty—for those who wonder, "Why is all of this not the complaints of the overfed and

overeducated, the resentful children of privilege who baste themselves in misplaced guilt attendant to life in a fallen world of sin and imperfection?" thank you for having reminded us of important obligations and norms. But these, I suggest, are the obligations and norms attendant to being a serf, a lackey, or a retainer. Allegiance for sale may well be reasonable in a world of rich and poor, of patron-client relations, where the latter are expected to bow and scrape and generally love their chains—but such is emphatically not how discipleship is meant to work. We Christians have seen this argument before—it's the same one that the second-century pagan philosopher Celsus used against the Church, saying it's a group of freeloaders and ingrates who refuse to serve in the army or sacrifice to the imperial gods. Our loyalty remains to God and to the Kingdom we're supposed to herald, however imperfectly—if that makes us crappy citizens, in Richard Goode's phrase, then so be it.[26]

6. *On Seeking the Welfare of the City*

My claim that the Church needs to renounce its support of the American empire bumps against some interpretations of a passage from the Old Testament that have enjoyed some popularity in our circles. I refer to this section of Jeremiah 29:

> Thus, says the LORD of hosts, the God of Israel, to all the exiles whom I have sent into exile from Jerusalem to Babylon: Build houses and live in them; plant gardens, and eat what they produce. Take wives and have sons and daughters; take wives for your sons, and give your daughters in marriage, that they may bear sons and daughters; multiply there, and do not decrease. But seek the welfare of the city where I have sent you into exile, and pray to the LORD on its behalf, for in its welfare you will find your welfare. (Jer 29:4–8, NRSV)

Much of the time, this verse has been used to counsel Christians to be good citizens in the nations they inhabit, asserting that the radical demands of being a Christian do not preclude being productive and useful in and for the countries we inhabit. We can work to benefit the places and countries in which we find ourselves without worry. This reading of

26. Goode, "The Calling of Crappy Citizenship."

Jeremiah 29 provides a way to assert our eschatological quality and mission without being—God forbid—separatists or something worse.

If we are finally going to come to terms with America as an empire, a world-striding creature built and blessed by Christian hands, we have to do better than this reading of Jeremiah 29 as a counsel to reliable and cooperative citizenship. One person whose ideas capture some of the rethinking I've done about this passage is Gary Hall, an Old Testament scholar who offers a reading less congenial to good relations with the empire:[27]

- First, he notes that Jeremiah's letter to the Israelites is conveying bad news, not good news, to them: they want to go home, but he says they have to stay put and weather the storm. The advice is not about making peace with one's oppressors but about going into survival mode—this time of exile and suffering is going to last a lot longer than you'd hoped.
- Marrying and having children are not permissions to relax and settle down, but rather are resistance strategies: rest, rebuild, and prepare for more struggle. It's not about making a bigger and better Babylon.
- The shalom they are to pray for is not for the sake of Babylon, so that it may become more powerful and prosperous, but so that the Israelites may revive themselves. Babylon remains the enemy of Yahweh and His people—remember the call for vengeance in Psalm 137, for example—and Israel's defeat doesn't vindicate the gods of Babylon. That Yahweh dares to invoke shalom on Babylon is a counterclaim, an assertion of Yahweh's sovereignty over a people that does not recognize Him.
- Rather than a call to pursue the common good, or a natural ethic shared by Babylon and Israel, Jeremiah 29 might better be read as a "love of enemies" text. They're still the enemy of God's people, and they're still not to be imitated or treated as objects of loyalty or allegiance. To say that the Church finds an exemplar in Jeremiah 29, or a recipe for harmonious relations or a picture of warm cooperation, is not at all an obvious or easily defended conclusion.

27. Hall, "Jeremiah 29," 52–62.

7. Traitors Again

Have you ever noticed that whenever the Christians stop playing church and get serious about matters, especially if it involves our refusal to kill, it doesn't take long for rumblings of treason to start wafting in the wind? Don't take my word for it—just ask some great Western leaders. Ask Theodore Roosevelt, who said, "The pacifist is as surely a traitor to his country and to humanity as is the most brutal wrongdoer."[28] Ask the celebrated George Orwell: "Pacifism is objectively pro-fascist. This is elementary common sense. If you hamper the war effort of one side, you automatically help out that of the other."[29] Ask the famed philosopher and theologian Alfred North Whitehead: "The absolute pacifist is a bad citizen; times come when force must be used to uphold right, justice and ideals."[30] When things get worse than they are now—when there are more and more vicious wars to stop refugee flows, to acquire or protect resources, to turn economic disadvantage into military advantage—you will be called traitors and perhaps treated like traitors. You should get ready and get your people ready for that.

To me, the rot in the American empire goes all the way down, root and branch, infecting everything—and I think the Church, or at least part of it, should say so. Stick a shovel into the ground anywhere in this country and out of it pours blood and water. We know that forming people into disciples, in allowing God to use us in this important work, has been a contested and controversial matter from the beginning. We know that saying that Christians shouldn't kill people was and is an intensely unpopular thing in a culture that glories in killing—public killing, private killing, sport killing, vicarious killing, re-enacted killing, remote killing, fantasized killing, righteous killing, beautiful killing, revolutionary killing, patriotic killing, and more. If we insist on it, and name it publicly in the coming time of imperial decline and increasingly ugly politics courtesy of climate change, our profile may change from being out of step to being an irritation to be removed. If you think the Constitution will protect you, we need to have a separate conversation—it most definitely will not.

In the 1960s, the Christian theologian and lawyer William Stringfellow wrote a book whose title resonates well today. It was something of

28. Roosevelt, *Roosevelt, His Life, Meaning, and Messages*, 871.

29. Orwell, "Pacifism and the War," 419.

30. Whitehead and Price, *Dialogues of Alfred North Whitehead*, 93.

an autobiographical reflection about race and war in America, and he entitled it *My People Is the Enemy*.[31] Like it or not, most of our country's population is an enemy of the gospel—and we are too, despite our desires to be otherwise. Most people can rattle off a list of warlike, jingoistic nations in world history without a lot of trouble—Sparta, the Mongols, Prussia, Nazi Germany, imperial Japan, and more—but who in this country would put the United States itself on that list other than a few fringe people? The United States has been at war, broadly defined, for 90 percent of its existence;[32] it lionizes military power and worships weaponry and glorifies its bloody past and present as much as any country ever has. To preach the gospel, to say that Christians shouldn't kill people—hell, to say that just-war people shouldn't kill on behalf of this empire—is to invite the ever-present charge of treason. And we have so much work to do, so much nationalist theology to undo. Ours is a country whose "Christianity" is so cosmetic that the president who dropped atomic bombs on civilians could declare with a straight face that the United States government is guided by the Sermon on the Mount. He said this twice, in a span of eight months, which was too much even for the liberal Christian patriotism of the *Christian Century*, who asked whether President Truman had read the Sermon recently.[33] For a more recent taste of how effective has been the Christian influence on the American empire, just a few weeks ago, the *Bulletin of the Atomic Scientists* published a study that found that more than one-third of Americans would support a first-strike nuclear attack against North Korea even if that strike killed more than one million civilians.[34] My people is the enemy indeed, and refusing to kill in such a culture makes one a bad citizen.

The Church has tried and failed countless times throughout its history, and God has forgiven us, and the Holy Spirit has dusted us off and Jesus has beckoned us to start back on the Way. But some failures have been more devastating to the gospel than others. We are still paying for the Crusades, for the Inquisitions, for conquest and slavery and many of the most glaring failures—such have driven countless people of good will and integrity away from God and the Church. My fear is that unless it finds a way to repent of its love of the American empire, the death throes

31. Stringfellow, *My People Is the Enemy*.

32. Sirvent and Haiphong, *American Exceptionalism and American Innocence*, 5–6.

33. See "Editorial"; "Mr. Truman's Spiritual Blindness."

34. Haworth, "What Do Americans Really Think about Conflict with Nuclear North Korea?," 182.

of this empire will take what little remains of the Church's credibility with it, to the detriment of the people who follow after us. It does us no good to sit secure in knowing that the Church will survive our own apostasy in the winding down of America, for, as I said earlier, we are also under orders not to put stumbling blocks in front of people who otherwise believe or could believe in Christ.

A long time ago, at the beginning of this talk, I mentioned how the founders of the American enterprise had a knack for drawing the wrong lessons from our scriptural legacy. I see one more ahead, one more image from the Bible that may come to describe the last days of America. I refer to the story of one of the Bible "heroes" whose story was fed to children like me and before me and after me—the story of one of Yahweh's mighty warriors who, in fact, was a ruthless and cunning killer, a vengeful and vain man who became leader of his people, one whose appetites and confidence led to his downfall and death. But not a quiet death, but rather a vengeful exit, taking thousands of people—more than he had killed in his entire bloody life—to their deaths alongside him.

This is Samson, and I see him as Uncle Sam's son. He is the heir to America. The American empire may well take much of the world down with it, like Samson between the pillars in the Philistines' temple. The Church should not help this modern-day Samson with whatever he does next—we have enough complicity for which to seek forgiveness and enough to do to find a better path along the Way.

CHAPTER 2

Send Lazarus to My Father's House: The Failure of US Catholicism as a Cautionary Tale for African Catholics

A lecture prepared for the Pan-African Catholic Congress, a first-of-its-kind gathering of church leaders from across the continent in December 2019. I was asked to explore what African Catholics might learn from the experience of Catholicism in the United States on matters of race and racism. The Congress modeled its exchanges around the "palaver method" of dialogue and interaction, emulating the traditional practices of village dialogue and communal reflection common in many parts of Africa. The proceedings have been gathered into three published volumes. More information on the Congress and its work can be found here: https://panafrican-theologyandpastoralnetwork.org/congress-2019/.

The Rich Man and Lazarus (Luke 16:19–31)

There was a rich man who was dressed in purple and fine linen and who feasted sumptuously every day. And at his gate lay a poor man named Lazarus, covered with sores, who longed to satisfy his hunger with what fell from the rich man's table; even the dogs would come and lick his sores. The poor man died and was carried away by the angels to be with Abraham. The rich man also died and was buried. In Hades, where he was being

> tormented, he looked up and saw Abraham far away with Lazarus by his side. He called out, "Father Abraham, have mercy on me, and send Lazarus to dip the tip of his finger in water and cool my tongue; for I am in agony in these flames." But Abraham said, "Child, remember that during your lifetime you received your good things, and Lazarus in like manner evil things; but now he is comforted here, and you are in agony. Besides all this, between you and us a great chasm has been fixed, so that those who might want to pass from here to you cannot do so, and no one can cross from there to us." He said, "Then, father, I beg you to send him to my father's house—for I have five brothers—that he may warn them, so that they will not also come into this place of torment." Abraham replied, "They have Moses and the prophets; they should listen to them." He said, "No, father Abraham; but if someone goes to them from the dead, they will repent." He said to him, "If they do not listen to Moses and the prophets, neither will they be convinced even if someone rises from the dead." (Luke 16:19–21 NRSV)

Introduction

The Catholic Church in the United States usually tells its story as one of triumph over adversity: having once been a despised group of outsiders, poor and marginalized and always under suspicion, it achieved social acceptance, positions of leadership and influence, and prosperity for most of its members. In the telling, it gives praise to the God who protected His Church, the steadfastness of its members, and the United States, where in His providence God created a land of freedom and a force for good in the world. Catholics in the United States now represent the single largest group of religious believers (larger than any Protestant denomination), are over-represented relative to population in the United States Congress and the United States Supreme Court, and are comfortably among the elite in corporate boardrooms, higher education, and civic and cultural life.

So compelling is this story that Catholics in the United States tell of themselves that it often occludes other, often less celebratory ways of narrating their past, present, and future. The story—usually told from the European immigrant experience—has been a powerful one, capable of absorbing the ugliness of indigenous genocide, the human breeding program that was racialized slavery, and an almost perpetual state of war against some peoples somewhere in the world. One would think such institutional atrocities past and present would render such a state unsuitable for Christian allegiance and loyalty—slave states and empires not self-evidently harmonious with the Prince of Peace and the incarnation of God murdered by an imperial slave state. On the contrary, that a political entity like the United States could change at all—however reluctantly and selectively—itself gets pressed into service as more proof of God's grace allowing the prodigal sinner to repent and return to the path of righteousness.

My contribution to our discussion is a modest one. I hope to bring some lessons from the inculturation and assimilation of Catholicism in the United States to my brothers and sisters in the faith in Africa. Far from being steps to be imitated, or a guide to replicating the success of American Catholicism, I offer instead a cautionary tale on inculturation and loyalties, and some reflections on not repeating the mistakes of the Church in the United States. I have never heard a sermon preached in the United States that situates the US Catholic Church as the rich man in Luke's parable—the successful insider condemned by his wealth and what it took to acquire it—but such seems appropriate for a discussion on the matters that concern us. Such is especially relevant when one considers what lessons might be derived from reflecting on American Catholicism, slavery, and race.

Inculturation as Ongoing

Far from being a settled matter, in the United States or across the African continent, inculturation is an ongoing process rather than a once-and-for-all achievement. The formation of human identities, allegiances, dispositions, affections, loyalties, and the like is a constant undertaking in which the Church is one actor—and not always the most powerful one—among many. States, economic actors, national and ethnic communities, political movements, and more all seek to shape who we are and whose we are. Inculturation does not end with the establishment of Africanized liturgies and personnel, just as it did not end in the United States with the creation of a thoroughly Americanized Catholicism with its own distinctive characteristics and nuances.

As is well known, concern for inculturation has been an enduring concern for Catholicism in Africa for decades, with institutional events of many sorts serving as benchmarks along the way. We have Pope John Paul II's statement in *Ecclesia in Africa* as one example:

> Just as in the Incarnation Christ assumed human nature in everything but sin, analogously through inculturation the Christian message assimilates the values of the society to which it proclaimed, rejecting whatever is marked by sin. To the extent that an ecclesial community can integrate the positive values of a specific culture, inculturation becomes an instrument by which the community opens itself to the riches of Christian holiness. An inculturation wisely carried out purifies and elevates the cultures of the various peoples.[1]

Similarly, Pope Benedict XVI reminded the world in *Africae Munus*:

> The Holy Spirit enables the Gospel to permeate all cultures, without becoming subservient to any. Bishops should be vigilant over this need for inculturation, respecting the norms established by the Church. By discerning which cultural elements and traditions are contrary to the Gospel, they will be able to separate the good seed from the weeds (cf. Mt 13:26).[2]

Inculturation as a process and a policy, as both theological and sociological, as a calling and a matter of contestation—such has been part of Christianity as the Way of Christ in the world since its inception. The spread of Christianity without a commitment to inculturation led to the evils of forced conversion, the imposition of cultural uniformity and Europeanization on the body of Christ worldwide, and the reduction of the gospel to a checklist of categories that elevated some peoples and cultures over others. Catholicism without inculturation is unworthy of the role Christ entrusted to the Church as the continuation of His ministry in the world, utterly incapable of being "a chosen race, a royal priesthood, a holy nation, God's own people, in order that you may proclaim the mighty acts of him who called you out of darkness into his marvelous light" (1 Pet 2:9 NRSV).

And yet, in ecclesial documents and most scholarly accounts, precious little attention has been given to inculturation done poorly or having been accommodated to the wrong values or wrong institutions or in ways antithetical to essential aspects of the gospel. While the major

1. John Paul II, *Ecclesia in Africa*, 87.
2. Benedict XVI, *Africae Munus*, 37.

documents contain the requisite cautions and disclaimers,[3] these documents also combine high levels of abstraction with assumptions that need to be demonstrated rather than assumed. The consequences of this are dangerous for the Church in each and every context, especially when one comes to accept that inculturation is not a once-and-for-all accomplishment, an achievement that once reached need no longer concern the present or future. Inculturation is always a matter of past, present, and future for a church that is essentially and irrevocably eschatological. And inculturation is always a political matter, always an arena of contestation.

Slavery, Racism, and US Catholicism: On Enculturating to the Wrong Things

What became the United States resulted from a process now known as settler colonialism, in which external actors displace the original inhabitants of a region and establish a new system and society. It differs from other types of colonialism, in which outsiders establish political control but leave much of a target region's population and society intact—soldiers, clerks, and ministers come from the colonial power, but not massive numbers of people seeking to displace indigenous communities in order to set up an altogether new polity by and for the newcomers only. While some sub-Saharan African countries underwent the settler-colonial type of invasion, the majority did not; ultimately, European settler colonialism failed in Africa.

But in the United States—as in Canada, Australia, New Zealand, Israel, Brazil, and other places—settler colonialism triumphed and remains in power. Settler colonialism in the United States combined ethnic cleansing—slaughter, displacement, forced assimilation, and dispossession—with human chattel slavery sufficient to exploit the massive amounts of land that speculators wanted to exploit. This combination—land to be settled and claimed, slavery to be enforced—gave rise to white supremacy as a material and ideological reality: a system based on the need for large numbers of people who could make effective the

3. See Benedict XVI, *Africae Munus,* 37: "By discerning which cultural elements and traditions are contrary to the Gospel, they will be able to separate the good seed from the weeds (cf. Mt 13:26)." See also John Paul II, *Ecclesia in Africa*, 62: John Paul II notes the African Bishops' conclusion that healthy inculturation requires "compatibility with the Christian message and communion with the universal church" and that "care must be taken to avoid syncretism."

dispossession of indigenous landholdings and large numbers of people with a vested interest in maintaining the permanent subjugation of a slave caste. The evolution of so-called racial science provided the underpinnings of white supremacy in the American settler colony—a system in which even the poorest of Europeans, having been displaced by early capitalist land expropriations, are given a place at the table in exchange for implementing and maintaining the structural wars against African slaves and indigenous communities.

The settler colony that became the United States was built on a near-universal consensus that white Protestantism was essential for building and sustaining this new "experiment in liberty"—one in which Catholicism was objectionable in every sense. Catholics pledged allegiance to a foreign monarch (the pope), so they could never be loyal to any other polity. They were people steeped in submissiveness and subordination and hence were unsuited for self-rule; they were superstitious idolaters for whom reason and enlightenment were implacable foes.

And yet, so great was the need for settlers who could occupy land and outnumber the slaves and provide even more labor for generating profits to capital that Catholics were granted entry—a process abetted by "borders" so porous that little could be done to stop those who came on their own, or so flexible as to be redrawn frequently and encapsulating previously Mexican communities or other Catholics in the process of military conquest and annexation. Catholicism could come to the United States, but only on terms set by rulers and rules designed to protect a racialized form of capitalism and a cultural ecology that affirmed it in every respect.

It remains no small irony that the papal justifications for the colonization of indigenous lands and the enslavement of Africans in the 1400s and 1500s (including *Dum Diversas* in 1452, *Romanus Pontifex* in 1454, Calixtus III's *Inter Caetera* in 1456, Alexander VI's *Inter Caetera* in 1493, and others) became central to the legal framework of law for the anti-Catholic United States of America. The secular legal justification for the dispossession of indigenous peoples built upon papal pronouncements in crafting the so-called "Doctrine of Discovery," even after those pronouncements had been modified, restricted, or superseded.[4] The United

4. Considerable disagreement exists between most indigenous communities and Catholic hierarchs about whether the Doctrine of Discovery remains in Church teaching and whether the pope or other Catholic leaders should issue a formal repudiation of it.

States Supreme Court relied on them in a series of decisions in the 1820s and 1830s that still stand, and the Doctrine of Discovery has been invoked to justify settler sovereignty over indigenous peoples ever since, as recently as 2005 in a decision written by Supreme Court "progressive" Ruth Bader Ginsberg.[5]

This is the original "inculturation" on offer to most of Catholicism in the United States: a conditional and partial access, with the need to prove one's compatibility with the settler project of the United States. Not a free and mutual exchange of gifts and cultural treasures, but a one-sided and power-laden ultimatum: our way or no way, take it or leave it.

Across the board, Catholic leaders in the United States took the offer. They chose to insist that Catholics embrace the United States with a degree of patriotism that would exceed that of the native born. If Catholics were suspect because of potentially divided loyalties—would they follow the pope or favor brother and sister Catholics elsewhere in the world, or would they give unquestioned loyalty to American leadership?—they would prove their nationalist credentials by killing their co-religionists as needed by the American state. They would prove that Catholics could be enthusiasts for capitalism just like their Protestant neighbors. And perhaps most decisively, in the inculturation that enabled and cemented all the rest, Catholics in the United States could and did embrace the racial ideology that secured the settler project in North America and the spread of the American empire around the world. All of this coalesced in something that, for lack of a better term, one might call US Catholic Nationalism.

> US Catholic Nationalism is used here to describe the ideological position that posits a harmony between living out one's Catholic religious convictions and the obligations of American citizenship and civic responsibility. More than positing a lack of conflict between religious and political loyalties, US Catholic Nationalism at its strongest maintains a special affinity between the two: the United States as the hope of the world, and the Church as the hope of the United States.[6]

I maintain that this sort of nationalism represents a temptation for the Church in all parts of the world. It is not limited by whether Catholics are a majority or minority, a senior partner in political life or a marginal

5. *City of Sherrill v. Oneida Indian Nation of New York*, 544 US 197 (2005).

6. Budde, *The Two Churches*, 74.

force. It remains a possibility for the Church regardless of the type of state or regime one encounters, whether that state is powerful or less so. As the great Jesuit Daniel Berrigan once observed:

> Every nation-state . . . tends toward the imperial: that is the point. Through banks, armies, secret police, propaganda, courts and jails, treaties, treasuries, taxes, laws and orders, myths of civil obedience, assumptions of virtue at the top.[7]

It is important to understand that the American identity on offer to Catholics in the nineteenth and twentieth centuries was very much a racialized one with a political economy and cultural ecology built upon stratifications and classifications that structured outcomes such that lower groups were exploited or excluded so that upper groups could enjoy long-term and self-sustaining advantages. One reason the American type of racialized capitalism has been so successful is that it has been remarkably adaptive; the meaning and contents of "race" have been fluid rather than static, and "inclusion" has meant different things at different times to different groups.

Scholars like David Roediger and Noel Ignatiev, among others, remind us about all the groups that used to fall outside the legal and cultural definitions of "white" in the United States as recently as the nineteenth and twentieth centuries—groups that included Italians, Irish, Greeks, Armenians, Hungarians, Serbians, Slovenians, Poles, Jews, Montenegrins, Croatians, Russians, Bulgarians, Czechs, Slovaks, and more.[8] The most absurd example, in my view, from the not-too-distant past was an attempt during the Depression to have Finns—people from Finland—in Minnesota defined as non-white and hence ineligible for citizenship. The argument was that Finns—because these were left-wing Finns interested in labor unions and anarchism—weren't really Scandinavian but, in fact, were derived from "Mongolian" ancestry and, thus, could be treated legally in the same categories as low-class reprobates like Native Americans.[9]

What this meant in practice was that Catholic immigrants from marginalized groups could and did improve their condition by embracing the racist tenets of the American system—they could "move

7. Berrigan, *The Nightmare of God*, 25.

8. Roediger, *Working Toward Whiteness*, 61; more generally, see Ignatiev, *How the Irish Became White*.

9. Roediger, *Working*, 61.

up" by becoming "white" as seen by the state and society, by affirming and incarnating the anti-blackness that sustained the entire edifice. No clearer example of such a transaction exists than the evolution of the Irish Catholics—who by the twentieth century had become stereotypical in their hostility toward the integration of white neighborhoods and white Catholic parishes. How far the Irish had come from their initial dispositions early in the 1800s, when many Irish groups proclaimed solidarity with enslaved Africans, seeing in their plight a copy of what the Irish had endured under the ruthlessness of British imperial rule of their homeland. Irish Americans supported and hosted people like Frederick Douglass in the 1840s; a century later, the descendants of those immigrants threw bricks and stones at Martin Luther King Jr. One sees similar dynamics among Italian immigrants to the United States, who earned "whiteness" slowly over time, and often at the expense of their African-American neighbors.[10]

While some students of race and law in the United States describe it as a system of "white supremacy," I find it more helpful to describe the system as one of "anti-blackness."[11] The latter is more adequate, I suggest, because it captures the extent to which non-white ethnic and cultural groups can and do improve their social positioning by embracing the notion that persons of African descent rightly constitute the bottom of the social and economic structure. One can be non-white but still superior to black people, and one can embrace and advance in the American system by affirming and enacting the laws and ideas that put black people at the bottom politically, economically, and culturally. One need not be white to prosper in the settler state of America—one need only be not-black. Such accords well with deeply rooted anti-black ideologies that exist throughout Latin America and Asia.[12]

So many of the fruits of having embraced the United States fully and unreservedly are contrary to any non-trivial sense of Christian discipleship. American Catholics throughout their history have supported and embraced the dispossession of indigenous peoples and their cultures. Catholics have embraced American imperialism with nary a second thought. The enthusiasm with which Catholics in the United States worship their nation's military power and ideology of power represents a

10. Staples, "How Italians Became White."

11. For one articulation, see Grimes, *Christ Divided*.

12. On Latin America, for example, see Gates, *Blacks in Latin America*.

form of idolatry that they identify easily when viewing other militaristic cultures (e.g., the Soviet Union, Nazi Germany) but are utterly incapable of recognizing in themselves. Having joined Catholicism and Americanism so thoroughly, it is little wonder that a majority of white Catholics voted for the sociopathic champion of predatory capitalism that is Donald Trump, who (protests to the contrary notwithstanding) may represent the coming to fruition of all the pathologies that have structured American history since its founding as a settler colony built on slavery.

I have painted an unreservedly dark picture for you, in large part because the propagandized version of America and its history still holds disproportionate sway—perhaps not with people outside its borders, but certainly among its domestic population. Those Catholics who opposed the absorption of Catholicism into Americanism—be it on matters of war, racism, capitalism, or conquest—deserve more attention than can be afforded in this brief contribution. From this too-abbreviated sketch, what message might the Rich Man of world Catholicism send to its brothers and sisters on the continent, were the Rich Man ever to repent of his shaving down of the gospel to fit the imperatives of the American Empire? I offer the following for your consideration.

From the Rich Man to His Brothers (and Sisters)

1. *Beware the Temptation of Nationalism*

Despite its universality in modernity, nationalism is a largely underdeveloped category in Catholic theological history.[13] No matter whether one discusses nationalism or patriotism (the latter often presented as a more benign and healthy version of the phenomenon), the Church embraces allegiance to a particular people or state at its own peril. The demands for allegiance required by nations or other so-called natural communities are strong and brook no rivals.[14] States, nations, ethnic communities, and other collective identities make demands on Christians that they should not always accommodate—most notably, demands to kill for the collective when it orders it. States as institutions are intrinsically violent

13. For some recent explorations, see Llywelyn, *Toward a Catholic Theology of Nationalism*; Budde, *The Borders of Baptism*; and Budde, *Beyond the Borders of Baptism*.

14. The literature on the constructed nature of nationhood and national identity is extensive; see, for example, Anderson, *Imagined Communities*; Smith, *Stories of Peoplehood*; Marx, *Faith in Nation*.

creatures and embracing them uncritically leads the Church into places it should not go.

2. Christendom Takes Many Forms

The history of Catholicism in the US demonstrates that one can still enact a form of Christendom even without formal religious establishment—indeed, without even being the dominant religious institution. American Catholicism effected a partnership of church and empire in which the mission of the Church became synonymous with protecting and extending the power of the empire, even in the presence of constitutional barriers between religious institutions and the structures of the state. Unlike many of our Orthodox brothers and sisters, I do not see the Church as a natural partner of empire, nor do I see the desirability of a Christian empire; the idea of *symphonia*, a partnership between church and state to advance the common good, has almost always meant the subordination of the gospel to the imperatives of state. The Church in Africa has been asked to take on many roles in relation to the nation-states of the continent; the American experience illustrates the ease with which the gospel becomes compromised by the state, even (or especially) during times of state breakdown or dysfunction. What is often described as "partnership" or being a "critical partner" with ruling institutions usually becomes something else, usually to the detriment of the gospel.

3. Racism Is Never Just about Race

Western imperialism has used racial stratification to help organize so many different aspects of life that disentangling them from one another is a daunting proposition. Even in places where white supremacy or anti-black ideology is thought not to hold sway, race continues to structure the operations of capitalism, state action, transnational organizations, and more. Places like the United States cemented a variety of capitalism in which racialization was essential to the construction and subordination of categories of vulnerable laborers, undermined solidarity among working people by playing racialized groups against one another, and employed selective incorporation into privileged "white" society in order to forestall challenges to property regimes and other systems of domination. In all of this, the Church through its history mostly deferred to the categories on offer as "natural" or outside the range of Christian critique; when it did speak against the worst manifestations of such, it often did so in ways that were so anodyne and cautious as to be irrelevant.

4. *Law Is Not a Neutral Technology*

In parts of the world where institutional corruption undermines nearly all areas of life, one may not want to hear that the "rule of law" or "law and order" may be goals that corrode the prophetic witness of the Church. Nevertheless, the experience of Christians in the United States gives evidence that the law remains an instrument designed for the self-preservation of the modern state and the political economy of capitalism. To the extent that these have presupposed and required the subordination of black bodies and lives for the past five centuries, so it is that the instruments of law circumscribe the good to be done even when persons of good will are the ones with their hands on the levers of power. The law will not abolish capitalism, nor will it put into jeopardy the self-preservation of the state that gives life to the law; given that capitalism and the state system require racism and economic subordination of the majority, law will stop short or frustrate those who attempt to use it in ways that conflict with its essentials.

This is a hard lesson to explore with Catholic thinkers. It may be necessary to put aside the Thomistic categories of law, or at least relax the assumption that these have purchase in the contemporary era. The history of Christian reformers who have assumed power in the United States and Europe seems to suggest that the system dilutes and castrates the gospel more than the gospel revolutionizes the operations of collective action and social power.

5. *Sowing Nationalism/Patriotism Leads to a Bitter Harvest*

The enthusiastic embrace that Catholic bishops, clergy, and lay people have given to "America" over the centuries has created a Catholic laity that is more deeply formed by American ideology than by the Sermon on the Mount (what Pope John Paul II described as the "Magna Carta" of Christian life). Catholic Americans are more deeply American than they are Catholic—in political ideology, in economic values, in racial socialization, and more. While much attention has been given to the collapse of Christian formation efforts in the contemporary era—and the inability of Christian communities to help newcomers and newer generations into the life of Christ—most of the scholarly literature sees the Catholic Church as the poster child for failed formation in the United States.[15]

What this has meant, among other things, is that Church leaders are afraid to confront lay Catholics with the sinfulness of their own practices, ideologies, and commitments. Having squandered their moral capital on corrupt deals with the devil with the Republican Party regarding the abortion issue and having failed so broadly on addressing sexual abuse by church personnel, the bishops are ignored when they do address matters within their competence. But rather than challenge white Catholics on the realities of white supremacy, and rather than challenge all American Catholics on the incompatibility of the gospel with American empire, the bishops sequester themselves behind reformist lobbying efforts, inoffensive and desperately apolitical statements on public issues, and laughable appeals to the "common good" in a context in which the common good does not exist because the interests of power do not (and cannot) correspond with the needs and legitimate claims of the poor and marginalized. As a result, the culture of race and empire continue to form American Catholics more deeply and determinatively than does the water of baptism or the reception of the Eucharist.

6. *More White than Catholic?*

Although reminders of the worldwide character of Catholicism surround the Church in the United States—from imported clergy to refugees—in too many ways the Catholic community remains a white community in perception and practice. This manifests itself in a variety of ways, none more clearly than in its treatment of African-American Catholics.

Black Catholics in the United States have long been neglected, mistreated, or ignored by the rest of the Catholic community, much of which is unaware that there are African-American Catholics to begin with. While black Catholics comprise a relatively small percentage of American Catholicism (approximately 5 percent), as a group the three million black Catholics in the United States would be the second-largest "denomination" of African-American Christians were they compared to other black Christian traditions in the United States (smaller than the

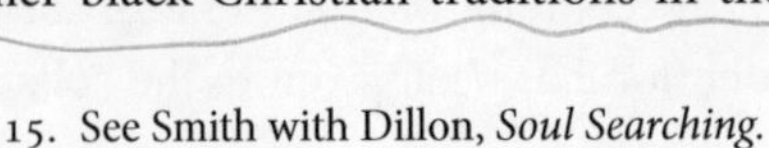

15. See Smith with Dillon, *Soul Searching.*

Pentecostal Church of God in Christ, but larger than denominations of black Methodists, Baptists, and other groups; indeed, there are more black Catholics than there are Episcopalians or Presbyterians of all races in the US).

Despite the presence in North America of black Catholics predating the "official" establishment of slavery in 1619, Catholics of African heritage have suffered enslavement, exclusion, segregation, hatred, neglect, and studied ignorance at the hands of the white Catholic majority. Where they once were shunted into all-black congregations and excluded from white ones, African-American Catholics nowadays have seen their distinctive parishes—in which they were able to develop and express their own traditions of worship, pastoral life, and social engagement—closed, their people dispersed and their cultures diluted by being forced into larger congregations in which black culture is mostly irrelevant. Even though black Catholics are more engaged with the faith by many conventional measures (church attendance, adherence to Catholic doctrine, etc.)[16] than are their white co-religionists, white (and now Latino) practices and norms dominate parish life. And the tradition of black Catholic commitment to social justice and anti-racism work seems not all relevant to the 59 percent of white Catholic voters who supported Donald Trump, certainly the most overtly racist American president since Woodrow Wilson.

As a barometer for measuring the real state of Catholicism and racism in the United States, the Church's treatment of its black Catholic members is useful, illuminating, and sobering. The gap between rhetoric and practice is large and shows few signs of shrinking.

7. Do Not Dismember the Body of Christ

It is no small irony that white supremacy, the modern state system, and the political economy of capitalism—arguably, three of the most powerful transnational forces of modernity—have succeeded in large part by dismembering the transnational quality of the Catholic Church. The rise of capitalism and nationalism in Europe both required and enabled the sundering of effective ties among Catholic communities around the world, to the extent that Catholic life and practice came to see national "Catholicisms" as normative rather than simply descriptive—that is, that

16. See Davis and Pope-Davis, *Perseverance in the Parish?*

"French" Catholicism is distinct and separate from "German" Catholicism, which in turn has only symbolic or inessential links with "American" or "Canadian" Catholicism.

When Pope Gregory finally spoke against the slave trade in 1839 (in *In Supreme Apostotalus*), after consultation with the College of Cardinals, he also denounced the institution of slavery itself. The response of the Catholic bishops in the United States was to deny (based on the English-language translation of a single word from Latin) that the condemnation was relevant to the practice of slavery in the United States, which had nominally outlawed the importation of slaves in 1808 (a law widely flouted since its inception). Led by Bishop John England of South Carolina, the US bishops claimed that the US experience of domestic slavery—which by then was sustained and expanded by large-scale breeding programs, selling off of children, and the breaking up of families—was not condemned and that Catholics need not oppose the institution. The US bishops met in council nine times between 1829 and 1849, and slavery went undiscussed—indeed, they did not speak on it at all before the Civil War of 1862–65.[17] The leadership of the Catholic Church chose to protect their position in the United States rather than stand with the pope and Catholic leaders elsewhere in opposing the buying and selling of human beings.

Make no mistake here: this is not an argument against rooting the Church in the myriad of local contexts, situations, and stories of the peoples of the world. Rather, it is a recognition that the powerful identity-forming capacities of nation and race have created a world in which US Catholics can kill Catholics in Central America without it being an outrage against their common baptism and membership in the one body of Christ. It means that Catholics in Rwanda and Burundi, Congo, and South Sudan can kill one another in the name of presumptively deeper and more important loyalties than to the one Prince of Peace. This should be a scandal in the Christian world, an embarrassment that cries to heaven.

To be clear, I do not think that Christians should kill anyone. But there is an additional level of distortion when Christians kill one another, a perversion of the sacraments and the idea of the Church as Mother to all. Race has been crucial in forming the national allegiances now assumed by all to be more important than one's membership in the worldwide

17. Capizzi, "For What Shall We Repent?," 783–84.

Church. Bear in mind that the deification of citizenship operates even where race plays no discernible role in constructing ideas of nationhood or political community. Citizenship by definition is as much a matter of exclusion as inclusion, a map of what groups may be treated less well than others; and for whom you will be expected to set aside Christian convictions in service of the political kingdom.

8. The End of Empire and Hope for Repentance

By most measures, the American empire has entered into a period of decline—economically, culturally, and diplomatically. What remains preeminent, alas, is its unmatched military machine—a network of more than seven hundred overseas bases, perhaps hundreds of secret deployments (including a rapidly rising number across Africa), and a military budget larger than the next seven countries combined. As the United States seeks to address its other weaknesses with ever-frequent military responses, especially given the multiple manifestations of climate change and resource conflicts, Catholics in the United States will again be expected to support the regime at all costs and against all rivals—especially the poor, the displaced, the refugees, and the vulnerable.

Given its history and allegiance to the United States, Catholics in the United States need fraternal correction from their brothers and sisters in the faith from around the world. Catholics in Africa and elsewhere can and should call upon their co-religionists to put their baptismal identity before their national citizenship. Despite the presence of significant numbers of poor and non-white Catholics in their midst, the Catholic Church in the United States may be incapable of reforming itself. It needs to be challenged, confronted, exhorted, encouraged, and inspired by those whose life of discipleship presents an alternative to the sort of political chaplaincy that has enfeebled the gospel in the United States, turning it into a tepid reformism that ignores structures of oppression. In this, you will be fulfilling Jesus' desire that a wayward member of the fellowship receive fraternal correction from brothers and sisters in the faith, so that the errant will repent of error and return to the true path (Matt 18:15–19). By doing so, you will be showing that death does not have the last word, and that truth can prevail even over the most entrenched of sinfulness.

CHAPTER 3

Killing with Kindness: Can a Plague Cure a Plague?

A lecture delivered May 4, 2019, for the 2019 World Catholicism Week conference, Put Away Your Sword: Gospel Nonviolence in a Violent World, sponsored by the Center for World Catholicism and Intercultural Theology (CWCIT) at DePaul University in Chicago. Information on CWCIT can be found here: http://cwcit.depaul.edu.

A revolution is interesting to the extent that it avoids
like the plague the plague it promised to heal.

—DANIEL BERRIGAN

Introduction

The world's been a mess for so long that it's understandable if you missed or have forgotten about one atrocity among others. On November 27, a report was made public—it spoke of the near-complete slaughter of a religious minority population yet again in the Middle East. These civilians had been attacked and plundered wholesale, and as one account summarized, "many had been brutally murdered; others had been taken prisoner and carried off into captivity."

These atrocities were designed to horrify and frighten people worldwide. The report continues: "When they feel like inflicting a truly painful death on some they pierce their navels, pull out the end of their intestines, tie them to a pole and whip them until, all their bowels pulled out, they fall lifeless to the ground . . . [For other victims, the attackers] see if they can manage to hack off their heads with one blow." The report continues by describing "the appalling treatment of women" with sexual assault practiced on a large scale

Massive human rights violations, ethnic cleansing underway, the systematic use of rape and torture against civilians—in the face of these crimes against humanity, the question of humanitarian intervention arises: whether to send soldiers into lands controlled nominally by another sovereign to put a stop to wholesale slaughter as quickly as possible. For many Christian ethicists, from a variety of traditions and regions, supporters of Christian pacifism and just-war traditions alike—for nearly everyone, in other words—the general presumptions against war and violence can and should be set aside. In such extreme circumstances, the protection of the innocent trumps the sovereignty of states under international law, as well as the explicit prohibition on killing found in the Gospel accounts of Jesus. Many of us here, I suspect, would share in the sense that given large-scale atrocities like this, using the military as a last resort to protect the innocent is an act of Christian love that we can endorse—such are the lessons of Rwanda, of ISIS, and countless other places. Many of us would support an armed intervention to protect civilians threatened by the atrocities just described.

The report in question became public on November 27, but you're excused if you missed it. It arrived on November 27, in the year 1095. In this case, support for humanitarian intervention endorsed the First Crusade, which sent a force of eighty thousand people to rescue persons being killed and endangered by Turkish soldiers as they engaged in conquest throughout what is now known as the Middle East. You may or may not find yourself echoing the affirmation of "Deus Vult!"—God wills it!—that issued from the crowd that heard Pope Urban II call for this rescue mission; you may not be encouraged by the pope's response back to them: "Let that be a war cry for you in battle because it came from God. When you mass together to attack the enemy, this cry sent by God will be the cry of all—'God wills it! God wills it!'"[1]

1. Frankopan, *The First Crusades,* 2, 8, 28.

I start with the Crusades not to complicate matters beyond clarity, but to remind us all that we as Christians have been here before. Amid the contemporary debates about using force to protect the innocent—to set aside our sense that following Jesus is incompatible with being a killer—it is important to provide a larger context than one beholden to the urgency and immediacy of contemporary examples and imperatives. And I start with this example not to impugn the intentions of those among my brothers and sisters whose Christian convictions lead them to support the constellation of practices and norms now known as the Responsibility to Protect (R2P). And it is not to agree with the killers in Al-Qaida and Boko Haram that by definition any military move against them constitutes another "crusade" or war of Christian military aggression. I start here, as I said, to remind us that we have been here before.

R2P and the Need to Be Realistic

I will spare you the background on the development of R2P doctrine and advocacy, which seems to be a requisite part of most presentations in the field. I am aware, and you should be aware, that R2P as a set of norms and as codified in international bodies like the United Nations is about much more than the use of military force. Indeed, the architects of R2P went to great lengths to add a host of preventative measures (and post-conflict policies) to responses to atrocities across borders in an attempt to distance the new norms from "humanitarian intervention," an earlier set of ideas and practices now suffering from public-relations problems of various sorts. I take these distinctions seriously and appreciate the attempt to make the use of lethal force only one tool in the box, and hopefully not the first one seized; these pre- and post-conflict imperatives are not without their own problems, but such is best left for another time.[2]

Instead, I will focus on how Christians as members of the body of Christ—as Christians, in other words—ought to think and act in response to calls for the use of lethal force to protect persons being victimized or threatened with large-scale crimes against humanity. Many of the normative and descriptive assumptions attendant to R2P are reflected in, and have been taken up by, some significant emerging Christian theological frameworks. These include those schools of thought and practice that

2. See, for example, Pandolfi, "From Paradox to Paradigm," 153–72.

are known as Just Peacemaking, Just Policing, and others.[3] I take these approaches seriously, both because I know the people developing them are persons of good will and because they are serious attempts to think Christian-ly about the difficult issues involved in using lethal force to protect innocent communities around the world.

Some of these efforts represent an attempt to apply a stringent version of just-war theory to attempts to prevent or stop crimes against humanity where the in-place state is unable or unwilling to do so.[4] It is also the case that some scholars argue for the disconnect and incompatibility between just war theory and R2P.[5] I respect those who have developed Just Peacemaking or Just Policing (for present purposes, I use the terms interchangeably, although I am aware they are not identical), but I do not endorse their conclusions. Some of these approaches build upon a distinction between military action and the "police function," with the latter being more compatible with a thoroughgoing Christian commitment to nonviolence.[6] I find this distinction to be untenable on historical grounds, but I can only note rather than defend my position given the limits of this essay. As much as I might want to find a way to fit some measure of lethal means into the Christian love due to neighbors and to enemies, I do not believe such should be done.

Persons like me, who insist that Jesus meant what He said in the Sermon on the Mount and elsewhere, that Christians shouldn't kill people even in a good cause, are generally regarded as unrealistic, detached from the realities of suffering and oppression in the world, and putting abstract purity of principle over the flesh-and-blood needs of the most vulnerable in society—leaving them to the wolves, in other words. One needs a bracing dose of realism, grounded in the experiences of at-risk others, lest abstract principle lead to the death of others.

3. Some leading spokespersons in these areas of Christian ethics attempt to distinguish R2P from their preferred frameworks, while others note the complementarity among frameworks. See, for example, Schlabach, "Just Policing, Responsibility to Protect," 73–88; Winright, "Just Policing," 84–95.

4. See, for example, Himes, "Just War," 10–15, 28–31; Hoppe, "Just Peace," 68–76; Schlabach, *Just Policing, Not War*; Winright and Johnston, *Can War Be Just in the Twenty-First Century?*

5. See Friberg-Fernros, "Allies in Tension," 160–73.

6. See Schlabach, "Practicing for Just Policing," 93–110; Schlabach, "Just the Police Function, Then," 50–60.

I take such claims seriously. In that spirit, let me start with a few realistic assertions that, for reasons of time, I am only able to mention rather than defend in the time at hand.

Here is some realism to consider:

- State actors (those whom we hope will listen to our talk about ethical limits on military action—before, during, and after) mostly don't give a damn about our ethics when the chips are down. Christian or semi-Christian ethics may be a public-relations card they can play when doing so is relative low-cost in terms of losses, but our ethical niceties will go the way of innocent civilians in Dresden, Nagasaki, Tokyo, and the rice paddies of Vietnam. If you have doubts, read Nick Turse's book *Kill Anything That Moves* for one set of cases.[7] The distinctions and discriminations made by Christians do not and will not materially shift the decisions made by persons engaged in military invasions. Theologians may call for higher-risk approaches to war, their aim being to minimize noncombatant deaths, for example, but these have been and will be overruled when the costs to intervenors threatens to exceed a fairly limited threshold, or one's comrades in arms are endangered.
- Military adventures, including those conducted under R2P auspices, will happen or not independent of what Christian leaders decide. Christianity hasn't been able to stop powerful countries from going to war in many centuries (some minor border disputes notwithstanding), and humanitarian invasions won't be launched or prevented to placate the demands of the churches. We have next to no influence in these arenas. To think otherwise is delusional. Whatever notions of justice, punishment, or compassion may be practiced by state actors in this area do not need Christian approval or grounding. In this area as in others, it's clear that the Christian tradition adds nothing much that secular states need in conducting their business.
- There have been some gains made in the area of gospel nonviolence in the past century—the delegitimation of war as an acceptable part of ordinary statecraft; opposition to some classes of tactics and weapons; the acceptance of conscientious objection; the elevation of Christian pacifism as a defensible position in the Church—but

7. Turse, *Kill Anything That Moves.*

whatever these gains and whatever advances one hopes to see in the future may well be wiped out should Christians endorse the use of killing in the "limited" and "constrained" contexts described in R2P and its theological cousins. The world will certainly see more wars in the years ahead as state actors worldwide are pressed upon by environmental collapse, mass expulsions of people, resource scarcities, and the like; military experts worldwide are building such assumptions into their strategic plans. More and more of these wars will be labeled as R2P occasions, inasmuch as such may be easier to sell to domestic and international audiences than are wars for water, for oil, for land (although one can envision interventions justified by invoking a "responsibility to protect" certain ecologically significant areas when such is in the interest of one or more powerful states). What look like rare cases today are likely to become more common in the future; should it sign on to these ventures, the Church will again be tarred with the brush of religiously sanctioned killing, and the gospel will be shown to be a sham yet again.

- R2P and its theological cousins presuppose the moral significance of scale: there is some magnitude of suffering and death sufficient to impel Christians to set aside their qualms about killing. The immediacy of threats to vulnerable populations further adds to the moral calculus—thousands, perhaps tens or hundreds of thousands, will suffer and die unless you bless the use of force. Afterward, however, the accounting may not be so simple. To whose account, for example, should one charge the 250,000 persons dead in Libya after the "successful" R2P intervention and overthrow of the Qadaffi regime?[8] Further, if protecting the vulnerable is the path by which the Church takes up arms, it may also be the path that leads to a renewed militarization of Christianity and more weaponized religion in the world. How does the moral calculus shift if the casualty count includes not only those at risk unless Christians kill to save them, but also those killed in later wars that the Church was powerless to resist, having already conceded the point to secular actors? Who will speak for those killed in later wars, who may have been spared had the Church not lost its moral credibility by blessing the kinder, gentler forms of war promised by R2P defenders?

8. See Davies, "Calculating the Millions-High Death Toll."

- There will always be actors and institutions that build some semblance of order using violence and coercion, but nowhere in the New Testament does it say that Christians have to help build or enhance the formal institutions of violent order-keeping—neither Romans 13 nor 1 Peter 2:13–17 nor anywhere else. Lethality-created order is like the weather: it's going to be here whether you like it or not, and sometimes—like a rainstorm that generates a flood, which can renew the soil—some good can come from it by the grace of God. It doesn't follow from that, however, that Christians are under an obligation to make the flooding more powerful, or to wash away one's enemies, just because these things happen sometimes on their own.
- Despite its obvious emotional appeal, upon inspection it is not obvious that the refusal of Christians to use lethal force to kill persons who are killing innocent persons is the same as being responsible for the death of those innocent persons. Such an assertion is more akin to gangster ethics—if you don't give me what I want, I'm going to kill this hostage and it will be your fault—than an unassailable chain of responsibility. By this logic, as Craig Watts notes, if the refusal of pacifists to take up arms in the name of rescuing certain innocent people is the ethical equivalent of killing them, then it must be conceded that everyone who has neglected to act in a way that could conceivably save someone's life anywhere is the ethical equivalent of a killer.[9]

Given the limits of space, here is what I will not do. For the most part, I will not develop some of the most important secular criticisms of R2P, even though I find them persuasive for the most part. These include:

1. the extent to which military interventions to "protect" at-risk populations have been the justification for colonial, neocolonial, and expansionist military attacks on weaker countries;
2. the degree to which R2P operates as an asymmetrical force in the modern world, a privilege held by the powerful and not the less powerful;
3. the impossibility of limiting the use of force in R2P adventures, or for managing the outcomes in ways that deliver on promises made. For example, despite protests to the contrary, it seems that one

9. Watts, "Just War, Pacifism, and the Ethics of Protection," 39.

cannot protect internal populations from a despotic regime without engaging in "regime change"—the disavowal of "regime change" is an important part of current R2P advocacy, in order that the use of force is seen as limited in scope and ambitions; and

4. the degree to which R2P extends and masks the intrinsic violence of liberalism as a system of political economy, and the dubious nature of distinctions its theological defenders make between war-making and (the presumably more benign) phenomenon of policing.

Additionally, I will presume for the moment that one is familiar with those parts of the scriptural tradition that point most directly toward the illegitimacy of lethal force employed by followers of Jesus. While such are important, by themselves they provide an incomplete sense of things. One needs to venture into the deeper waters of ecclesiology and eschatology to get a deeper sense of why lethality and Christian discipleship remain incompatible with one another. We lack time for this at present.[10] Instead, I want to examine only one feature of the theological case in favor of R2P—one shared by most theologians, even if not explored as deeply as some others.

The Importance of Right Intention

Christian advocates of R2P, just policing, and just peacemaking continue to make reference to St. Augustine as part of the project to defend military force as part of peacemaking or police functions.[11] While many of his criteria have received considerable attention—legitimate authority, proportionality, and last resort, for example—I want to draw attention to one feature that receives relatively little attention in the theological reflections on just war as it relates to R2P—namely, the matter of right intention.

Lest anyone feel that focusing on one aspect only of just-war theology is a poor test of the framework—getting four out of five or five out of six should be good enough, for instance—I am following the guidance of some of the best contemporary advocates of the tradition. Tobias Winright, for example, speaks for many who describe themselves as "strict

10. For one exploration, see the following chapter in this book on eschatology and ecclesiology.

11. I am aware that just-war thinking admits of several formulations and articulations and that what is emphasized in one may be muted in another.

constructionist" in their approach. Each criterion must be met, and one must be willing to reject a proposed course of warfare if all of the obligations of just war theory are not met. This is to take things beyond a "minimal or negative checklist" approach, serving instead "along the lines of a discipline that involves commitments, duties, and virtues as well as categories, criteria, and principles."[12]

Augustine's most famous passage on the matter, in which he claims that death and killing in warfare are not the worst things that can happen to a Christian, appears in *Contra Faustum Manichaeum*. It's often referred to as *Quid culpatur*:

> For what is culpable in warfare? Is it because some men, who will die anyway, are killed so that others may be tamed to live in peace? This censure is one of cowardly, not conscientious men. The desire to harm, the cruelty of vengeance, warlike and implacable intention, ferocity of rebellion, lust for domination, and similar motives, these are what are culpable in warfare.[13]

Not only does Augustine place intention and one's interior disposition at the center of whether war is just—or is simply murder—this move shapes what he does with the injunctions against violence in the Gospels (e.g., "do not resist evil," Matt 5:39; "turn the other cheek," Luke 6:29). These commands of Jesus are to be observed only in one's heart, only in one's intention and attitude toward one's adversaries. Killing can be an act of charity, and torture can be an expression of corrective love. As one commentator summarizes Augustine:

> Now the intention rather than the hostile act itself becomes the criterion of righteous warfare. Practically any hostile act was justifiable provided it was motivated by love. The good Christian could suffer injury and yet retaliate, could love his enemy and yet kill him, both forgive and punish him. The evangelical precepts were transformed so that love was no longer an inhibition on warfare. In some cases, it even necessitated it.[14]

So central is intentionality to Augustine's understanding of just war that crusading warfare—war ordered by divine command, an aggressive warfare to avenge offenses against God—is valid because such is fought without the will to power, and with a properly ordered sense of love and

12. Winright, *Can War Be Just in the Twenty-First Century?*, xx.
13. Augustine, *Contra Faustum Manichaeum* XXIII.74.
14. Russell, "Love and Hate in Medieval Warfare," 111–12.

internal disposition.[15] Those who build upon Augustine's just-war thinking in crafting maxims of just policing and just peacemaking reaffirm the importance of intentionality in their theological projects.[16]

The matter of war making with love in one's heart strikes modern people as curious, if not downright nonsensical. And in fact, some contemporary defenders of just-war theory radically circumscribe this notion of love in battle by elevating the notion of "callousness," a necessary "military virtue," needed alongside love toward one's target.[17] Yet Augustine's idea of intentionality is crucial if one is to maintain that just-war making or peacemaking is to be something consistent with Christian convictions, and not merely an ideological window dressing provided for the dirty secular business of human slaughter. The need to create and sustain the virtue of love would seem to be even more important in the context of just policing or just peacemaking, in which deployed personnel are meant to operate with greater limits and restrictions than are operant in all-out warfare.

Lethal Means and the Means at Hand

Which raises a critical and unevenly explored question: Who will be the agents of lethal force employed in matters of Christianly-inflected R2P and protection of the vulnerable? What institutions will provide these agents, and how have they been trained, socialized, and formed into the attitudes, dispositions, and convictions necessary to be efficient soldiers?

In some formulations, the agents of military intervention are to come from the United Nations, or from some other multistate institution like the African Union, or from regional security organizations. In reality, of course, national military institutions are the primary means of deploying military force, even for groups like the UN or African Union, who do not have their own military forces but instead rely on units loaned to them by member states (the latter is attempting to construct its own forces, the so-called "African Standby Force"). These are the institutions

15. Russel, "Love and Hate in Medieval Warfare," 113–14.

16. Schlabach, *Just Policing, Not War,* 75; "Schlabach, "Practicing for Just Policing," 95; Pfeil, "Whose Justice?," 115, 127.

17. Biggar, *In Defence of War*, 148; see also O'Driscoll, "The Heart of the Matter," 273–79.

that will be charged with acting with right intention and love in the process of exerting lethal force on behalf of at-risk persons around the world.

And these institutions—national or multilateral—have their own ideas about intentionality, and about the formation and socialization necessary to create soldiers. These priorities predate the ideas of humanitarian interventionists and R2P advocates and take priority over whatever formation of persons one might want to see for just-peace interventionary military forces. Foremost for modern military institutions is the formation of young people into efficient killers—people able and willing to kill upon the orders of others, to kill on their own initiative, and to do so under stressful conditions. On one level, this is a statement of staggering banality—of course soldiering requires teaching people how to kill—it's the job description. On another level, however, the matter is nowhere near as straightforward or obvious as it may appear.

In fact, conventional wisdom notwithstanding, it is very difficult to compel most people to kill other people. It's a problem that has occupied the best of military minds, of military psychologists, for decades, even centuries—contrary to the stereotypes, there seems to be a deeply ingrained aversion to killing another human being, even in conditions of combat and self-defense.

Some of you are familiar with the work of David Grossman, a retired Army colonel and psychologist whose book *On Killing* brought into public view how difficult it is for military forces to socialize young people into killers (Grossman now trains US police forces how to kill more quickly and with fewer hesitations).[18] Among other things, he reminded contemporary readers of the work of Brigadier General S. L. A. Marshall, the official combat historian of the European theater in World War II. Marshall's research discovered that only 15 to 20 percent of individual riflemen were able to fire their weapon at exposed enemy soldiers—the vast majority were unable to do so, even at risk to themselves. This extreme reluctance to kill—even in the "most just" of just wars—confirmed earlier research from the Civil War and World War I on high rates of refusal-to-fire and has been confirmed by subsequent research and experiences.

None of this has been lost on those who create and deploy armies. The cross-cultural aversion to militarized killing is a problem to be solved, an obstacle to state action and ambition. Starting in 1946, the United

18. See, for example, McLaughlin, "One of America's Most Popular Police Trainers."

States Army led the way in pioneering new approaches to military formation and socialization designed especially to overcome this aversion. These new approaches are constantly evaluated and refined, adjusted and abandoned, as needed, all with the aim of solving the problems seen in World War II of soldiers' reluctance to kill. David Livingstone Smith, discussing the Marshall study, draws the following conclusion:

> Although it sounds very nasty, and Marshall never put it quite this way, his observations imply that military training should concentrate on overriding the recruit's moral integrity, so that he or she will have no scruples about killing on command. Moral reservations are—in Marshall's words—a "handicap" that prevents the soldier from doing his job. . . . The US armed forces overhauled their system of military training to try to solve the problems that Marshall identified. . . . Apparently as a result, US soldiers' ratio of fire increased during the Korean conflict, and by the time the Vietnam War rolled around, American troops had become much more efficient killers. But this situation created a whole new problem. The troops did better in battle, and the ratio of fire skyrocketed, but so did the incidence of combat-related psychological disorders.[19]

It's a fascinating topic, but one that can be summarized as involving more intensive psychological de- and re-construction of recruits (taking apart their sense of self and replacing it with loyalty to the military and especially to their small unit); systematic indoctrination in what many participants describe as dehumanization of others, and a hyper-masculinity that generates sexual predation (among male and female recruits alike); and a profound disdain for civilian life and culture as weak, corrupted, and unworthy of the virtuous service of soldiers. These processes of formation begin in basic training, are sustained by military culture, and are deepened for those undergoing specialized training (e.g., elite forces of various types).

The literature is extensive, and the personal testimonies from those who have experienced it are extensive (even as a powerful code of silence discourages sharing with outsiders the nature and depth of the dehumanization necessary to make modern soldiers). From physical brutalization and sleep-deprived exertions to countless repetitive drills—complete with racist and sexist cadences, invectives and insider-outsider language, and combat conducted while using powerful stimulants and psychotropic

19. Smith, *Less Than Human*, 230.

drugs—the modern soldier is different from the romanticized citizen-soldiers of Hollywood war films and July Fourth parades.

A sampler from Matt Young, a Marine Corps veteran who served in the recent imperial wars in Asia:

> I get it. The military fashions itself as the last bastion of true manliness, and in a world that feels unstable, it promises four years of a steady job, decent pay, health care and moral high ground over those who didn't serve.
>
> Then, they'll tell you, at the end of your active service you'll be left with a marketable set of skills so desirable employers will be lining up outside your door begging for you to take their jobs. You'll be wanted, a provider.
>
> The Marines have "How to Become a Man 101" down to a science. My fellow recruits and I suffered together. We were given a common language that sought to bond us, ensconce us in groupthink and separate us from the outside. We weren't allowed out in the civilian world without a partner to watch our backs, a "battle buddy." We were at war even when we were at home. We were never alone. I had more fathers than I knew what to do with.
>
> I shaved my head like one of my drill instructor's [*sic*] and copied from my senior Marines hard turns of phrase that relayed disgust of everything feminine, anything vulnerable. They called our girlfriends Susie Rottercrotch and told us fictional bull studs back home were having their way with them—women were not to be trusted.

The result of all of this, according to Young:

> The infantry taught us to use language like "haji" and "raghead" and "target" and "towelhead" to dehumanize not just enemy combatants, but every Iraqi and Arab person we encountered. We screamed "kill" for every repetition of cadence during stretching exercises and calisthenics—"1!" "KILL!" "2!" "KILL!" "3!" "KILL!"—to make the thought of killing commonplace. Our senior Marines joked about raping Iraqi women, so we did too. They called Iraqi children terrorists in training and meant it. So did we.
>
> I developed ethnocentric thoughts that I shared without shame. I'd only been in the Marines for eight months before my first deployment. But by then I was no longer a quiet, lost, empathetic kid . . . I was bloodthirsty. I wanted to kill.[20]

20. Young, "I Hope the Military Doesn't Change My Brother Like It Did Me."

With widespread reports of military personnel raping, abusing, mutilating, and killing civilians in conflict zones around the world—involving the armed forces of rich and poor countries alike—military leaders in general have attempted to blame so-called "bad apples" for such behavior. One study (from scholars supportive of the military enterprise) concludes, alas, that "most violations of the laws of war cannot be traced conveniently back to some pre-existing psychological or physical pathology" among isolated soldiers. Important for the purposes of my argument, the authors of this study suggest that it is the dehumanization of military training, combined with "asymmetric conflicts involving insurgencies and unconventional warfare" that put troops at higher risk of committing atrocities.[21] Asymmetric conflicts, of course, are precisely the conditions in which R2P comes into play.[22]

These same experts on the psychological costs of dehumanization offer a telling admission relevant to precisely what one agrees to once one buys into just-war theory.

> [O]ne response would be to suggest that all forms of dehumanization should be resisted, rather than being incorporated into military training. However, this view is also problematic for anyone who is not a pacifist. If we accept some version of Just War Theory, and therefore endorse the view that violent military force is sometimes required in defense of a just cause, then we are cornered by the reality that troops do need to be trained to kill. Indeed, for justified military actions, there is a strong moral argument that military training should, first and foremost, be directed at enabling our troops to kill in the most effective and efficient manner possible. We doubt this can be accomplished without allowing some form of dehumanization of the enemy.[23]
>
> On the modern battlefield, our troops are asked on the one hand to be ready to fight an enemy with clear-sighted and dispassionate efficiency, and, on the other hand, we expect them to be sensitive to the mores of a foreign culture, enabling them to win the hearts and minds of its citizenry while forming strong and mutually trusting working relationships with members of its military. In other words, we ask them to be both highly analytic and highly empathetic. Hence, at first sight, it might appear

21. French and Jack, "Dehumanizing the Enemy," 169–70.
22. French and Jack, "Dehumanizing the Enemy," 170.
23. French and Jack, "Dehumanizing the Enemy," 177.

> that the demands of the modern battlefield are simply impossible to manage: they are bound to drive our troops insane.[24]

In the face of manifest problems generated by socializing people into overriding the aversion to killing, the military solution has become this: even more psychological manipulation and formation of soldiers by their own military. The goal is something that, for lack of a better term, might be called a humane dehumanization—which is about as logical as Augustine's killing as an act of love. First, dehumanize one's enemies and one's own soldiers, then rehumanize them at the end of their service.[25]

Finally, in an admission that sits awkwardly with Augustine's view and that of just-war and just-peace advocates after him, the authors of the study note:

> It strikes us that any attempt to square empathy or humanitarian concerns for an individual with committing acts of extreme intentional violence against that person represents a mindset that is too tortured and dysfunctional to condone. Troops should not be asked to love their enemies while inflicting suffering and death upon them. This is the mindset of an abuser, not a mindset we wish to encourage in troops who will return to civilian life.[26]

As if all of this were not enough, one ought also explore the literature on "combatant socialization," or the ways in which violent conflict builds company morale and efficiency. Much of this literature deals with the ways in which rape is used or tolerated by military forces as a way to bond soldiers to one another, as a form of compensation for soldiers' efforts, or as ways for soldiers to prove their masculinity.[27] A significant portion of this literature focuses on those areas where military forces have been deployed in peacekeeping operations, with troops from regional neighbors as well as from the industrial north. The prevalence of rape within a given military unit is another product of military socialization, both via training and combat exposure—lowering inhibitions, building appetites for violence and cruelty, and displacement of guilt onto victims.[28]

Then, there is the literature—from the United Nations, and from journalistic, NGO, and academic sources—about sexual violence and

24. French and Jack, "Dehumanizing the Enemy," 180.
25. French and Jack, "Dehumanizing the Enemy," 191.
26. French and Jack, "Dehumanizing the Enemy," 192.
27. See Cohen, "The Ties That Bind," 701, 704–5.
28. See Wood, "Rape as a Practice of War," 518–19.

widespread civilian abuse perpetrated by UN peacekeeping forces.[29] Some of this occurs in places where sexual violence against civilians prompted calls for external intervention in the first place. At this point, it bears mentioning that I do not think that all soldiers are sociopaths, nor that all perpetrate heinous crimes in casual fashion as a result of military training and socialization. The wonder is that, given the power of these formative processes, there are not more incidents than there seem to be (although significant underreporting and secrecy remain powerful).

Still, even this cursory dip into the waters of military socialization should be enough to suggest that one cannot—cannot—hold on to even a shred of Augustine's regard for intentionality as constitutive of a just war and expect such to be operationalized by the modern military systems of the world. To the extent that just peacemaking, just policing, and R2P aspire to any sort of connection to Augustinian principles, to that extent they cannot but fall short.

In other words—these are your rescuers, these are your saviors, these are the instruments you are entrusting with the lives of civilians and innocents who are themselves at risk from other militaries and armed groups. Especially given the emphasis put on external invaders also providing humanitarian assistance after the end of armed conflict—and these soldiers will be crucial in the so-called *jus post bellum* stage of things—these dehumanized and dehumanizing human beings are your only means of conveying Christian-sanctioned violence and killing. There are no other options now available.

Is there anyone else able to fight the wars of just policing? What institutional forces will be deployed to rescue innocents at risk in other countries, in ways that meet the strict conditions Christian ethics hopes to maintain for R2P and related armed interventions? Powerful states have too much history to be reliable—too many bloody incursions made in the name of lofty values and selfless assistance. One would similarly feel uneasy about calling upon terrorists or mercenaries to conduct humanitarian violence (although the idea of using mercenaries has been raised several times in recent years). Multilateral institutions have no significant armed forces of their own. And all armies around the world, in countries great and small, take great pains to instill dehumanization, hatred, and prejudice into the character of their members so that they will kill on command. Who are the actors capable of implementing just

29. For one example, see Moncrief, "Military Socialization," 715–30.

policing/peacekeeping in ways that uphold the requirements of this school of thought?

Theological defenders of armed intervention acknowledge the deficiencies of available means in the way they recommend the development of international police forces to implement their vision—and if one is to have international police, one also needs real international law and courts, regional enforcement agencies, and extensive cooperation with civil society organizations.[30] And yet, without the existence of such infrastructure—the problems with which I will overlook for now—one is left to advocate the pursuit of military interventions using the only tools at hand—the armed forces of states, as presently formed and socialized.

Even if one assumes for the sake of argument that things like international policing and courts with plenary jurisdiction are good things, the Church can't make them or bring them into being. What options can the Church implement in the here and now to construct the institutional capacities necessary to pursue the types of humanitarian intervention called for by Christian ethicists in these areas?

I have a proposal. If one is serious about conducting armed interventions in ways that respect the Christian convictions described herein, I suggest that you have no other choice than to bring back religious military orders—explicitly Christian armies. You heard me right—Christian military orders like the Knights Templar, the Knights Hospitallers, and more. The only way to make sure that one conducts war—excuse me, fulfills police functions—in ways consonant with just peacemaking or with R2P compatible with Christian just-war principles, is to have soldiers deeply formed by Christian convictions and practices; just the opposite of the formation steeped in bloodlust, misogyny, xenophobia, and enemy-hatred typical of secular military institutions. While they may have done so imperfectly, Christian military orders attempted to engage in simultaneous deep formation and socialization of members—into martial dispositions and practices and into Christian sensibilities and ways of inhabiting the world. Who else can kill with love, who else will be adequately prepared to sacrifice persons under their command in the interest of Christian principles, who else can be trusted to refuse orders given by self-seeking secular rulers who would exploit a humanitarian crisis for crass political or economic advantage?

30. See Winright, "Community Policing," 144–48.

I see no way around it. Unless one is willing to entertain the prospect of specialized military forces capable of acting in accord with the principles of Christian just-peace/policing approaches, one is merely play-acting. It is absurd to believe that the powerful states of this age will conduct themselves in anything resembling the standards held by Christian ethicists looking to make room for violence of a highly constrained sort. They will ignore those cases where intervention is needed but not in their self-interest; they will ditch limits on their warfighting options when the cost becomes too high, and especially if defeat becomes a real possibility; and they will use the ideological cover provided by well-meaning Christians to legitimize a range of objectives, some far beyond those countenanced by those well-meaning Christians.

So, we have returned full-circle to the beginning—to a call for humanitarian intervention in the year 1095, to be answered best by reconstituted Christian armies. If either or both of these seem distasteful to you, if they violate some deep religious intuitions, I suggest one should be attentive to these reactions and take them seriously. They suggest that killing for Christian reasons remains a bridge too far, a contradiction at the level of visceral reaction that should be explored rather than buried under piles of exculpatory discourse. That, I suggest, is what *Deus Vult*—God wills—means in our time and place.

CHAPTER 4

An Interlude

Eschatology, the Church, and Nonviolence: Some Provisional Claims

This is less a chapter than an interlude. In 2017–18, the Catholic Nonviolence Initiative (a project of Pax Christi International) convened a group of several dozen scholars and peace practitioners from around the world to explore foundational issues in Christian nonviolence and peacemaking. There were five working groups tasked with different issues and sources; I participated in a group given the task of exploring "a foundational theology of nonviolence." This interlude—more a research note than a traditional published paper—is my contribution to the group: an overview of eschatology and ecclesiology, and why they matter in what it means to be a Christian and the Church. While it may seem to end without a conclusion, it stands as an overview of how and why I think eschatology should matter for what it means to "be the Church" and to "be a Christian." It makes explicit some of what is alluded to or assumed in most of the other chapters. More information on the Catholic Nonviolence Initiative can be found at https://nonviolencejustpeace.net.

Introduction

Despite all appearances to the contrary throughout most of its existence in the world, the Church is not a permanent institution. Theologically speaking, it is an interim community,

> although in worldly, institutional terms its endurance and stability through two millennia lend it an air of intransigence . . . The Church is on its way to its promised end, the consummation of all things, the fullness of God's reign in and over all things.[1]

It is an odd thing to be reminded that the Church—seemingly the most tradition-laden institution of the modern world, one rooted in the formative stories and experiences of its past—is fundamentally defined by the future. Rather than a barge being pushed from behind by a tugboat, the Church is a vessel guided into the future by a lodestar, a magnetic attraction to what lies ahead.

In the Christian world, what lies ahead is the Kingdom of God. It was the beginning of the consummation of the Kingdom that Jesus proclaimed and inaugurated, and it is the reconciliation of the created order with God that Christians point to as the ultimate direction of history. It is the arrival of a "new heaven and new earth" (Isa 65:17; Rev 21:1), in which sin and its effects have been effaced, and in which peace and love flow from unity with a loving and benevolent God.

Christians reaffirm these hopes every time they recite the Lord's Prayer, every time they celebrate the Eucharist, and every time they are mindful that in caring for the poor and outcast they are projecting the past love exemplified by Jesus into our present *en route* to the future.

All too often overlooked or marginalized, however, is the role of the Church in the unfolding of the Kingdom that began with Jesus and reaches completion when He comes again. Returning attention to the eschatological role played by the Church is not an exercise in the esoteric or fanciful—on the contrary, it speaks to lived realities in all parts of the Church's common life and presence in the time in which the Kingdom is not fully realized.

This task—of reviewing the eschatological mission and quality of the Church, even in its everyday, pedestrian activities and practices—is worthwhile on several levels. The prevailing tendency in history has been to trim off the future-oriented nature of the Church, ignoring the power of the Spirit to create human community in ways that do not require compulsion, violence, or radical self-interest. By minimizing the degree to which the mission and actions of the Church should be constituted by what God intends all humanity to become, the Church instead settles into dull conformity with the ends and means of the old age, that age

1. Mostert, "The Kingdom Anticipated," 5–6.

whose end is proclaimed in the Resurrection and completed in God's future time. When the role of the Church in the unfolding of the new era of God is properly reconfigured, many contemporary assumptions and habits stand ready for review and reconsideration.

One area that stands to be transformed by a returned sense of the Church's eschatological role is in the area of peace and nonviolence. For all the ink and blood spilled over the centuries in debating whether Christians can kill, relatively little of it engages deeply with the eschatological nature of the Christian community. As a result, the debate often seems stuck in place, akin to the theological equivalent of trench warfare without end, without resolution, and without broad support. The grooves in Christian social ethics have been cut so deeply into the ground that nothing changes, no new insights emerge, and no new possibilities are suggested.

This paper has modest aims. It offers a brief overview related to the eschatological nature of the Church, including attention to significant considerations and cautions attendant to "eschatological ecclesiology." It then moves into a discussion about how peacemaking and nonviolence are reconceptualized when the future-directed nature of Christian life is given its due. Finally, it reflects on some of the implications that follow from seeing the Church as part of God's plan to bring the Kingdom into being—not in an overbearing or determinative way, but as something of a rough draft of what God intends for all human sociability and interaction.

1. An Absurd View of the Church

It seems too ridiculous to believe. That God would intend the Church (that historic repository for the mundane and the compromised, the source of great hypocrisy and venal pursuit of power) to be a central part of the plan to redeem the universe—such seems too absurd to be true. Centuries of sin and failure have left most of us with minimal expectations regarding the role of the Church in the world. Sometimes all we ask is that it not bring further scandal or embarrassment to the cause of Christ.

And yet, when we look up from the dust of our own failures, we sometimes see reminders of what the Church is called to be, and the role it is to play, in heralding the Kingdom of God. Our Scriptures testify to it, the best among us have testified to it, and in our more clear-headed moments we see glimpses of it through the fog of human life.

Eschatology is the area of Christian theology that points toward the role of the future in the present. It describes the end toward which God moves history—from the sinful and wounded humanity and created world we know toward the healed, redeemed, and remade heaven and earth promised by God.[2] It points toward the consummation of the Kingdom of God, which broke into the fabric of history with Jesus—His life, death, resurrection, and proclamation. It is this new era, with a new way to live and keep score in life, that Jesus begins and which His followers are to exemplify as creation moves ever closer to its complete restoration.

While the Church does not build the Kingdom of God, nor is it itself the Kingdom of God, it nonetheless has an irreplaceable role in the unfolding of the Kingdom. This understanding of eschatology is widely shared across the Christian landscape (with the exception of some corners of the fundamentalist world), even as it has been eclipsed in lived Christianity across that same landscape. The effects on how Christians live, and think they are supposed to live, are many and damaging; it cannot help but be so if, as one contemporary theologian writes, "Ethics is lived eschatology."[3] Christian ethics without eschatology becomes a matter of propriety and good manners in a world both unchanged and unchangeable.

2. Deeper into Eschatology

The Church as an eschatological reality appears as an important consideration in the work of many contemporary Catholic theologians, including Balthasar, de Lubac, and others.[4] In this, of course, they are retrieving important themes from earlier in church history, and in this they are accompanied by some significant Orthodox and Protestant theologians.

One of these is John Panteleimon Manousssakis, who notes that the epistemological emphasis on protological logic (that which comes first determines what comes later) in conventional logic becomes upended by the axial moments in Christian history—creation, incarnation,

2. See, for example, Isa 65:17 and Rev 21:1–3.

3. Middleton, *A New Heaven and a New Earth*, 24.

4. Waldron, "Hans Urs von Balthasar's Theological Critique of Nationalism"; Weinandy, "Henri de Lubac."

crucifixion, and resurrection. These events make no sense when seen as results of prior actions, but instead make sense only looking backward from the future (the cross is meaningful only in light of the Resurrection, for example):

> Theologically speaking, then, the cause of the things that happen and have happened lies not in their beginning but "in the end," for they come *from* the kingdom of God: it is the kingdom that is, properly speaking, their origin. . . . Eschatology . . . reverses naturalistic, essentialist, and historicist models by making the seemingly improbable claim that I am not who I am, let alone who I was and have been, but rather, like the theophanic Name of Exodus (3:14), I am who I *will* be. Eschatological theology is deep down a liberating theology . . . The shadow now does not follow but rather precedes reality, so that, in Christian typology, the present condition of things as things-themselves is merely an adumbration of things to come.[5]

Eschatology is not, contrary to many commonplaces in Christian thought, concerned primarily with the end of the world, or about a post-historical utopia with no purchase on life today. Such dispositions serve as:

> the perfect alibi for getting all too comfortable with the world in its current state. We have found the ideal justification for forgetting that this is not our home, our goal, our destination; that the categories of this world are not and should not be the paradigms and concepts of our thought. By exiling eschatology to a time beyond time, we have precluded ourselves from the wonderfully subversive effects of the future, of the reversals that the new might bring. Without an eschatological awareness in our interaction with the everyday, we cannot but be immune to surprise, and, therefore, to the kingdom of God, which has surprise as its very mode of manifestation (Matt 24:27; Mark 13:36; Luke 12:40; 17:24).[6]

The eschatological reality of the Church flows from the mission of Jesus, for whom the gathered apostles and disciples were to be a new chosen people, alongside the people of Israel, in giving witness to the now-arriving Kingdom of God. Whether thought of as a "demonstration plot," a prototype, a first-draft, or a beachhead, the thrust of an ecclesiology mindful of its eschatological nature emphasizes that, within the Church,

5. Manoussakis, "The Anarchic Principle of Christian Eschatology," 31–32.

6. Manoussakis, "The Anarchic Principle of Christian Eschatology," 33.

people are supposed to start acting as if the Kingdom has already begun, and that the Church is called to show the world that a different way to live is possible *here and now*, even as the old order seeks to preserve itself against the onslaught of the coming Kingdom of God. In this, as one contemporary theologian writes:

> The final decisive Christian distinction is not between the sacred and the profane, the cult and the world, the just or unjust, or even between good and evil. The decisive distinction is between the *old* and the *new*.[7]

Similarly, Alexander Schmemann reminds us that "The Church is not a natural community which is 'sanctified'; rather, it is the actualization in this world of the 'world to come,' in this *aeon*—of the Kingdom."[8]

The eschatological nature of the Church has often been caricatured by those seeking a more comfortable accommodation with the world, a task made easy by the many chiliastic movements and end-times prophets that litter the landscape of Christian history. Debates about the extent to which Christianity ought embody a fully realized eschatology (the Kingdom in its fullness is already here, and all is transformed), or a deferred eschatology (the Kingdom has yet to arrive, so nothing has changed), too often overlook the sense in which a healthy eschatology recognizes that the Kingdom has begun (and at least some things have been forever changed) and is yet to be fully realized (which happens in God's time, even as Jesus' followers have been given a new role in this current era).

Among the most crucial things that have been forever changed, according to Christians, is that death is no longer the final word. The resurrection of Christ marks an irrevocable change in the created order, here and now, if only people had the courage to believe it and act as if it were so. If Christ has been raised, the fear of death—the ultimate limit on human hope and aspirations—should no longer hold sway. If all who follow Jesus will be taken up into God at some point in the future, the grave need not serve as a check on our life and work and most noble predispositions. If life is held only when it is freely given away (Mark 8:35; Matt 16:24; Luke 9:24), then we need not kill any longer to protect it; in fact, by seeking to protect life with violence, we may be foregoing the experience of eternal life first exemplified by the resurrection.

7. Guorian, "Liturgy and the Lost Eschatological Vision," 229.

8. Schmemann, *Liturgy and Tradition*, 16–7, quoted in Guorian, "Liturgy and the Lost Eschatological Vision," 231.

When the Church is properly aware of its eschatological character, it sees that following Jesus—His practices and priorities, dispositions and affections—is itself a crucial aspect of the Kingdom's unfurling in history. The Church does not cause the Kingdom to advance, but it is meant to show the world what human community starts to look like as the Kingdom becomes a lived reality. It does this in and through its sins, mistakes, wrong turns, and reversals—it does this through showing what penance and reconciliation can make possible, by showing that the past need not have a death-grip on the present and future, and by imitating however it can the self-giving love of God toward one another and those outside its community.

3. Living the Eschaton: Time and the Sermon on the Mount

Catholic theologian Gerhard Lohfink, in drawing on the commonalities between political revolutionaries and the radicalism inherent in Christianity, draws attention to the significance of different time horizons:

> [A]ll revolutionaries have one basic problem: they are short of time. Individual lifetimes are limited, and the masses are inert. If they want to see the new society of their dreams within their own lifetime revolutionaries have to change the old society in a relatively short period of time, and that they can only do by violent means. In fact, the usual concept of revolution includes at least three elements: (1) that the masses are involved, (2) that the social overthrow happens relatively quickly, and (3) that it is brought about by open and direct violence.[9]

By contrast:

> God's principle is different. God, like all revolutionaries, desires the overturning, the radical alteration of the whole society—for in this the revolutionaries are right: what is at stake is the whole world, and the change must be radical, for the misery of the world cries to heaven and it begins deep within the human heart. But how can anyone change the world and society at its roots without taking away freedom?
>
> It can only be because God begins in a small way, at one single place in the world. There must be a place, visible, tangible, where the salvation of the world can begin: that is, where the

9. Lohfink, *Does God Need the Church?*, 26.

> world becomes what it was supposed to be according to God's plan. Beginning at that place, the new thing can spread abroad, but not through persuasion, not through indoctrination, not through violence. Everyone must have the opportunity to come and see. All must have the chance to behold and test this new thing. Then, if they want to, they can allow themselves to be drawn into the history of salvation that God is creating. Only in that way can their freedom be preserved. What drives them to the new thing cannot be force, not even moral pressure, but only the fascination of a world that is changed.[10]

This "new thing," to Lohfink, is what God does first through Israel and later through the Church. This new approach to the world operates on a different timetable and scores by a different metric: for example, the book of Genesis talks of a wandering Aramean (Abraham), even as the world's problems seem huge.

> From the standpoint of the world the hands of the clock are always close to twelve. And yet God continually provides humanity with more time, even opening gigantic periods before them, because God does not use force like a revolutionary in a blind rage. God favors a "silent revolution" that has time to see, to understand, and to repent.[11]

In understanding the inauguration of this silent revolution, Lohfink draws attention to Mark:1–15 (citing Isa 57:7–12), and the need for greater clarity in translation. As provided in the NRSV, Jesus says "the time is fulfilled, and the kingdom of God has come near; repent and believe in the good news."

> It is true that "has come near" contains an element of "not yet," but this has to do not with God's action but with Israel's response. At this moment Israel has not yet repented. It must still decide for or against the gospel. Hence the *basileia* is indeed near, but not yet present. It has been offered to the people of God; it has been laid at their feet. It is at their disposal, there for the taking. But as long as it has not been accepted it is only near, and it is still necessary to pray: "Thy kingdom come" (Matt 6:10).[12]

10. Lohfink, *Does God Need the Church?*, 27.
11. Lohfink, *Does God Need the Church?*, 29.
12. Lohfink, *Does God Need the Church?*, 134–35.

This is strikingly different from the sense of the Kingdom as yet to arrive, as something dangled in front of the world but entirely out of reach. The Kingdom has been rejected, and most have refused Jesus' invitation to repent and believe that things are now changed—instead, the Kingdom is pushed into the future, and sometimes into some sort of other world. Doing so misperceives both God and Jesus, according to Lohfink:

> Ultimately, Jesus' present eschatology is about who God really is. Jesus lived in a revolutionary new relationship with God. For him God is so powerful in graciousness and so present in power that *as far as God is concerned* there is nothing lacking, nothing still wanting. Because Jesus lived in complete union with the will of his heavenly Father, he knew that when God comes it is not by halves, but totally. And God does not come sometime, even if that sometime be tomorrow; God comes today. We simply do not do justice to Jesus' message if we speak as if God gives the *basileia* but not altogether at this moment, as if God would allow it to dawn, but only partially, as if it were revealed, but only in anticipation. We cannot say such things any more than we can say that God was revealed in Jesus, but only in anticipation, only partially, and certainly not entirely and definitively.[13]

The Church maintains that the fullness of divine revelation is found in Jesus Christ—all that God wanted to convey to humanity is found in Jesus, and no other source of information or revelation can contradict what is revealed in Jesus Christ. For the Church to see what it means to live as an eschatological community of witness in the world, it need go no further than the Sermon on the Mount and the Beatitudes (the latter is described by Saint John Paul II as the "Magna Carta" of Christianity).[14]

On the one hand, such a statement is fairly uncontroversial. The Sermon has long been considered to be a summary statement of Christian life and practice, and has drawn the attention of saints, scholars, and common people since the earliest days of the Church. At the same time, the Sermon has proved to be a stumbling block to Christians who recoil from its assertions and imperatives. The injunctions against violence, revenge, and killing in Matthew 5 are among the cornerstones of a Christian ethic of nonviolence, grounded as it is in the new era announced by Jesus and instantiated by His Church.

13. Lohfink, *Does God Need the Church?*, 138.

14. John Paul II, "Address at 17th World Youth Day."

According to at least one biblical scholar, "the fifth chapter of Matthew appears more often in their works [the ante-Nicene writers] than any other single chapter, and Matthew 5–7 more frequently than any other three chapters in the entire Bible."[15] The Sermon was seen as coming from Jesus "and prescriptive for the life of the Church": while there were some attempts to soften some of its features, "the question of practicability never directly arose during this period."[16] Another notes that in the first two Christian centuries, the Sermon was "the most quoted and cited of Jesus' teachings. It is the largest block of Jesus' teachings in the New Testament."[17]

Those tendencies to soften, evade, or avoid the radical implications of the Sermon—especially its prohibitions on killing—become more widespread, especially after the consolidation of the Church into the imperial system. While the literature on this dynamic is extensive, a brief summary suffices for present purposes. Augustine relegates the demands of the Sermon to the interior attitudes of the Christian, freeing the Christian to kill people when necessary. Aquinas says that Christians must not kill to protect themselves, but they are to do so in serving the common good or protecting others.[18] Aquinas further insulates matters by arguing for a two-tiered ethic in which the Sermon is normative for a spiritual elite called to the "counsels of perfection," while the majority of Christians are held to a lower standard beyond the Sermon's reach.[19]

Martin Luther found a way to oppose both the dual ethic of Catholicism and the claim by the Anabaptists that the Sermon should be normative for all Christians. To him, Christians lived in "two kingdoms," with the norms operative in one part of one's life separate from the other. Christians might follow the nonviolent call of the Sermon in their spiritual life and among fellow Christians, while using all the violence necessary to fulfill the requirements of office one holds in the worldly kingdom.[20]

15. Kissinger, *The Sermon on the Mount,* 6, cited in Guelich, "Interpreting the Sermon," 118.

16. Gueilich, "Interpreting the Sermon," 118.

17. Stassen, "Healing the Rift," 92.

18. Clough, "On the Relevance of Jesus Christ," 201–2.

19. Aquinas, *Summa Theologica* I, IIae, cvii-cviii, cited in Gueilich, "Interpreting the Sermon," 118.

20. See, for example, Gueilich, "Interpreting the Sermon," 119; Luther, *Luther's Works*; Prill, "Martin Luther, the Two Kingdoms, and the Church."

For his part, John Calvin also rejected the dual ethic of Aquinas. His refusal of the Anabaptist option followed on his claim that they refused to interpret the Sermon in light of the rest of the Bible, especially the Old Testament. Doing so allowed him to discipline the reach of the Sermon in ways that did not affect the public roles and actions of Christians, especially Christian magistrates.[21]

The marginalization of the Sermon continues into contemporary times, through luminaries like Reinhold Niebuhr, Paul Ramsey, John Milbank, Peter Leithart, and others. David Clough offers a summary statement:

> For Augustine, Aquinas, Luther, Calvin and Niebuhr, therefore, the teaching of Jesus about violence is irrelevant to most Christian judgments about the use of violence: for Augustine, Jesus' teaching concerns inner dispositions rather than outward actions; for Aquinas it is irrelevant where the welfare of others is a factor; for Luther it is irrelevant except among Christians; and for Calvin and Niebuhr it should never be a restraint on what is necessary for public order. We must recognize that these judgments of the relevance of Jesus' teachings are made in the context of a conviction that other parts of the teaching of Christ require Christians to be violent. In particular, each of these authors share the conviction that Jesus' commands to love one's neighbor sometimes require violent actions. What we have here, therefore, is a judgment that a particular interpretation of Jesus' teaching on love (love of neighbor necessarily means sometimes being violent) shows that Jesus' teaching on violence that contradicts this interpretation of neighbor love (don't resist evil, turn the other cheek, don't retaliate, love your enemies) is irrelevant for most Christian judgments about the legitimacy of violence.[22]

The power of these interpretations allowed Niebuhr to justify the atomic bombings of Hiroshima and Nagasaki as defensible in Christian terms.[23] Even more remarkably, the Sermon on the Mount was cited as the policy guide of a prominent Christian layman: President Harry Truman, responsible for the nuclear attacks, referred to the Sermon as "what we [the United States and Great Britain] try to live by" in a 1949 meeting, while assuring another group in 1950 that American policymaking was guided

21. See Gueilich, "Interpreting the Sermon," 120.

22. Clough, "On the Relevance of Jesus Christ," 204.

23. Clough, "On the Relevance of Jesus Christ," 203.

by the Sermon. This was too much even for the pro-American *Christian Century*, whose editors wrote: "Does he really know what's in the Sermon on the Mount? Has he read it recently, and does he still think it is reflected in American policy?"[24]

Clearly, a more adequate understanding of the Sermon is needed. Such an understanding moves nonviolence from one aspect of the Christian message to one of its central features. As a first step, doing so requires seeing the essentially communal aspect of the Sermon—it is not best seen as an individualistic, private obligation, but rather as the blueprint and lodestar for a community moving forward to and in the Kingdom of God.

Such an eschatological understanding of the Church presupposes a special kind of Christian formation, one that creates dispositions, habits, and affections capable of embracing the Sermon as good news for the world begun anew. In this, one sees continuity in the drama of salvation. As the Chosen People of God, Israel was called to exemplify God's ways among the nations, and ultimately to lead the nations into harmony with creation and their creator. Similarly, Jesus created a new people—called the Church—as part of the Kingdom of God that arrived with Him and that now defines the new age of creation. The Church is to act as a beachhead, a pilot project, of the Kingdom—showing what it means to live as if the Kingdom has already begun even while the old order grinds slowly to an end. The Kingdom people gathered around Jesus come from all nations and cultures and give proof of human community and mutuality that does not require coercion or force to maintain itself. It has the Sermon on the Mount as its guide to living. As people who believe that the resurrection did happen, and that death no longer has the final word, members of the Church strive to illustrate, however imperfectly, what life looks life when no longer oriented around the fear of death.

Christian formation, when it's done well, is always a lifelong effort to push against interpretive frameworks not rooted in the word become flesh, in the Christ that brings the Kingdom of God among us and that calls us to live in the world as if that Kingdom has already begun. Putting on the armor of God is as much perceptual as intellectual, as much a matter of changing the operating system of our hearts and minds as it is a matter of accepting new propositions about creation, history, and destiny. It means that the process of making disciples is about taking down the scaffolding of some interpretive frames and replacing them with those of

24. See "Editorial"; "Mr. Truman's Spiritual Blindness."

the Church and the followers of Jesus—dismantling the complexes that make nationalism seem normal, subverting the conventional wisdom that might makes right, and giving people new eyes with which to see and new ears with which to hear all that's been going on around them all the while, but to which they've been oblivious so long as they lacked the right equipment with which to catch, retrieve, and act upon this God-soaked reality.

A renewed attention to the constructed nature of Christian identity and practices is among the more salutary developments in recent years, driven in no small measure by the wholesale ineffectiveness of Christian formation compared to other powerful processes of formation, socialization, and identity creation.[25] All Christians, in other words, "are formed by the stories, symbols, songs, and exemplars of the Christian experiment. In particular it involves the internalization of the priorities, affections, and dispositions of Jesus of Nazareth, he through whom God reveals most fully who God is and what God desires of us."[26]

Theologians and pastoral leaders have long recognized the centrality of the sacraments—especially the Eucharist—in the formation of Christian communities and disciples of the gospel therein. It is captured in Augustine's well-known reminder that the Eucharist is unlike all other sorts of food inasmuch as transformed bread and wine does not simply metabolize into the human body, but in fact changes the recipient into part of the Body of Christ ("nor shall you change Me, like the food of your flesh, into yourself, but you shall be changed into Me").[27]

> The Eucharist makes the memories of Jesus alive and transformative among the faithful. More than a simple remembrance, the sacrament collapses the barriers between past, present and future—Christ becomes present among us today, we become part of his body moving forward toward the exemplification of His completion of history. No matter how small the gathering, how scattered are the communities who celebrate His presence in the Eucharist, all are united in a common worship and incorporation binding all of us to Christ and to one another. The Eucharist is meant to bring to life and sustain a new people, unlike any ever seen in human history—one built on love and mutuality, forgiveness and other-regardedness. It is meant to make real

25. See, for example, Smith with Dillon, *Soul Searching.*

26. Budde, "Collecting Praise," 125.

27. Augustine, *Confessions* VI.10, 16.

> the outrageous divine promise that coercion and self-interest, domination and subordination, are not the ways that God wants human community to be built and sustained; the eucharistically generated body of Christ is meant to be a foretaste of the Kingdom, a prototype that shows what God intends for all forms of human association when the Kingdom is fully manifest.[28]

As interpreted by the eschatological community called Church, then, the Sermon forms part of a constellation that pushes lethal force outside the orbit of Christian discipleship. Reading the Sermon outside of an eschatological understanding of the Church makes it something other than what it should be for Christians in all times and places.

28. Budde, "Real Presence and False Gods," 285.

CHAPTER 5

The Church after Development

A lecture on political economy and ecology delivered April 12, 2015, at the 2015 World Catholicism Week Conference, Fragile Earth: Ecology and the Church, sponsored by the Center for World Catholicism and Intercultural Theology (CWCIT) at DePaul University in Chicago. Information on CWCIT can be found at http://cwcit.depaul.edu.

Introduction

A word of background to what I will talk with you about today: prior to joining the Department of Catholic Studies in 2010, I spent twenty years in departments of political science—one at DePaul, a Catholic university, another at a large state institution with strengths in agribusiness, science, and technology. In both, my work focused on political economy, especially on matters of global economics and development theory. My interest in environmental issues, development theory, and political economy began during my undergraduate years in the 1970s, where I first encountered important figures like Nicholas Georgescu-Roegen, William Ophuls, and the pre-World Bank, pre-process theology work of Herman Daly.

All of which is to say that, for me, thinking about ecology and theology always presupposes some decisions about the political economy of capitalism in general and the postwar field of development theory in particular. Let me start with a few statements that I will assume rather than argue for in this paper/conversation—I lack the time and you cannot be expected to have the patience required for me to defend them in this context, although to me they have been defended sufficiently well to be persuasive. That others disagree with me is beyond question, so let the conversation begin.

1. Among the most contested terms in the Western lexicon, "development" cannot be understood adequately unless one accepts that it is a violent, coercive process—always has been, always will be. It involves the coerced reorganization of societies, peoples, lands, and practices. Sometimes that coercion is obvious, in the form of soldiers or police or private violence that pushes people off their land, prohibits them access to needed sources of food and materials, or kills people who disagree with the ends and means of actors who drive the development process. In other times and places, the coercion takes less easily perceived forms, from changes in tax structures designed to push people from self-provisioning activities, to those dependent on wage markets, to legal processes that replace traditional land tenure systems with those that benefit the favored agents and outcomes of development processes. Moreover, this violence is not an originating practice that, once its grim work is accomplished, can be replaced by a more civilized sort of cooperative or voluntary set of interactions—such doesn't end with "primitive accumulation" stages of economic transformation, but is a necessary and ongoing function throughout.

2. Development has and continues to be an unrelenting war on the ability of peoples to provide for their most basic needs—food, water, shelter, and more. It has been called the war on subsistence, and this five-hundred-year battle continues to push people further into depending for their survival on labor markets they do not control, investment policies they do not control, and ideological systems they do not control—all of which presuppose the intrinsic inferiority of subsistence activities relative to modern market relations in terms of efficiency, productivity, and freedom. However much they disagreed on other things, the need to destroy subsistence systems made allies of liberal capitalists and authoritarian state socialists, investment bankers, and most well-intentioned nonprofit

organizations throughout most of the modern era. As Adam Smith knew but refused to say—it was left to his contemporary, Sir James Steuart, to say it explicitly—people first had to be made desperate by the destruction of subsistence activities before they would "voluntarily" agree to sell their labor power to the wealthy on whatever terms they could manage.[1]

3. Development is tied to a conception of state governance that, regardless of regime type (liberal, authoritarian, electoral, etc.), assumes that in principle economic expansion is without limit. Indeed, it is not an exaggeration to say that the assumption of unlimited economic expansion is among the essential material underpinnings of political liberalism—explicitly so in John Locke and his labor theory of property, and simply assumed by generations to follow. For Locke, and for the liberal tradition that followed, the right to extract from nature and make private property presumed that "there is enough, and as good" left over in nature's bounty for everyone else to do the same.[2] The promise of liberal democracy in general, and of "development" as the name of a package of interventions designed to broaden and deepen liberal economic relations and spaces, needs the promise of unrestricted growth as a fire needs oxygen.

This is so because the expansion of goods and services promised by development allowed politics to focus on the allocation of future resources, of pieces of a pie growing ever larger, to borrow the tired economics metaphor—this, instead of politics focusing on redistributing existing wealth and access to resources. The politics of redistribution are, and always have been, politics of the most brutal sort—for those on the bottom to gain, those at the top have to lose. Those at the top do not surrender their privileges lightly, and the resulting zero-sum politics has no room for the niceties of civil liberties, meaningful democratic processes, or presumptions of political legitimacy that make for social peace or quiescence. This is not news—C. B. MacPherson described with economy and elegance how processes of political participation (e.g., voting, office-holding) in Great Britain were not expanded beyond the propertied classes until those processes were structured and limited in ways that

1. See, for example, Perelman, *The Invention of Capitalism.*
2. Locke, "Second Treatise," 27.

made wealth redistribution impossible at a later date.[3] More than thirty years ago, Alan Wolfe explored how the underlying politics of Western democracies was built upon a shared, inviolate agreement on economic growth as the end of politics—parties, factions, and movements disagreed on means to that end, but the end was shared.[4] Regimes that could not deliver growth were dismissed or overthrown, and even authoritarian regimes built legitimacy on their ability to deliver the goods even (or especially) without the promise of political freedom. The specter of redistributive politics—ugly, uncompromising, and unrelenting—was the wolf at the door that kept the chimera of economic expansion as good beyond all goods, no matter how improbable or costly that good might reveal itself to be over the years. When Pope Paul VI defined development as "the new name for peace" in *Progressio Populorum* in 1967, he was right in ways he may not have understood fully even as he bequeathed to the Church a powerful slogan that continues to make it difficult for us to see that development may also be a new name for warfare.[5]

4. Development as practiced and understood has put the ecosystem into a long-term spiral that has already inflicted irremediable harm and has already generated significant suffering on people worldwide, especially the poor and others incapable of protecting themselves from the damage done to soil, water, air, and other systems of the biosphere. Things will get worse, in ways foreseen and unforeseen; political and economic elites are not up to the task of addressing or fixing the problem, there is no technological fix capable of undoing what has been and continues to be done, and politics will grow more authoritarian and coercive regardless of purported ideologies and political beliefs. From the left, center, and right come alarms for protection—of natural resources and systems, of property and security, of ways of life and assurances for the future—that require systems of surveillance, discipline, violence, and interventions both hard and soft. I reject that this reflects undue pessimism or a projections of an otherwise gloomy personality; indeed, people with

3. MacPherson, *The Life and Times of Liberal Democracy.*

4. Wolfe, *America's Impasse;* before this, see the important work by Ophuls, *Ecology and the Politics of Scarcity.*

5. Paul VI, *Progressio Populorum*, 76.

sunnier dispositions than me have reached the same conclusions, which are not limited to the nihilistic or the apocalyptically inclined among us.

Of course, all of this is confounded by the conceptual and ideological incoherence of the term "development" itself. It admits of so many definitions, it has undergone so many reforms and permutations and adjustments over the past seventy years that to define it is to privilege an array of claims in advance. In fact, the sheer resilience of the term, the ability of its believers to redefine it, recast it in the face of criticisms, to deflect such criticisms away from core convictions and onto understandings that can be disclaimed as "outdated," "incomplete," "misspecified," or not the newest and most improved version—bright shiny, new development, not to be confused with last year's product model—is itself an important part of the story. Such deflections and off-loading have served to keep development's essentials immune from criticism even as it absorbs and co-opts much of its opposition. All of which is to say that I am aware of the ambiguity surrounding the term, and that the ambiguity itself is part of the ideological and political power of the discursive world of development. It remains simultaneously ethereal and profoundly material, as hard to pin down as is smoke yet seemingly as obviously good as the air itself.

In most scholarly gatherings, this would be the place at which I offer the "real" definition of development, or a genealogy of the term, or my preferred reform of the term in ways that to me represent a more adequate, less flawed understanding of the ends and means in question. I will resist the temptation to do so here because my aims are different. I invite you today to ask larger questions about what is assumed, performed, and justified in the practices we describe as "development." However noble or virtuous our intentions, eventually one reaches a point in discussions of development—here is my picture of "good" development, and here is my picture of "bad" development—where the primary effect is to replenish the legitimacy of the category for the benefit of those powerful actors that constitute the determinate forces shaping what "development" accomplishes in the world. The rest of us, for the most part, neither control nor own the powerful mix of ideas and practices that constitute "development," but by continuing to reform or moderate or redirect it, we may be doing little more than renewing its legitimacy even as its fundamentals continue unabated.

Freeing the Church from Development

Separating the good work of the Church and Christians worldwide from the development machine is like freeing a host organism from a malicious parasite—the Christian works of mercy, church efforts for justice and peace, laudable initiatives to address poverty and immiseration, solidarity among churches and mutual assistance—all of these and more have become so intertwined with the institutional, conceptual, and ideological apparatuses of development that it becomes difficult, if not dismaying, to envision them except in a context framed by development discourse. The separation must be made, however, especially if the Church is serious about its commitment to the poor and to those today and tomorrow who will be made worse off by the workings of capitalist development in a context of ecological crisis. In fact, the language of crisis as "future" is itself an ideological apparatus of some comfort to the wealthy nations of the world, inasmuch as ecologically derived suffering has been part of the day-to-day reality of untold numbers of people worldwide for some time.

If one restricts oneself to examining the genre known as Catholic Social Teaching—that is, the formally promulgated body of ideas and declarations on Christianity and social issues in the recent past (1891–present), as embodied in papal encyclicals and apostolic exhortations and Vatican II documents—one finds a discourse on politics, economics, and church sharing some long-term continuities. Some of the strengths and virtues of this tradition have already drawn attention here. I would like to remind us of some of its more salient limitations when discussing development and, by extension, ecological matters. These continuities in Catholic Social Teaching include:

- an overemphasis on the autonomy of the individual decision-maker relative to the limits and barriers on decision-making presented by structural and institutional processes;
- presupposing a consensus model of social organization in which class conflict is ignored or minimized whenever possible. In much of this literature, there are no intractable conflicts, no deep and unavoidable incompatibilities between one group and another—all differences can be solved by rich and poor, strong and weak, coming together in harmonious social engagement;
- a methodological and epistemological strategy, in the sense that while most of the documents in this genre contain explicitly

Christian justifications and theological reflections, the heavy work of analyzing and recommending matters of public life is left to natural law philosophy and related approaches available presumably to all persons, with or without Christian conviction or formation. Using reason and human intelligence, people of any, all, and no faith can and should converge in a pursuit of the "common good," itself a term of broad applicability that is thought to be readily apparent to persons of good will regardless of material circumstances, ideological formation, epistemological presuppositions, or any other contextual factors;

- a circumstance in which all of these choices, taken together, all too often result in social analyses that seem disconnected from the more radical implications of the theological analyses that undergird them; in approaches to politics that can be most charitably described as "civics-book" or utopian in style, and (most important for our immediate purposes today) a consistent unwillingness to contemplate any sort of structural analysis of capitalism, or of political economy, the effects on investment on political agency and its limits, or anything similar.

What you get, as typified in what I believe to be the worst papal encyclical of my lifetime—*Centesimus Annus* (1991)—is a wish-list approach to political economy and Christian ethics. Simply make a list of all the good things you want from capitalism (wealth, material advancement, increased liberty, prosperity) and a list of the bad things you don't want (inequality, poverty, exploitation, plunder) and tell politicians and business elites to give you one without the other. That document reflects no sense of linked dynamics—that one might not be able to avoid inequality and exploitation in the generation of wealth, for example; no sense that it is asking for things that are impossible to achieve simultaneously; no sense that one cannot order *à la carte* from the menu of capitalism any more than one can order *à la carte* from the menu of aging or finitude. (I would like the wisdom of old age without the pain of experience, or a toned physique without the inconvenience of exercise; similarly, I would like the goodies of capitalism without any of the political, economic or ecological bad things. I would also like a pony—at least I did when I was a child.)[6]

6. For an extended discussion, see Budde, *The Two Churches;* Budde and Brimlow, *Christianity Incorporated.*

Around the world, the Catholic Church has developed a massive stake in development theory and practice, its discourse and ideological legitimacy. And it has usually followed, rather than led, critiques and reappraisals in the intersections that define development—when secular scholars and activists in the 1960s attacked the notion of development-as-GNP growth, the Church responded with the language of "integral development." More recently, as the world's attention has shifted to grasp the enormity and interconnectedness of environmental crisis, Cardinal Turkson has responded with the language of "integral ecology."[7]

In speaking of the buzzwords of development theory—terms like "participation," "empowerment," and "poverty reduction"—Andrea Cornwall and Karen Brock describe an intellectual apparatus that could also be said to describe Catholic Social Theory on matters of development, power, and conflict:

> Many of the familiar terms of recent years evoke a comforting mutuality, a warm and reassuring consensus, ringing with the satisfaction of everyone pulling together to pursue a set of common goals for the well-being of all. Participation, poverty reduction, and empowerment epitomize this feel-good character: they connote warm and nice things, conferring on their users that goodness and rightness that development agencies need to assert their legitimacy to intervene in the lives of others.[8]

As they note, many of these terms, which "once spoke of politics and power," have instead "come to be reconfigured in the service of today's one-size-fits-all development recipes, spun into an apoliticized form that everyone can agree with. As such . . . their use in development policy may offer little hope of the world free of poverty that they are used to evoke."[9]

All of this is important, I suggest, because the era of "development"—however much it has benefited me and people like me, however many its blessings—has been built upon massive levels of "borrowing" (to use a genteel term). It has been built from the lands and resources of indigenous peoples and the poor, from the minerals and soils of persons abroad, from the life support systems needed by future generations, and from the non-human sectors of creation. The buzzwords of the present day—"sustainable development," "integral development," "local/

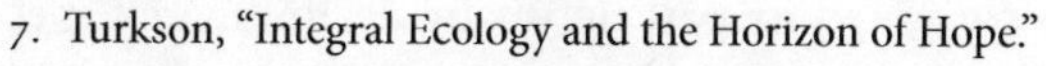

7. Turkson, "Integral Ecology and the Horizon of Hope."

8. Cornwall and Brock, "What Do Buzzwords Do," 1045.

9. Cornwall and Brock, "What Do Buzzwords Do," 1043.

participatory development"—seem on balance to be fresher fig leaves on the extractive and coercive practices of capitalism, in which the adjectives (sustainable, integral, local, participatory) provide ideological cover for the same old things that have created the worlds we inhabit today. Doubtless, such is far from the intent of many, if not most, people committed to such modified, tamed, or governed versions of development. Nevertheless, these intents are having and will continue to have little to no power to transform the institutional and ideological power of the development machine. As an illustration, consider that Jeffrey Sachs, the prime mover of "shock treatment" economic policy that destroyed Bolivia, Russia, Poland, and other places in the 1980s and 1990s, is considered a visionary in the field of "sustainable development," and that his massive new tome, *The Age of Sustainable Development*, will likely become required reading in academic centers for years to come.[10] That no one laughs out loud at this absurdity testifies to the power of development discourse to swallow, disarm, and redeploy criticisms that leave it stronger for the effort.

The Church has hitched its star to development theory and practice in the modern world—through its institutions, its rhetoric, and its social standing. We are in need of a divorce, or at least an annulment, if the integrity of the gospel and the well-being of the poor are to be carried into the future.

Still, one must not be too cynical regarding the Church's internalization of development ideology—for most people in the Church, it has represented the best, most efficacious way to live out the Church's imperative to feed the hungry, house the homeless, and care for the sick. Not being a sectarian redoubt of anti-intellectualism or scholarly know-nothingism, Catholicism listened to the best and the brightest, the accomplished leaders in finance, public administration, sociology, and the sciences. The needs of the world were and are many, the means to alleviate many of them seemed to be at hand in the form of industrialization, capitalism, and the modern state. All it would require is concerted action to transform societies to make them more productive, less backward, and more capable of delivering the goods and services needed for a humane and dignified existence.

It would have been wrong to ignore what considered opinion suggested was best, especially in an era of ecclesial humility after Vatican II, in which the Church confessed its past hubris by declining any special

10. Sachs, *The Age of Sustainable Development*.

competence in science, economics, or government. It would be even worse to refuse the offer of development if one had no "better" idea, no alternative ways to address human suffering and poverty in a world newly optimistic in the years after World War II regarding the ability to get things done given the right formula for social engineering. The power that turned back fascism, rebuilt Europe and ended the Depression (so the narrative held) could surely—given adequate resources and authority—send world poverty into retreat while advancing the march toward prosperity, security, and freedom. That such was defined, driven, and contextualized by deep anticommunist convictions is also no small matter. Whatever the costs to be borne (By whom? How severe? For how long?), surely development would be worth it and surely would deliver on its promises—if not to us, then to our children. Such promises represent the "pyramids of sacrifice" of both left and right that Peter Berger criticized before his full embrace of capitalism later in his career.[11]

Furthermore, part of the reason the Church finds itself painted into a corner on development is a result of its legitimate desire to protect the poor and weak from the neo-Malthusianism of the world's powerful actors, past and present. From the population bomb to lifeboat ethics and more, the Church looked for ways out of resource traps and shortages by focusing on human ingenuity, the capacity of science to generate more from less, and the plenitude of creation already available. Such were also accompanied by entreaties for the rich countries to share more equitably by some modest forms of redistribution; responses to these ranged from deafening silence to shrill denunciation, which made the emphasis on existing and future plenitude more palatable (and less controversial) politically and culturally. Some of this was also motivated, no doubt, by a misplaced concern to protect Catholic strictures on contraception; still, one can discern a critical awareness of how environmentalism, conservation, and the like could become weapons of the strong against the weak, legitimating authoritarian violence (overt and genteel) in the name of necessity and survival even as the wheels of development grind on.[12]

11. Berger, *Pyramids of Sacrifice.*

12. For one example, see Dowie, *Conservation Refugees.*

Being Church after Development?

Being opposed to the idea of development seems to many to be such a stupid idea as to be beneath exploration, akin to being against a self-evident good like mom or apple pie. To some, reflections like these will be heard as just another comfortable white man seeking to deny others the privileges he already enjoys; sacrificing the poor and weak on the altar of language games and semantics; counseling the retreat of the Church from the messy world of poverty and human suffering toward something more insulated and abstract; or a self-fulfilling pessimism that ignores the reality of human ingenuity and resiliency and the ongoing generosity of God.

While I resist those sorts of dismissive assertions, I am also aware that it would be presumptuous of me to attempt to dispel them too vigorously if such requires telling the Church in other parts of the world, facing difficult choices and tradeoffs that are simultaneously unique and widespread, what should be done. More modestly, but perhaps more helpfully, might be a few points to consider as we begin thinking through how to love our neighbors and the created order in the era after development. Christians worked to feed the hungry, house the homeless and clothe the naked well before "development," after all—presumably it will still be possible and necessary to do so after development crashes on the rocks of ecological limits and social breakdown.

Fortunately for me, I am not alone in asking questions about the ongoing utility of the development machine for the Church, especially in poorer countries. Writing in the *Journal of Theology for Southern Africa*, David Field describes an emerging view of ecological ecclesiology that explores the return of the Church to being a producer of human essentials, not merely a consumer entity or a cultural adornment.[13] Such is apparent in the recent decisions by the Catholic Diocese of Nairobi, and the Pontifical Mission Societies (both in Kenya) to begin using church land for food production, for church distribution and for sale in local markets.[14]

Similarly, in critiquing the dominant flavors of development and the Church's experience in them, the late Steve DeGruchy grasped for something better, which he described as a "sustainable livelihoods framework," an approach that attempts to move outside the development matrix by

13. Field, "The Gospel, the Church, and the Earth," 67–68.

14. Nzwili, "Kenya's Catholic Church to fight hunger by farming its vast land reserves."

looking at the assets of a community—social, physical, and natural—from which people draw in constructing their ability to feed themselves. As he explains:

> A household is said to have a sustainable livelihood when it can cope with and recover from shocks and stresses and can maintain its capacities, assets and existing livelihood activities without undermining its natural resource base. By diversifying their activities in order to reduce their vulnerability, poor people can improve their quality of life . . . This approach respects the freedom of people to make choices between different strategies available to them and empowers them in the process of identifying and addressing different livelihood strategies. It builds on people's strengths rather than focusing on their problems or needs. Those who are poor are agents of their own development.[15]

In this, De Gruchy references the asset-based understanding of livelihood and provisioning described by John Kretzman, John McKnight, and—my addition here—Ivan Illich. This notion of building on strengths is different in teleology from that articulated by someone like Amartyta Sen, for whom building capacities privileges incorporation into the global economy and market system.

For applied expressions of this willingness of Church and allied actors to reprioritize matters crushed or denigrated by the development consensus (be it "sustainable" or "integral" or some other adjectival modifier without power), consider the example of the "Communities of Peoples in Resistance" in Guatemala. These are indigenous Mayan groups (including some church communities and allies) who, since the 1996 accords that ended the government's war on the indigenous population, have resettled their former lands and insisted on rebuilding subsistence rather than market-driven communities. They developed co-operatives pursuing local subsistence rather than export maximization or selling their labor to outside landed elites.[16] This is one of many sites of experimentation and new direction being explored, especially by indigenous groups who are among those looking to revitalize notions of subsistence provisioning (even as one must not be uncritically enthusiastic about all things indigenous in the matters of development—the capitalistic

15. Quoted in Warmback, "'Bread and Butter' Issues," 29.

16. Kuokkanen, "Indigenous Economies," 231.

absorption of Alaskan Native groups into global capital markets via the Alaskan Native Corporations is one cautionary tale among many).[17]

Another expression of this move of church leaders into a world after development was one I witnessed last year as one of the few external participants in a study group of East African church leaders—Protestant and Catholic—drawn from across East Africa. Our seminar group focused on questions of land—land tenure, land use, matters of ecology and development, subsistence and justice, and more—and it included current and former officials in Church-based development initiatives, Protestant and Catholic pastors from urban and rural areas, government bureaucrats, and persons steeped in the diversity of East African agricultural practices. What was evident in that gathering was the two prominent divisions there. On one side were those advocating more and more effective church participation in NGO and state development projects (under headings ranging from conservation and eco-tourism to increased agro-exports). On the other side of the discussion were those who had experienced quite enough of these things and who wanted to try some different things. These included reclaiming land for subsistence production, and creating demonstration farms to teach people, both in rural and hyper-urban sections of the region, about ecological interactions and appropriate human practices therein (most of which would fall under the "permaculture" umbrella). This latter group also wanted to explore expressions of Christian discipleship that were at once more communal (focused on the poor and vulnerable) and in opposition to efficiency norms that pushed people into more commodification of the natural beauty of their lands, into unforgiving labor markets and away from their preferred vision of a life worth living.[18]

Some of what is going on is already known to persons in this room or to persons conversant with pastoral practices and the dizzying number of local initiatives that engage this large question in countless small ways. Some examples include:

- watershed preservation and shared-use ventures;
- local and regional labor and producer co-operatives;

17. For one articulation of this, see Kuokkanen, "Indigenous Economies," 231.

18. Author's observations at the meeting of the Great Lakes Initiative Leadership Institute, January 12–18, 2014, in Kampala.

- numerous efforts to create restored or partial subsistence activities adjusted to new circumstances;
- the myriad versions of "local food" practices; solidarity production and consumption activities (e.g., church-to-church production exchanges, community supported agriculture); and
- demonstration initiatives and training in permaculture and similar types of local food provisioning (e.g., the remarkable St. Jude Institute of Organic Agriculture and Sciences, founded by Catholic laywoman Josephine Kizza in Masaka, Uganda).

Two things are apparent from a list like this: first, that none of them are unfamiliar to people in this room, at least in general terms, since none of them are novel in themselves, and second, that the dominant development industry can tolerate any and all of these practices so long as they remain insignificant, marginal, or peripheral. When they begin to impinge on local labor markets, commodity production levels (e.g., food exports to cities and foreign markets), or access to resources (water, topsoil, minerals, and energy), then they must be attacked as inefficient, backward, or threats to national progress, priorities, and security. Should the Church ever move beyond development, it can expect to be accused of national disloyalty and neo-feudal power-seeking.

Killing for Sustainable Development? What is at Stake for the Church

The final stage for development as commonly practiced and understood, I submit, is Mike Davis's *Planet of Slums*, a book chilling in its detail even as it is restrained in its rhetoric.[19] Published in 2006, Davis explores the past, present, and future of hyper-urbanization—the proliferation of megacities whose populations number in the tens of millions, most of these populated by persons forced into substandard sprawling cavalcades of informal settlements with no urban services like water or sanitation—overcrowded, unsafe, ecologically devastated, and devastating blast zones of modernity. Of the twenty largest cities in the world as of 2012, more than half of them are in areas where urbanization occurs largely devoid of effective infrastructure or zoning or anything resembling even minimally

19. Davis, *Planet of Slums*.

livable housing.[20] In the next thirty years, the fastest-growing urbanization complexes will be in slums of varying size and distribution in places with which you are familiar like Karachi, Manila, Jakarta, and Lagos. But this will also be happening in thousands of what used to be considered huge cities but are now thought of as of only modest size—only a few million people—like Conakry, Lumumbashi, Douala, and places like Mbuji-Mayi, a small diamond trading town of twenty-five thousand in 1960 that, mostly within the past twenty years, has become a metropolis of two million people.[21]

The explosion of such squatter towns should not be seen as among the failures of the modern world to be remedied, but as a predicted and predictable aspect of its successes. The dominance of megacities—and I can do justice neither to Davis's narrative on this point, nor to the underlying realities—is a product of the development policies and "improvements" that have animated states, NGOs, corporations, and other actors since the 1940s. As Davis notes, the growth of slums worldwide was driven in no small measure by

> policies of agricultural deregulation and financial discipline enforced by the IMF and World Bank [which] continued to generate an exodus of surplus rural labor to urban slums even as cities ceased to be job machines . . . At the same time, rapacious warlords and chronic civil wars, often spurred by the economic dislocations of debt-imposed structural adjustment or foreign economic predators (as in the Congo and Angola) were uprooting whole countrysides. Cities—in spite of their stagnant or negative growth—have simply harvested this world agrarian crisis. Rather than the classical stereotype of the labor-intensive countryside and the capital-intensive industrial metropolis, the Third World now contains many examples of capital-intensive countrysides and labor-intensive deindustrialized cities. "Overurbanization," in other words, is driven by the reproduction of poverty, not by the supply of jobs.[22]

When war planners and militarily corporations think about future conflict, especially conflict related to ecological dislocation and displacement, one of the places of central concern to them are these sorts of

20. See *World Atlas 2014* for the 2012 population estimates: http://www.worldatlas.com/citypops.htm.

21. Davis, *Planet of Slums*, 8.

22. Davis, *Planet of Slums*, 15–16.

megacities. Military strategist and diplomat David Kilkullen describes the "new normal" of megacities worldwide in these terms:

> [A] woman born in Dhaka in 1950 would have been a toddler in a midsized town of roughly four hundred thousand people. Today, Dhaka's population is almost 15 million—nearly a twenty-eight-fold expansion in a single lifetime. This breakneck growth puts immense strain on governance: fire, ambulance, and health services are overstretched, local government is plagued by corruption and inefficiency, and the police have ceded whole districts to gangs and organized crime . . . Like 80 percent of cities on the planet, Dhaka is in a littoral zone. The vast majority of its people live less than forty-two feet above sea level, making the city extremely vulnerable to coastal flooding. Floods in 1998 put 60 percent of Dhaka's districts underwater, killed more than a thousand people, and caused more than $4 billion in damage . . . Even if you assume no climate change effects whatsoever, the city will become steadily more vulnerable over time, as more people move to low-lying areas in the next generation. If, on the other hand, Bangladesh experiences any sea level rise, the effects will be catastrophic—five feet of rise would put 16 percent of the country's land area and upwards of 22 million people underwater, prompt massive refugee movement, and leave vast areas of cropland too salty to farm.[23]

Kilkullen is among many who note the deep militarization of "development" worldwide—the integration of humanitarian works and projects within a larger set of military interventions, objectives, and strategies. He describes the work of one "Provincial Reconstruction Team," or PRT, in Afghanistan (a PRT is a handful of civilian development persons incorporated into larger military units, charged with providing development/pacification in areas controlled by the military). This PRT took the form of what was called an Agribusiness Development Team (ADT), run by the Missouri National Guard, bringing the technical and corporate partnerships established by land-grant universities in Missouri into rural Afghan districts.[24]

Ryerson Christie from the University of Bristol describes these Provincial Reconstruction Teams as one visible example of what he calls "liberal interventionism," in which humanitarian goals are invoked to justify new and ongoing military incursions of strong states into weak

23. Kilcullen, *Out of the Mountains*, 234–35.

24. Kilcullen, *Out of the Mountains*, 8–9.

ones. This is the "new rescue industry" that is reflected in contemporary counterinsurgency doctrine as a positive codependency joining high-legitimacy NGOs and the armed forces in ways that advance the interests of both, but especially those of the military power. While there are some debates within the NGO world about the wisdom of partnering, even provisionally, with military institutions (armed groups often choose to reject the distinctions aid workers would like to make between the benevolent developers and the dangerous soldiers, and target both of them in similar fashion), the explicit acceptance of these partnerships in most parts of the development industry helps us to see through the barriers that have previously obscured the structural violence that has always infused development—social transformation driven by force, persuasion, and coercion.[25]

We know that the future will be even more militarized than is the present and that ecological problems—movements of people, crises of flood and drought, wars to control necessities and assets, and more—will figure centrally in much of this. We also know that the development machine has and will continue to respond to all of this even as it presents itself as the only way out—the "new name for peace," as Paul VI described it. How is the Church to respond to this sort of violence, and these sorts of rationalizations, in the years ahead?

A worthwhile set of questions, I submit, even as I am unable to do anything more than raise them for reflection here. To have a Christianity worth inhabiting in the years ahead, I submit, means practicing a sort of discipleship that is both costly and unromanticized, in the rich and poor provinces of the Church alike. For example, the debate over whether killing is ever a legitimate option for Christians, a long and contentious dance, takes on a new flavor in the years ahead. I wonder whether the just-war tradition as traditionally understood—the majority position among most Catholics and Protestants—is up to the challenges of the new day ahead. I also wonder about the implications of all of this for the pacifist traditions within the Church, but those are less pressing inasmuch as Christocentric pacifism has so little influence on Christian life in most sectors of the Church.

I wonder if the traditional Catholic notions of just war (which themselves have been appropriated by state actors and used with disregard of Church judgments on the justness of causes, conduct, and post-conduct

25. Christie, "The Pacification of Soldiering."

aspects of warfare) will be joined to patristic and Thomistic defenses of appropriating the resources of others in extremis (that is, when a person at risk of starvation takes bread from someone better off, it isn't actually "theft"). While such were articulated to protect the right of the poor to survival needs despite prohibitions on theft, I can see already the redescription of that sentiment in the context of ecological scarcities on both the input and output sides of the equation (resources and absorptive capacity). We need water, especially our poor people; over there is more water, or underutilized water, or wastefully administered water, or water used for purposes other than those we would support. Therefore, we are justified in appropriating that water without having to call it theft or plunder or conquest. Our people provide essential services to the world community or to the common good—therefore, when we protect access to the wherewithal to protect those people and their well-being, such is both right and just. Use of force in advancing those claims or the relations that support this people cannot be considered unjust. It takes no great imagination to consider the sort of world that emerges when such rationalizations become self-evidently true and legitimate as justifications for armed action by all parties in the world, all of which unfolds amid rising demands for the means of life and disposal of waste by hitherto poor countries and regions, and the defenses of the status quo by those whose wealth-construction generated much of the so-called ecological crisis in the first place. I wonder what the churches of the industrial North will do when the bill comes due—in terms of even more war and even more armed intervention—from George H. W. Bush's famous declaration at the Rio environmental conference that "the American way of life is not up for negotiation,"[26] to the declaration by the UK's chief scientific advisor in 2006 that governmental policy could not be built on questioning the "comfort level" the British electorate has come to expect.[27]

Similarly, the militarization of both development and ecology are a *fait accompli* in most parts of the world. Armed forces of state and nonstate actors all incorporate development within their campaigns of conquest and control, and ecological justifications are and will continue to be integrated with military functions—from armed units killing poachers in game parks, even when the poachers are persons who once lived off the plants and animals now sequestered for ecotourism and multinational

26. Quoted in many places; see, for example, "A greener Bush."

27. Sir David King quoted in Scott, "The Future as God's Amnesty?," 317.

travel conglomerates, to humanitarian interventions and deepening of deals-with-the-devil like the R2P doctrine in response to climate and resource-related instability and suffering around the world. All of this is justified, and will expand, as the politics of "emergency" and "crisis" override notions of sovereignty and nonviolent problem-solving, even as they presuppose and deepen power imbalances in the world. (Powerful states conduct humanitarian war in weak ones, not the other way around—although it would be interesting to see how the US Catholic bishops made sense of an external power invading the United States to defend racial minorities victimized by ecological disregard and poisoning by corporate and government entities. Such might be an interesting test for whether just-war thinking has any merit in the current and emerging era, or whether it simply provides an ideological fig leaf for the pursuit of self-interest.)

None of us knows what the Church after development might look like, what might be required of those who aspire to follow Jesus in a time that can no longer assume the illusion of growth without cost or limit. I do know that the ordinary human aversion to death—against which Christianity has positioned itself as a bulwark (fear not, death is not the end of the story or the goodness of God's creation)—becomes supercharged and steroidal with the powers of industrialism, capital, and the modern state available to enable a material and spiritual vampirism on hitherto unimaginable scales.

Caring for a particular place means not despoiling or acquiring someone else's place, even if that means we and our children do not live as long or as well as would be possible at the expense of others. One of the contributions that Christianity is uniquely positioned to make in all of this is to the deep Christian sensibility that it may be better to die than to kill—a sensibility that needs to be nurtured or reinforced, given that the trumpets summoning us to war will only grow in volume and power in the years ahead. A hard prospect, to be sure—surely a suggestion to be received as folly and scandal for Christians and not merely for Jews and Greeks (1 Cor 1:23). Who knows whether it may be a sensibility deepened and renewed in the years to come. Whatever comes next, I hope Thomas Merton was correct when, in the darkest days of the Cuban Missile Crisis, he wrote that "Christian hope begins where every other hope stands frozen still before the face of the Unspeakable."[28]

28. Quoted in Myers, "From 'Creation Care' to 'Watershed Discipleship,'" 251.

CHAPTER 6

The Patron Saint of Anarchism: Dorothy Day and the Construction of Ecclesial Memory

A lecture prepared for the Faith, Justice, and Testimony Conference sponsored by the Pontifical Catholic University of Rio de Janeiro on October 22–23, 2013. The conference focused on what the Latin-American Church might learn from the life and witness of US Catholic lay woman, Dorothy Day. A companion conference at DePaul University in the United States explored what Catholics in the United States might learn from the Brazilian Dom Hélder Câmara, archbishop of Recife, Brazil.

Introduction

Dorothy Day was neither the first nor the last to make the case that Christian discipleship ought to entail an anarchist disposition toward the powers of government, especially in the case of the modern state. Making the case for something called "Christian Anarchism" has never been easy, given the resistance to the category flowing from anarchist and Christian camps alike. Suggesting that Catholicism, of all things, can and should adopt an anarchist critique of the state flies in the face of centuries of theologizing about the legitimacy of the temporal sword, untold numbers of examples of cross and sword joined in common ventures, and more than a hundred years of papal teaching about the state as responsible for the common good. Catholic anarchism presents itself as the very exemplar of an oxymoron, a contradiction in terms not deserving of serious attention or respectful consideration.

Such is the status of the anarchist sensibilities of Dorothy Day. As one of the most influential lay persons in twentieth-century Catholicism in the United States—someone now championed for sainthood by persons left, right, and center in the US Catholic world—the process of constructing the dominant picture of Dorothy Day is well underway. Which stories about her will be told? Which of her ideas, practices, and positions—and there were many, spread out over eighty-three of the most tumultuous years in the modern era—will be upheld as worthy of imitation, adoption, and instruction? For Catholics with progressive political instincts, Dorothy is the one-time communist and socialist whose conversion to Catholicism never weakened her commitment to social justice and life among the poorest of the poor. She blended the corporeal works of mercy with a consistent critique of war, economic injustice, and racism. For the Catholic right, Dorothy is the former bohemian who repented of an early abortion, sacrificed her common-law marriage in favor of life in the Church, and someone who rejected the temptations of the welfare state in favor of charity done through the non-governmental sector.

To be sure, none of this is unusual or exceptional. What Craig Hovey says about how martyrs entrust their legacy to the Church is equally true of the life of exemplars like Dorothy Day. They hand themselves over

> to the church's memory with no guarantee that the church will discern the meaning of their death in its continued existence. This is not because they might be betrayed by the church but because even in death they openly subject themselves to the church's discipline. After all, the way the church narrates the past is a work of disciplining its tendencies toward self-deception and learning to speak truthfully, especially about those things at which it has failed.[1]

To be sure, not everything in the life, work, and thought of Christian exemplars, even those like Dorothy Day, can or should be emulated or recommended to subsequent believers. As Dorothy herself said, paraphrasing one of her spiritual mentors, one could go to hell imitating the imperfections or wrong qualities of the saints.[2] Thirty-three years

1. Hovey, *To Share in the Body*, 51.
2. Day, "About Cuba."

after her death, much of the Catholic memory machinery seems to have decided that whatever else is to be carried forward from the witness of Dorothy Day—her commitment to the sacraments, her fearless defense of the poor and the victims of social injustice, her commitment to Christian community and an ecological sensibility years ahead of its time—the anarchism she lived, advocated, and recommended throughout her life is better left in her grave, a gift refused, an optional and deficient addendum to an otherwise serviceable life worth institutionalizing via formal canonization and informal commemorations.

My own view is otherwise. The anarchism that Dorothy Day practiced and preached, rather than being peripheral to her remarkable life of witness, is central to it. Far from being a deficient or utopian bit of flotsam that can be discarded without consequence, her "theory of the state," to use the terms of contemporary political theory, in fact is a serious and important contribution to ongoing questions of how Christian discipleship can or should relate to the principalities and powers that govern the temporal world. The anarchism of Dorothy Day, contrary to the assertions of her enemies and the demurrals of some of her friends, deserves more attention, not less; more imitation, not less; more experimentation and risk, not less.

Whose Anarchism? What Sort of Christianity?

One reason anarchism seems like such a poor political posture is the fractious nature of its adherents—the anarchism of Proudhon is not the anarchism of Bakunin, which is not the anarchism of Malatesta, which is not the anarchism of Tolstoy. The Spanish anarchists are not the Mexican anarchists, and the IWW (Industrial Workers of the World, a radical anarchist labor movement) is not the same as the Situationists. There are pacifist anarchists and violent anarchists; anarchists who despise capitalism and anarchists who idolize capitalism; anarchists who privilege the pre-industrial past and anarchists who embrace a hyper-technological future. An old joke among some Jews is that one can put the same question to two Jews and get three opinions; Charles de Gaulle asked famously, "How can anyone govern a nation that has two hundred and forty-six different kinds of cheese?" Anarchism as a tradition is not alone in being diverse to the point of occasional distraction, but it is noteworthy, nonetheless.

Similarly, the universe of opinions regarding what makes for "real" Christianity is such that it need not be explored among this audience. Christianity sometimes seems so divided that it makes anarchism by comparison look like a coherent, unified tradition of thought and practice *par excellence*. That these two traditions are fissiparous matters. What matters even more is that Dorothy Day, incorporating and extending the contributions of her mentor, Peter Maurin, derives coherence, consistency, and something compelling from both traditions by the equation she fashioned linking the two. I am not a mathematician, but Dorothy Day's formula is fairly straightforward: *Christian pacifism + personal commitment to the works of mercy = Catholic anarchism*

The notion that Jesus meant what the Gospels report Him saying about loving one's enemy, turning the other cheek, returning evil for good, putting away the sword—none of this is original to Dorothy Day and, in fact, has a long and venerable lineage in the Christian tradition. Political power—the property of Satan offered to Jesus in exchange for worship (Matt 4:8–10)—is incompatible with following a Messiah who would die for His people but not kill for them; the sort of power typical of the world, which dominates and lords it over others, is forbidden for the followers of Jesus (Luke 22:26). The insistence that loving one's neighbors precludes killing them no matter the cause (whose cause could have been more just than that of Jesus, after all?) gives a definite shape to Christian discipleship, the purposes and nature of the Church, and how Christians construe the social, political, economic, and cultural implications of the here-but-not-consummated Kingdom of God.

At the same time, Dorothy believed that all Christians were to practice the Church's traditional works of mercy. As she wrote:

> Christ commanded His followers to perform what Christians have come to call the Works of Mercy: feeding the hungry, giving drink to the thirsty, clothing the naked, sheltering the harborless, visiting the sick and prisoner, and burying the dead. Surely a simple program for direct action, and one enjoined on all of us. Not just for impersonal "poverty programs," government-funded agencies, but help given from the heart at a personal sacrifice. And how opposite a program this is to the works of war which starve people by embargoes, lay waste the land, destroy homes, wipe out populations, mutilate and condemn millions more to confinement in hospitals and prisons.[3]

3. Day, "We Go On Record."

To understand Dorothy Day's politics, it is important to keep sequences and priorities straight. Her commitment to the Jesus of peace, the suffering servant who accepted the cross and not the sword, undergirds whatever politics she espoused. All political parties, policies, options, and dispositions were tested against the ends of the Kingdom of God and the means of the nonviolent Jesus. She could accept commonalities across divisions; she could recognize shared ends and disagreements among means. But for her, unlike many, it was her theological convictions that drove her political choices and not *vice versa*. Being a disciple of Christ was more important than being a socialist, an anarchist, a communist, or anything else. She carried much from those movements into her life as a Christian but only those aspects that she judged compatible with the love of the poor, the hunger for something better for the oppressed, and the coherence between ends and means that gave credibility to the gospel as Good News to a world of wars, empires, and capital.

Dorothy's version of anarchism accepted that the modern state, in its essentials and not merely in its contingencies, was a tool of violence and lethality. It required the sacrifice of everything by all for its continued existence—its self-preservation is the *summum bonum*, which could not be questioned. Moreover, the modern state was itself tied inextricably to the workings of capitalism, an anti-Christian ideology that robbed most people of their means of subsistence and pushed them into a proletarianized and degraded existence. The forced expulsions of millions from the land, the growth of cities made inhumane by their scale, the degradation of work from a means of human enrichment down to the level of factories that destroyed people, body and soul—all of this was tied to the violence of the state. The state created and enforced the property laws that dispossessed the majority of people. The state wrote the laws that enabled the wealthy to exploit the poor and that maintained the police and the prisons that created "order" of a most odious sort. The state waged war, always war, to expand the reach of capital and the strivings for power—always for noble and righteous purposes, of course—that made talk of peace a hoax perpetrated on the working class and the poor even as they were conscripted, propagandized, and shipped off to die by the millions.

Dorothy's views on the connection between these things were on display countless times in the pages of *The Catholic Worker* and elsewhere; her April 1948 column was distinguished by its eloquence, not its content:

> If we are to accept the materialistic and atheistic philosophy of the capitalist state which holds sway in the United States, then there can be but little objection to this state of affairs. If our values are derived from the stock exchange, if we are to join in the psychopathic mania that has made war an end in itself, which has made it the norm of the American economy . . . then we are on the right track.
>
> . . . [T]o go to war means to go against every decent sentiment and against all cries for justice and against all love of man for his neighbor. The policy of the United States is anti-Catholic because it is atheistic. God does not enter into it for in place of Him there is EXPEDIENCY. It has become expedient that we murder, it has become expedient that we ignore the precepts of Jesus Christ laid down in the Sermon on the Mount and applicable to ALL MEN, not just to a chosen few who are to be perfect. It is expedient that we preach hatred of Communists to the people, that we fasten signs of hate on Church doors and sell comic strip hate books in the Church vestibule. Christianity has been reduced by the theologians to a rule of expediency, Christianity has been made to identify itself with Americanism, with the scum of the Right![4]

Put simply, the unholy blend of capitalism and war-mongering pushes Christians into making choices:

> We are against war because it is contrary to the spirit of Jesus Christ, and the only important thing is that we abide in His spirit. It is more important than being American, more important than being respectable, more important than obedience to the State. It is the only thing that matters . . . [I]t is better that the United States be liquidated than that she survive by war.[5]

The sort of anarchism Dorothy espoused was that of Proudhon and Kropotkin, focused on de-proletarianization, on providing the means of production directly to people via cooperative farms, factories, credit unions, communal enterprises, and initiatives. She and Peter Maurin saw capitalism and state socialism as members of the same family of economics, one that presumed the inherent superiority and inevitability of processes of mass industrialization, and a division of labor made possible by forced dispossession of persons from means of subsistence. With both feet firmly planted in the misery of both the urban proletariat and

4. Day, "We Are Un-American: We Are Catholics."
5. Day, "We Are Un-American: We Are Catholics."

the impoverished rural communities—sharecroppers, migrant workers, landless refugees from industrial agriculture, exploited migrants—Dorothy saw the illusory nature of the "progress" offered by modern capitalism, as well as how the direct and indirect violence of the state both created and sustained the dispossession required for such an oppressive system to operate.

This is not the sort of anarchism that glorifies individualism or castigates the state in order to liberate capitalism from the restraints of regulation or restriction. This is the sort of libertarian socialism advocated by popularizers like Rudolph Rocker and Noam Chomsky in Europe and North America; it prepares the ground for many currents in ecological economics, including Catholic thinkers like Ivan Illich and E. F. Schumacher. It owes much to the Distributist movement of the late-nineteenth and early twentieth centuries—names like Eric Gill, G. K. Chesterton, and Hillaire Belloc come to mind, who in turn built upon the work of John Ruskin, William Godwin, Proudhon, and Kropotkin. Dorothy remained a student of communal alternatives to the political economy of capitalism throughout her entire life, studying and visiting secular and religious experiments around the world.

As Dorothy often quoted Peter Maurin as saying, this sort of anarchism involved creating a new society "to be built in the here and now, *within* the shell of the old."[6] Peter himself echoes Bakunin, who distinguished communism and (anarchist) collectivism on precisely these grounds:

> I am not a communist, because communism concentrates and swallows up in itself for the benefit of the State all the forces of society, because it inevitably leads to the concentration of property in the hands of the State, whereas I want the abolition of the State . . . I want to see society and collective social property organized from below upwards, by way of free association, not from above downwards . . .[7]

As one scholar notes, in Bakunin's view, "workers should strive to create their future world in the very heart of the existing bourgeois world,

6. See, for example, Day, "Peter the Materialist."

7. Carr, *Michael Bakunin*, 356; quoted in Cutler, *From Out of the Dustbin*, 26.

alongside but altogether separate from it," using cooperative organizations to produce and distribute goods and services in a more equitable fashion.[8]

Its critics to the contrary, Dorothy's anarchist sensibilities aimed at practicality and realism even while confronting the institutional and mental fetters of the state and corporate capital. She refused to pay federal income taxes as a way to resist the imperial warmaking machine, yet she paid local taxes on the grounds that such provided useful services like fire protection and had the potential to be less obviously in the thrall of the military state. Over a period of many decades, she refused to vote as a sign that her allegiance was to God and God's people rather than to the nation, the state, or the party—this from a woman arrested in women's suffrage protests in her youth. She welcomed those aspects of Catholic social teaching that stressed the common good, the virtues of decentralization, the value of life on the land, and the imperative to serve the poor; she calmly ignored those aspects of it that seemed naïve in their embrace of industrialization and the capacity of the state to serve the common good. She supported striking labor unions and the right to organize for decades, even as she disagreed with the conservative forms of unionism that came to dominate the US labor movement. To her, the IWW continued to have much to say even as it shrank as a result of government oppression and the co-optation of the rest of the labor movement.

Whether capitalist or socialist, industrialism represented a dead end that condemned the masses of people worldwide to a life of servitude, insecurity, and poverty—except during wartime, when production boomed and workers learned to submerge the teachings of Christ lest they interrupt rising wages, benefits, and employment.

Dorothy's anarchism was aware of its bad reputation—as bomb throwers and killers of clerics in the view of the right, as anti-industrial agrarians in love with an idealized picture of the Middle Ages according to the left. What gave her framework both coherence and credibility was its rootedness in a holistic practice of discipleship in all aspects of life. Scores of arrests protesting war and its many seductions protected her from anarchism's association with violence, and a lifetime living with the inner-city poor and championing their needs gave the lie to any charges of being a deluded medievalist or romanticizing rustic.

8. Cutler, *From Out of the Dustbin*, 19.

She was familiar enough and confident enough among communists and socialists, her former comrades and lifelong friends, to ignore charges that her endorsement of property made her an apologist for the petty bourgeois. As she once wrote, "When we talk about property we do not think of stocks and bonds, shares in coal mines, the property of the hunters in their red coats [on a fox hunt of the wealthy]. They have no respect for property" inasmuch as they denied even basic rights to land or productive resources to the poor.[9] She saw through the hypocrisy of the right's charge that she was a communist opposed to property rights; referring to the United States in the 1940s, she said,

> There is no respect for property here. So why do we talk of fighting communism, which we are supposed to oppose because it does away with private property? We have done that very well ourselves in this country. Or because it denies the existence of God? We do not see Christ in our brothers the miners, in our brother John L. Lewis [leader of the United Mine Workers of America union]. We live in an age of war, and the turning of the wheels of industry, the very workings of the mines, depends on our wars.[10]

Dorothy's equation (Christian pacifism + personalism = anarchism) was a costly matter. Her refusal to endorse World War II cost her untold supporters, including among some of the leadership circles of her movement.

An Anarchist in Solidarity with Revolution

Like Bakunin, Dorothy denied to the Marxists the right to call themselves the only true advocates of revolution. Dorothy maintained a lifetime of support and solidarity with revolutionary causes around the world, especially in Latin America. In this she was unlike many self-styled progressive or liberal Christians in North America and Europe who had a sentimental affection for pacifism but bristled at the thought of violent revolution, reluctantly endorsing counter-revolutionary policies or condemning revolutionary movements for "going too far."

As a young woman, Dorothy worked for the Anti-Imperialist League, a communist organization that supported Augusto César Sandino in his revolutionary efforts in Nicaragua; she interviewed Sandino

9. Day, "Reflections on Work."
10. Day, "Reflections on Work."

himself on at least one occasion[11] and voiced support for the intentions of the Sandinista movement that overthrew the Somoza regime the year before she died. She took great interest in revolutionary movements and leaders in Africa and hoped for good things from Catholic revolutionaries like Julius Nyerere of Tanzania.[12]

But it was Cuba that held a special place in Dorothy's heart and writing. Writing in 1961, Dorothy acknowledged the difficulty in expressing her views on Cuba and its revolution, since, on the one hand, "we are religious in our attitude with a great love for Holy Mother Church; and we are also revolutionaries, in our own fashion."[13] Not content to settle for the propaganda output of the US government, its media allies, or the Catholic hierarchy, Dorothy made her own trip to Cuba in 1962—knowing full well that she would be considered a dupe by one side and insufficiently revolutionary by the other. She wrote a lengthy, four-part report on her travels—a blend of close, detailed observations and reflections on big-picture questions of politics and faith.

Fidel Castro and his revolution presented Dorothy with a juxtaposition of several of her life's priorities and her core theological convictions: authentic change that sought to improve the lot of the poor, a rejection of capitalism and neocolonialism, millions of oppressed people infused with hope for a better day—as well as reports of persecution of the Church she loved, large-scale imprisonment of political opponents, and a militarized state and society with no pretense of nonviolent or pacifist sympathies. So she went, she saw, she interviewed, she studied, and she reflected. She took issue with reports of wholesale persecution of the Church:

> Let me insert there that I went to Mass and Communion daily, that churches, but not schools are open, that almost two hundred priests remain and more are coming in for those who left voluntarily (intimidated, insulted, in some cases threatened, but not coerced to go), that two minor seminaries are open, active catechism classes continue and the presence of sisters and an active secular institute of women rejoices the heart.[14]

11. Day, "On Pilgrimage."
12. Day, "On Pilgrimage."
13. Day, "About Cuba."
14. Day, "On Pilgrimage in Cuba—Part II."

She noted that while Catholics at that time had "complete freedom of speech and there was criticism as well as praise of the regime,"[15] it was with regard to education that Catholic parents were caught in a bind. The question, as she noted, was this: "How can we let our children go to schools where Marxism-Leninism is taught?"[16]

In all of this, Dorothy worked to discern rightly and weigh her counsel with care. She told some of her Cuban Catholic partners in dialogue that the pope encouraged people to find "concordances" rather than "heresies" and "to work as far as one could with the revolution, and to always be ready to give a reason for the faith that is in one."[17] Her example of such in practice focused on the singing of the *International*, "most of the verses of which can be joined in with enthusiasm," including "Arise, poor of the world / On your feet, slaves without bread / and let us shout all together / all united, Long Live the International. / Let us remove all shackles / that tie humanity / let us change the face of the earth / burying the bourgeois empire."[18] She adds, however, that it is at the third verse "where I would recommend that the children sit down. It is—'No more Supreme Saviors / no Caesar, no bourgeois, no God. We ourselves have our own redemption.'"[19]

Dorothy was aware that the critical support she gave the Revolution was bound to draw criticism upon her:

> Of course, I know that the island is an armed camp, that all the people make up the militia. It is too late now to talk of nonviolence, with one invasion [by the United States] behind them, and threats of another ahead of them. And according to traditional Catholic teaching, the only kind Fidel Castro ever had, the good Catholic is also the good soldier.
>
> Several of our old editors have accused us of giving up our pacifism. What nonsense. We are unalterably opposed to armed resistance and armed revolt from the admittedly intolerable conditions all through Latin America as we ever were . . . We are against capital punishment whether it takes place in our own country or in Russia or Cuba. We are against mass imprisonments whether it is of delinquents or counterrevolutionaries . . .

15. Day, "On Pilgrimage in Cuba—Part III."
16. Day, "On Pilgrimage in Cuba—Part III."
17. Day, "On Pilgrimage in Cuba—Part III."
18. Day, "On Pilgrimage in Cuba—Part III."
19. Day, "On Pilgrimage in Cuba—Part III."

> No one expects that Fidel will become another Martin of Tours or Ignatius and lay down his arms. But we pray the grace of God will grow in him and that with a better social order, grace will build on the good natural, and that the Church will be free to function, giving us the Sacraments and the preaching of the Man of Peace, Jesus.[20]

A few months later, still with Cuba on her mind, Dorothy wrote:

> There is still much I wish to write about Cuba and why we are so mightily interested, though we are both pacifist and utterly opposed to all state control. It is because the zeal and enthusiasm of the young in Cuba increases our hope for man—that he can undergo a great transformation, that he can be converted to a heart warming zeal for the common good. Of course, I see the tragedies that inevitably accompany every great change, and more so when those changes are brought about by wars. I hate the arms buildup in Cuba as I hate it in my own country, the waste of intelligence, the waste of resources. Incredible sums are poured into destruction that should be used for schools, hospitals, the development of new and better institutions. I hate to think of prisoners still in Cuban prisons, and of the "shanty towns" which have sprung up in the gardens of the embassies where fugitives full of fear are also imprisoned . . . I hate to see women especially proudly bearing arms. These things, and these things only, I found to criticize and condemn, but I shall continue to try to write of all the good which is happening . . .[21]

It was not only the Catholic Worker folks that were challenged by the Cuban Revolution, both in its origins and as it evolved through the crises and pressures of the Cold War. While not abandoning her commitment to nonviolent politics, neither did Dorothy renounce her revolutionary sensibilities; the tenor of her critique of the United States, the powerful hegemon, remained much more aggressive than did her criticisms of the Cuban revolution and its instantiation of Marxist-Leninist authoritarianism. The tensions between incompatible commitments remained and were pushed deeper by Christians in the Americas throughout the remainder of the twentieth century.

20. Day, "Pilgrimage to Cuba—Part I."
21. Day, "More About Cuba."

Indigestible Anarchism?

Dorothy Day is notorious for having rejected the idea of her being declared a saint someday because she didn't want people to dismiss her so easily. Proclaiming someone a saint, whatever else it is meant to do, all too often meant designating someone as qualitatively different from the mass of human beings—so pious, so dedicated, so strong in faith as to be unlike the rest of us. No wonder someone like that can do great things for God, goes the thinking; the rest of us have to settle for doing less because we're on a lower level of spiritual existence across the board. As she once said, "When they call you a saint, it means basically that you are not to be taken seriously."[22]

The scrubbing of Dorothy's life and witness is already well underway—it began with the work of John O'Connor, the cardinal archbishop of New York, who first introduced the cause of her canonization in the year 2000. In his February 7, 2000, letter to the Holy See opening the cause of her canonization, O'Connor stepped nimbly through Dorothy's long and controversial life in constructing the picture of her he urged upon the universal Church. This was the Dorothy who had an abortion and regretted it, the Dorothy who was theologically orthodox and immersed in the sacraments and the lives of the saints. When it came to dealing with her politics, O'Connor marked off her pre-conversion life among socialists, anarchists, and communists; after her conversion, according to O'Connor, "she was neither a member of such groupings nor did she approve of their tactics or any denial of private property."[23]

His political reconstruction of Dorothy the anarchist, opponent of American imperialism in all its forms, becomes something altogether different:

> Yet, it must be said, she often held opinions in common with [communists, socialists and anarchists]. What they held in common was a common respect for the poor and a desire for economic equity. In no sense did she approve of any form of atheism, agnosticism, or religious indifference. Moreover, her complete commitment to pacifism in imitation of Christ often separated her from these political ideologies. She rejected all military force; she rejected aid to force in any way in a most

22. Reported by Robert Ellsberg in Martin, "Don't Call Me A Saint?"

23. O'Connor, "Dorothy Day's Sainthood Cause Begins."

> idealistic manner. So much were her "politics" based on an ideology of nonviolence that they may be said to be apolitical.[24]

This is scarcely a picture of Dorothy that she would have recognized, nor would it have resonated with her contemporaries, defenders and critics alike. But it makes sense coming from O'Connor, for whom Day was a figure to be domesticated and neutralized. As journalist Colman McCarthy reminded people:

> Cardinal O'Connor was a Navy chaplain for twenty-seven years, serving the military establishment so obediently that he retired in 1979 with the rank of rear admiral. He worked on submarines, destroyers and cruisers, including a tour in Vietnam in the mid-1960s when the US killing machine was in full throttle . . . After the slaughter ended, O'Connor was appointed Navy chief of chaplains, serving from 1975 to 1979.[25]

O'Connor later led the entire Military Vicariate for the US Catholic bishops. He also attempted to undermine the bishops' statements critical of nuclear weapons and capitalism in the 1980s and provided ideological cover for Reagan Administration policies in Central America.[26]

The political and ecclesial right continues to scrub the anarchism off Dorothy Day's portrait, most recently after the United States Conference of Catholic Bishops endorsed her canonization cause in November 2012. Many in the hierarchy attempted to enlist Dorothy as an ally against the Obama administration's policies on contraception and health care; as Francis Cardinal George of Chicago said, "As we struggle at this opportune moment to try to show how we are losing our freedoms in the name of individual rights, Dorothy Day is a good woman to have on our side."[27]

In a similar fashion, Dorothy's insistence that care for the poor is an obligation for all Christians, and not something to be left to the impersonal bureaucracies of the welfare state, has been used by groups seeking to dismantle what remains of government policies to aid the poor in the United States and elsewhere.[28] Her critique of the New Deal and other programs, and her insistence on the centrality of the works of mercy

24. O'Connor, "Dorothy Day's Sainthood Cause Begins."

25. McCarthy, "Cardinal an unlikely champion of 'St. Dorothy,'" 22.

26. McCarthy, "Cardinal an unlikely champion of 'St. Dorothy,'" 22.

27. Quoted in Gibson, "St. Dorothy Day?"

28. See, for example, Kauffman, "Flashback: Saint Dorothy"; Finnegan, "Was Dorothy Day a Libertarian?"

performed by Christians directly—at personal sacrifice, in ways that treated the poor as Christ Himself—has made her legacy an attractive one for conservatives seeking ideological cover from someone venerated by liberals and the left.

Time constraints prohibit an extensive discussion on this point, but one thing seems clear: despite her commitment to personal service and life with the poor, Dorothy had no interest in a libertarian dismantling of state programs that aided the poor. While her experience with unfeeling bureaucracies and miserly state programs convinced her that state relief would almost always be inferior to person-to-person service done from Christian love, she was no fellow traveler with today's neoliberal opponents of all state help for the poor. Like the communists, she saw the introduction of social welfare policies in the 1930s as an attempt to save capitalism by buying off some of the discontent that the Great Depression engendered everywhere.

In the late 1940s, Dorothy reflected on the question of state help for the poor, noting that while the Catholic Worker had never accepted government money, "[n]evertheless, as the Holy Father has said, in times of crisis it is necessary for the State to give help and relief to the poor, to aid victims of famine, flood, pestilence or disaster, etc."[29] The nature of modern capitalism and its state enforcement is to make everyday life a state of emergency—people pushed off the land unable to support themselves, the instabilities of wage and factory work rendering it impossible for millions to feed their families, the degrading conditions of poverty destroying families and dignity on a daily basis. Dorothy was unstinting in her criticism of government relief programs for the poor, but she did not advocate for their immediate abolition for the sake of principle or purity of vision. Such an approach would typify those defenders of unfettered capitalism that now seek to enlist her in their cause.

The left has had its own troubles with Dorothy; ironically, much of it also focusing on her anarchist disposition. Not for nothing did Marx devote so much of his time in the 1860s attempting to destroy the anarchist currents within the working class. Bakunin's critique of the dictatorial nature of state socialism—what it means to seize the state and what it means to exercise state power—was withering then and is still valid today. As he wrote concerning Marx's idea of the proletarian revolution,

29. Day, "On Pilgrimage."

> Do you know what this means? Nothing more or less than a new aristocracy, that of the urban and industrial workers, to the exclusion of the millions who make up the rural proletariat, and who . . . will in effect become subjects of this great so-called popular State. *Class, power, and State,* these three terms are inseparable, each of them necessarily implying the other two, and summed up in aggregate by these words: *the political subjugation and economic exploitation of the masses.*[30]

In Christian circles, Dorothy's anarchism—coming as it does from a pacifist vision of Jesus and Christian discipleship—sits uneasily with "progressive" movements of social change, in both their reformist and revolutionary expressions. Dorothy Day calls into question what to progressive Christians is self-evident: that to advance justice on earth Christians must seek political power and influence with all that entails. When the powers that be are so oppressive as to be beyond reform, Christians should take up arms against such regimes in the pursuit of a just revolution.

Such is not a new debate, and one hopes that the processes of image-construction among Dorothy Day's friends on the left will not wash it away. One thinks, for example, of the serious but respectful debate via letters between Ernesto Cardenal, the priest founder of the Solentiname community in Nicaragua, and his Jesuit friend, the US antiwar activist Daniel Berrigan. In the course of the Nicaraguan revolution, Cardenal set aside his pacifist views and joined the armed Sandinistas fighting the Somoza regime. For his part, Berrigan had been arrested countless times for protesting against the US war in Vietnam, even imprisoned for several years for burning draft records; he would serve several more years in prison for damaging nuclear warheads and pouring blood on them during the 1980s "Plowshares" movement for nuclear disarmament.

While Dorothy Day remained ambivalent about the use of violence against property—Berrigan's form of nonviolent protest in the late 1960s—she nevertheless recognized him as continuing her own work for peace and against the Catholic legitimization of killing. Cardenal would later be straightforward in his defense of armed struggle: he and the Sandinistas did not take up arms

> for any principle—no matter how high—but to avoid the shedding of blood of those children who were assassinated by this dictatorship and those adolescents and those men and those

30. "On Marx and Marxism," in Lehning, *Michael Bakunin,* 253–54.

> women and those old people who day after day were assassinated. These arms were not to kill, but to give life.[31]

He added that

> One can't compare weapons of common people in Nicaragua, with their .22 caliber guns or machetes and sticks and stones, to the heavy arms of Somoza's National Guard, supplied by the United States and Israel. And one also cannot compare the blood the Sandinista Front had to spill, which was only that of National Guard soldiers, whom the Sandinistas shot and killed in combat, to the numerous assassinations by the National Guard . . .
>
> This war was fought to end violence. The Sandinista Front has been very generous in its victory and is not killing any of those who are criminals who truly deserve death . . . The church is very involved in this revolution, understanding the church to be not only those bishops of Nicaragua but all God's people of Nicaragua.
>
> One cannot make the separation in the case of Nicaragua between the church and the revolution. The church is God's people, who have made this revolution. It has produced changes in the people: it has made the people be generous, brotherly.
>
> For this we have made the revolution. Those who have taken up arms have done it for compassion. They have done it because of vested interests. They have done it for the benefit of others. And those who died have followed the precepts of Christ in giving their lives for others.[32]

Ironically, Berrigan's contribution to the discussion preceded Cardenal's remarks above. The Jesuit offered the following thoughts:

> One religious paper here published your words [on taking up arms] under the following headline: "When they take up arms for love of the kingdom of God." How sublime, I thought, how ironic. We have had "just wars" of the right, a long history of blood, the blood of colonials and natives and slaves and workers and peasants.
>
> But we are through with all of that. Now we are enlightened. We are to have "just" wars of the left! So, the young men of Solentiname resolved to take up arms. They did it for one reason: "on account of their love for the kingdom of God." Now here we certainly speak within a tradition! In every crusade that

31. "Fortieth Anniversary: Berrigan Debates," 34A.

32. "Fortieth Anniversary: Berrigan Debates," 34A.

> ever marched across Christendom, murder—the most secular of undertakings, the most worldly, the one that enlists and rewards us along with the other enlistees of Caesar—this undertaking is invariably baptized in religious ideology: the kingdom of God.
>
> Blood and iron, nukes and rifles. The leftists kill the rightists, the rightists kill the leftists; both, given time and occasion, kill the children, the aged, the ill, the suspects. Given time and occasion, both torture prisoners. Always, you understand, inadvertently, regretfully. Both sides, moreover, have excellent intentions, and call on God to witness them.

Later, he adds:

> Thou shalt not kill. Love one another as I have loved you. If your enemy strikes you on the right cheek, turn to him the other. Practically everyone in the world, citizens and believers alike, consign such words to the images on church walls, or the embroideries in front parlors.
>
> We really are stuck, Christians are stuck with this Christ, the impossible, unteachable, irreformable loser. Revolutionaries must correct him, set him right. That absurd form, shivering under the crosswinds of power, must be made acceptable, relevant. So, a gun is painted into his empty hands. Now he is human! Now he is like us.[33]

Berrigan, like Dorothy, refused to cede to the state the power to bring in the Kingdom of God. Like Dorothy, he refused to trim down Jesus or the gospel to make it more realistic and effective in confronting death-dealing with more death-dealing, even that sort purer in intention and more limited in its range of victims. Like Dorothy, he recognized and affirmed the sense of outrage and love that would move other Christians to set aside the gospel of peace for the more practical tools of warfare. But also like Dorothy, he believed that Christians should not fail to confront one another in love over such questions of means and ends, love and suffering, and the ultimate nature of God's plan for creation.

Dorothy Day's anarchism continues to challenge and inspire; rooted as it is in the personal call to love and the uncompromising renunciation of the sword exemplified by Jesus, it is not an incidental or contingent part of her witness. May it remain part of her story, regardless of who tells that story.

33. "Fortieth Anniversary: Berrigan Debates," 31A–32A.

CHAPTER 7

Real Presences and False Gods: The Eucharist as Discernment and Formation

A lecture on the Eucharist and the ecclesiology delivered April 17, 2012, at the 2012 World Catholicism Week Conference, Real Presences: Eucharist, Society, and Global Catholicism, sponsored by the Center for World Catholicism and Intercultural Theology (CWCIT) at DePaul University in Chicago. Information on CWCIT can be found at http://cwcit.depaul.edu.

Introduction

One need not be an expert in Eucharistic or liturgical theology to notice the greater emphases in such circles on the formative character of Eucharist—its relationship to the cultivation of affections, dispositions, and aspirations appropriate to life lived in Christ. Similarly, one need not be an expert in Eucharistic or liturgical theology to notice the retrieval of eschatology as a central aspect of the Eucharist, a fundamental orientation to the ends of creation and divine will with implications for church, world, and the very cosmos.

It's a good thing that one need not be an expert in such matters, otherwise I would have precious little to share with you today. With these disclaimers, I would like to explore with you some of what appears to me—someone whose interests revolve around ecclesiology broadly construed—as important considerations in thinking about the Eucharist in relation to matters of formation, eschatology, and discernment. I would then like to think about extra-ecclesial factors and forces that frustrate the practice of the Eucharist in contemporary Catholic circles, focusing on one particular constellation of practices that constitute a counter-liturgy that deforms the body of Christ in the service of a rival vision of the eschaton.

I. Eschatology, Formation, and the Eucharist

In an insightful reflection on the life and work of Alexander Schmemann, Michael Plekon helpfully draws attention to the tight connections this important Orthodox theologian makes between the Eucharist, the Church, and the eschatological Kingdom of God. A full and complete retrieval of the constitutive interactions among these three features of Christianity is necessary to mend the "reductions" that have hindered Christian life and practice in our time.

As Schmemann notes:

> The Church first of all and before everything else is a God-created and God-given reality, the presence of Christ's new life, the manifestation of the new "aeon" of the Holy Spirit . . . an eschatological reality . . . In and through the Church the Kingdom of God is made already present, is communicated to men.[1]

He adds that the world appears differently once the Eucharist is seen in relation to God's purposes in creation and the Church as created and sent by God in service to His mission:

> The Church, the sacrament of Christ, is not a "religious" society of converts, an organization to satisfy the "religious" needs of man. It is *new life* and redeems, therefore, the whole life, the total being of man. And this whole life of man is precisely the world in which and by which he lives. Through man the Church saves and redeems the world. One can say that "this world" is saved and redeemed every time a man responds to the divine gift, accepts it and lives by it. This does not transform the world into the Kingdom or the society into the Church. The ontological abyss between the *old* and the *new* remains unchanged and

1 Schmemann, *Church, World, Mission*, 211–22, cited in Plekon, "The Church, the Eucharist, and the Kingdom."

> cannot be filled in this "aeon." The Kingdom is *yet to come*, and the Church is not *of* this world. And yet this Kingdom to come is already present, and the Church is fulfilled *in* this world. They are present not only as "proclamation" but in their very reality, and through the divine *agape*, which is their fruit, they *perform* all the time the same sacramental transformation of the *old* into the *new*, they make possible real action, real "doing" in this world.[2]

In another context, Gloria Schaab reminds us of the transformative aspects of Eucharist, of the creation of a new people in and through the Eucharist who are charged with continuing the mission of Christ in the world—an eschatological picture of the Church in every respect. As she notes:

> To be Eucharistic people is to be the presence of Christ, transformed by the whole of the Eucharistic event to take on the mind of Christ and to make the mission of Christ our own . . . [T]he encounter with Christ in the Eucharist, far from being confined to the ecclesial or liturgical context, challenges those who partake of the Body of Christ in the context of the culture, the society, and the world in which the person of faith lives and moves and has being. In so doing the community of Christ's disciples carries forward the mission which Christ embodied in his own person, words, and actions.[3]

In reflecting on the Eucharistic thought of John Paul II, Schaab draws attention to the essential connection between the historical Jesus and the mission of the Kingdom that the Church is called to live out by way of its Eucharistic formation and transformation. Such is critical to maintaining a Christology capable of sustaining its radical particularity against pressures to substitute a more diffused and generic humanitarianism that falls short of the Kingdom-oriented mission of Christianity. It is in this sense that Schaab identifies the Eucharist as "paradigmatic of self-emptying humility, radical inclusivity, and self-giving service through which Jesus lived his mission of proclaiming the reign of God."[4]

The retrieval of the eschatological nature of the Church is not limited to Catholic theologians. The Australian theologian Christiaan Mostert,

2. Schmemann, *Church, World, Mission,* 216.
3. Schaab, "As Christ, So We," 171.
4. Schaab, "As Christ, So We," 172.

drawing upon Pannenberg, Moltmann, and others, echoes themes found in a variety of Catholic thinkers:

> The formation of the church was understood as one aspect of the kingdom's dawning. The first Christians saw themselves as "the provisional gathering of the fellowship that, awaiting God's future, would find its definitive realization in the fellowship of men and women in the kingdom of God."[5] The inclusion of Gentiles in the Christian community was a vital element in this eschatological self-understanding. In this way the church could be seen, at least in part, as a fulfillment of the destiny of humankind as a whole in the kingdom of God. The church's relation to the reign of God is then a constitutive element in ecclesiology. The church is a function of the kingdom rather than the kingdom being in some sense a function of the church.[6]

This new people, created by the Holy Spirit from across the deep divisions of race, political status, gender, and wealth, is found and created anew most fully in the practice of the Eucharist:

> In the Eucharist the church enacts and celebrates its identity as the eschatological community, *anticipating* the lordship of God in and over the whole creation and the eschatological reality of reconciliation with God. Here the church becomes what it essentially *is* in its anticipatory role in the *oikonomia* of salvation. Here the future breaks through into the present, as God's future salvation is mediated to the gathered assembly and it in turn becomes an instrument of the reconciliation of people with each other and with God. As the Eastern Orthodox Church makes more explicit than the rest of the church, in the celebration of the Eucharist the church is the "image of the eschaton."[7] Here, the church again and again becomes God's eschatological community, the anticipatory sign of the eschatological reign of God.[8]

And lest one worry that attention to the origins of the Christian community as relevant to contemporary ideas be dismissed as naïve "primitivism," John Paul II reminds us that

5. Pannenberg, *Systematic Theology*, 28.

6. Mostert here references Jurgen Moltmann, *The Church in the Power of the Spirit*; the quote here is Mostert, "The Kingdom Anticipated," 26.

7. Zizoulas, *Lectures in Christian Dogmatics*, 160.

8. Mostert, "The Kingdom Anticipated," 36.

> at each Holy Mass we are called to measure ourselves against the idea of communion which the Acts of the Apostles paints as a model for the Church in every age. It is the Church gathered around the Apostles, called by the word of God, capable of sharing in spiritual goods but in material goods as well.[9]

II. Formation, Eucharist, and Church

A renewed attention to the constructed nature of Christian identity and practices is among the more salutary developments in recent years. Much of this reflection uses the language of "formation"—of desires, affections, dispositions, imaginations, and more—in ways that make clear that all Christians (not merely members of religious congregations, for whom the language of "formation" historically has been more typical) are made, not born. All Christians, in other words, "are formed by the stories, symbols, songs, and exemplars of the Christian experiment. In particular it involves the internalization of the priorities, affections, and dispositions of Jesus of Nazareth, He through whom God reveals most fully who God is and what God desires of us."[10]

Theologians and pastoral leaders have long recognized the centrality of the sacraments—especially the Eucharist—in the formation of Christian communities and disciples of the gospel therein. Relevant here is Augustine's well-known reminder that the Eucharist is unlike all other sorts of food inasmuch as transformed bread and wine does not simply metabolize into the human body, but in fact changes the recipient into part of the Body of Christ ("nor shall you change Me, like the food of your flesh, into yourself, but you shall be changed into Me").[11]

The Eucharist makes the memories of Jesus alive and transformative among the faithful. More than a simple remembrance, the sacrament collapses the barriers between past, present, and future—Christ becomes present among us today, and we become part of His body moving forward toward the exemplification of His completion of history. No matter how small the gathering, how scattered are the communities who celebrate His presence in the Eucharist, all are united in a common worship and

9. John Paul II, *Mane Nobiscum Domine*, 22, cited in Okonkwo, "The Sacrament of the Eucharist (as Koinonia)," 94.

10. Budde, "Collecting Praise," 125.

11. Augustine, *Confessions* VII.10, 16.

incorporation binding all of us to Christ and to one another. The Eucharist is meant to bring to life and sustain a new people, unlike any ever seen in human history—one built on love and mutuality, forgiveness, and other-regardedness. It is meant to make real the outrageous divine promise that coercion and self-interest, domination and subordination, are not the ways that God wants human community to be built and sustained; the eucharistically generated body of Christ is meant to be a foretaste of the Kingdom, a prototype that shows what God intends for all forms of human association when the Kingdom is fully manifest.

One of the enduring drawbacks of some of these reflections on the formative power of Christian discipleship and the centrality therein of the Eucharist and liturgical practice more generally is the more-or-less automatic efficacy sometimes accorded the latter. Reading some of this literature, it's almost as if many theologians assume that the Eucharist works in a more or less automatic way: more Eucharist, more serious Christians . . . more unity, more charity, more love, more real-life incorporation of the example of Jesus of Nazareth. People who know better continue too often to assume that the formative power of sacramental life operates in such a fashion, as if restating its supernatural efficacy—*ex opera operatore*—is sufficient in addressing real-world complexities and limitations.

Such is an unfair exaggeration in many respects, of course. Scholars and pastoral leaders alike are well aware of the sad state of congregational life for most Catholics in the United States, for example,[12] and theologians refer regularly to the cautions of St. Paul regarding the conditions under which communion fails or becomes a parody of itself (1 Cor. 11:17–33 NRSV). When the Eucharistic gathering reflects deprivation and opulence among those gathered, when the divisions of the world undermine the unity and new life of the gathered community, then what results is the consumption of body and blood in a way that brings condemnation rather than blessing. Better not to share the table of the Lord at all than to do so in an unworthy fashion that brings only condemnation upon oneself. Paul requires that those gathered must "discern the body" of the Church—taking its measure, ensuring that it testifies to what the Eucharist testifies, working to prevent becoming a scandal and embarrassment to the transformative, future-directed nature of the holy feast. The community as the body of Christ is called to be a discerning body, for whom

12. See, for example, Smith and Dillon, *Soul Searching*.

discipleship means vigilance against practices, relationships, and desires that reflect rivals to the sort of new creation inaugurated by Christ in the breaking of bread.

For the Eucharist to be a properly eschatological endeavor, for it to create and guide a new people toward a new heaven and new earth, these people must be a discerning people. They must be a people attuned to the conditions that have brought them into being and continue to give them life and to conditions that would thwart this pilgrimage into the future by keeping it rooted in the world's past, one typified by formative systems of power, domination, division, and enmity. To the extent that this latter sort of formation exercises power, it erects formidable barriers to the mission of Christ and the Church. God ultimately triumphs over such obstacles and sin, to be sure, but followers of Christ are also called to remove those obstacles where and when they can. Not to do so, to allow them to run riot through the assembly of the people of God, is for Christians to "eat and drink judgment upon themselves" (1 Cor 11:29 NRSV).

III. False Liturgy and False Gods: One Illustration

States are not churches, and the actions of states are comparable to those of churches only by analogy. While modern states engage in ritual behaviors of all sorts, many with religious overtones and associations (with a significant literature now exploring such matters), most do not instantiate something as central to political life as Eucharist is to Christian life and practice. To say that states engage in Eucharistic or liturgical action is to make the claim that language often used in the realm of religion and ritual can provide insights and perspectives not available via other traditions of discourse and analysis.

I count myself among those who make such claims, and who argue that such is of great importance to the Church today. The manifold expressions of human sinfulness frustrate the outworkings of Christian witness in the world, a circumstance that will perdure until God completes the coming in fullness of the Kingdom. This side of that completion, the Church is called to discern and name—and resist—those things that impede its discipleship and undermine its capacity to reflect, even imperfectly, the sort of love and mutuality that God incarnates in Jesus and that Christ continues through the Church and the Holy Spirit.

Let me illustrate what I mean by starting at the end, rather than the beginning, of the process of sacramental formation by the modern state. One end product of this process, I would suggest, is the hagiography of the "Greatest Generation": the veneration in American politics and culture of World War II and those who fought in it. It stands as a shining example of what can be produced by processes of liturgical and sacramental construction oriented toward the kingdom of Caesar rather than the Kingdom of God. As such, it deserves to be seen by the Church as working in opposition to the unity of the faithful created and sustained by the Eucharist; more specifically, a sense of Eucharist rightly inhabited would make the processes that produce idolatries like the Greatest Generation become apparent and worthy of resistance.

By now, a helpful literature exists on the ways in which state actions parody the liturgical functions of religious communities; these actions aim to build identities, allegiances, and obedience.[13] In several respects, these resemble Eucharistic processes involving the elision of past, present, and future; matters of remembrance and repetition; the calling into being of a people with an eschatological role, identity, and mission; and much more. Several scholars have observed how matters of warfare and militarism are particularly vivid and powerful examples of sacramental—even Eucharistic—practice by modern states whose survival requires the creation and sustenance of people in sufficient numbers willing to kill for them, die for them, and pay for them.[14]

Given time constraints here, I presuppose the helpfulness of these analogies rather than argue for them. I would like to spend a few minutes reflecting with you on the ways in which one feature of this secular worship creates an important field of discourse and power, one that inhibits clear Christian thinking about sacramental theology, social ethics, and ecclesiology. To raise criticism of the so-called Greatest Generation is to risk exclusion from the field of acceptable discourse in American public life; nonetheless, it may be instructive to spend a few minutes with the topic here.

13. See, for example, Marvin and Ingle, *Blood Sacrifice and the Nation*; see also, O'Leary, *To Die For*.

14. In particular, see an outstanding article by a young Catholic scholar, Iafrate, "Destructive Obedience"; see also Hauerwas, *War and the American Difference*.

1. The Greatest Generation Industry

The marriage of information technology and cultural monopoly means that when I recently bought a copy of Tom Brokaw's bestselling *The Greatest Generation*, I was provided with a printout with my sales receipt, suggesting I might also want to purchase *The Greatest Generation Speaks: Letters and Reflections, The Time of Our Lives: A Conversation About America,* or *The Greatest Generation* with DVD. If I'm more in a movie-going mood, my appetite whetted by the *Greatest Generation* DVD, I can avail myself of the most recent of cinematic glorifications of World War II: *Saving Private Ryan*, perhaps, or *Band of Brothers*, *The Big Red One*, or *Pearl Harbor*, which stand as but a few contributions over the past seventy years of big-screen praise for the war, the nobility of those fighting on the Allied side, and the lessons learned about valor, sacrifice, and national unity. If I want to take a trip with my family, I can take them to the World War II Memorial in Washington, DC, the D-Day Memorial in Virginia, the Pearl Harbor Memorial in Hawaii, or any number of other state-sponsored exercises in veneration and formation.

The men and women who fought the war and held down the home front, even those who merely lived through the era, are object lessons for all of us who come after them. To Brokaw, "they gave us the lives we have today,"[15] "[t]hey answered the call to help save the world,"[16] and ultimately, they were "the greatest generation any society has produced."[17] The celebration of the World War II generation is itself a subset of the glorification of World War II, the so-called "Good War"—an evocation of incredible power and significance ever since.

In reflecting on the Greatest Generation and the Good War, Paul Duke notes:

> Because it was so easy to single out the good guys from the bad guys, World War II has always been seen as a classic study in good versus evil, virtue versus depravity. It is also remembered as a time when the country rallied from a lethargy of innocence and marched forth in a spontaneous sense of national unity in the cause of freedom. The disciplined, can-do spirit of the early 1940s not only paid off in victory for the Western Allies, but sent a resounding signal that the United States had arrived as a

15. Brokaw, *The Greatest Generation*, xii.
16. Brokaw, *The Greatest Generation*, xxvii.
17. Brokaw, *The Greatest Generation*, xxxviii.

> prominent player on the world stage. In short, it was America's finest hour.[18]

The erstwhile cultural historian Studs Terkel, while noting the ironies in the notion of the "good war," nevertheless found a deep fondness for the war and its era among his conversation partners. One former serviceman remembered it as a time "when buddies felt they were more important, were better men who amounted to more than they do now. It's a precious memory."[19] For another,

> You had fifteen guys who for the first time in their lives were not living in a competitive society. We were in a tribal sort of situation, where we could help each other without fear. I realized it was the absence of phony standards that created the thing I loved about the army.[20]

Or, as one Red Cross worker put it:

> The war was fun for America. I'm not talking about the poor souls who lost sons and daughters. But for the rest of us, the war was a hell of a good time. Farmers in South Dakota that I administered relief to and gave 'em bully beef and four dollars a week to feed their families [during the Depression], when I came home were worth a quarter-million dollars, right?[21]

Another veteran reported that

> [i]n a short period of time, I had the most tremendous experiences of all of life: of fear, of jubilance, of misery, of hope, of comradeship, and of endless excitement. I honestly feel grateful for having been a witness to an event as monumental as anything in history and, in a very small way, a participant.[22]

Or, as one soldier who later became a United States Senator remarked, "The one time the nation got together was World War II. We stood as one. We spoke as one. We clenched our fists as one."[23]

To Brokaw and others, the Greatest Generation was modest, not given to boasting of its accomplishments, and not perfect—he mentions

18. Duke, "The Greatest Generation?," 20.
19. Terkel, *The Good War*, 3.
20. Terkel, *The Good War*, 5.
21. Terkel, *The Good War*, 10.
22. Terkel, *The Good War*, 16.
23. Daniel Inouye, quoted in Brokaw, *The Greatest Generation*, 349.

the shortcomings of their age on occasion, as if to dispose of the charge of a one-sided picture by mentioning some of the undeniable failings of American life and culture. Their quality as "ordinary people" serves to elevate them further in his view, and the postwar power and wealth of the United States is seen as the product of their commitment to the ordinary, hard-working quality of this generation's character:

> It may be historically premature to judge the greatness of a whole generation, but indisputably, there are common traits that cannot be denied. It is a generation that, by and large, made no demands of homage from those who followed and prospered economically, politically, and culturally because of its sacrifices. It is a generation of towering achievement and modest demeanor, a legacy of their formative years when they were participants in and witness to sacrifice of the highest order. They know how many of the best of their generation didn't make it to their early twenties, how many brilliant scientists, teachers, spiritual and business leaders, politicians, and artists were lost in the ravages of the greatest war the world has ever seen.[24]

The cultural project of nationalism and state-building makes war and killing on behalf of one's country a powerful and oftentimes inescapable imperative. While matters of lethal force and war have long been a central concern of Christian ethics—just war and pacifism, questions of war and peacemaking, and much more—such questions have drawn less frequently from Eucharistic theology and practice. If such a deficiency does in fact exist, I suggest that it is important that it not continue unchallenged in the years ahead.

Let me identify a few areas in which an adequate theology of Eucharist challenges the easy acceptance of war and lethality typical of mainstream Catholic and Protestant social ethics. It may not be too much to say that, in the post-Vatican II era, the Catholic Church in particular finds its ongoing legitimation of war on a collision course with a renewed sense of Eucharistic and baptismal unity championed by the Council and afterward.[25]

24. Brokaw, *The Greatest* Generation, 11.

25. For example, the *Catechism of the Catholic Church*, 2310, describes being a soldier as an admirable form of Christian life: "Those who are sworn to serve their country in the armed forces are servants of security and freedom of nations. If they carry out their duty honorably, they truly contribute to the common good of the nation and the maintenance of peace." Similarly, see Pontificium Consilium de Iustitia et Pace, *Compendium of the Social Doctrine of the Church*, 502: "*The requirements of*

2. Creating or Fracturing the Body of Christ?

James Massa is among many who suggest that the notion that "we become the body of Christ by consuming the body of Christ" has become the dominant Eucharistic ecclesiology in many Catholic and ecumenically Protestant precincts today. What this means is that

> [a]t every eucharist, all of redeemed creation unites in praise of the eternal God. Christ gathers to himself his elect of every time and place, tearing down the walls of enmity that separate human beings from God and human beings from one another (cf. Eph 2:14). No barriers can obstruct the Eucharistic mystery, not even those that exist between heaven and earth or the invisible realm of grace and the visible realm of historical action. The dead join hands with the living; the divisions among tribes and classes fall asunder; and the distances between one local church and all others disappear.[26]

For its part, the rhetoric of the Greatest Generation and World War II is about creating, sustaining, and empowering another sort of unity—a political body built upon exclusions (non-citizens, enemies, traitors, ethnic/ideological "others"), cementing allegiances and unities based upon the willingness to kill and die for the political collective. The renewed enthusiasm for World War II, especially during times of perceived national fragmentation or insufficient patriotic fervor, works to raise nationalism above all other claims on identity and belonging, including the Church. As noted by Barbara Biesecker, the outpourings of World War II material

> together constitute one of the primary means through which a renewed sense of national belonging is being persuasively packaged and delivered to US audiences for whom the question what does it mean to be an American has, at least since the Civil War, never been more difficult to answer.[27] [T]hese extraordinarily well-received reconstructions of the past function rhetorically as

---

legitimate defense justify the existence in States of armed forces, the activity of which should be at the service of peace. Those who defend the security and freedom of a country, in such a spirit, make an authentic contribution to peace." These quotes are found in Iafrate, "Destructive Obedience," 4, n. 3. One wonders how such can be reconciled with a robust theology of Eucharist that does not limit itself to excessively localized or nationalized theologies, nor a sense of Eucharist that reflects even a modest awareness of the eschatological nature of the church as described herein.

26. Massa, "The Priority of Unity," 589–92.

27. Biesecker, "Remembering World War II," 394.

> civics lessons for a generation beset by fractious disagreements about the viability of US culture and identity. By manufacturing and embracing a particular *kind* of American, a certain idea of what it means to be a "good citizen," these popular cultural texts, best understood as technologies of national cultural transformation, promote social cohesion by rhetorically inducing differently positioned audiences—by class, race, ethnicity, and gender—to disregard rather than actively to seek to dismantle the inequitable power relations that continue to structure collective life in the United States.[28]

While Biesecker omits consideration of religion, not to mention the Church, as among those audiences expected to subordinate themselves to the superior category of "American citizen," Hauerwas makes the point explicitly:

> War is a moral necessity for America because it provides the experience of the "unum" that makes the "pluribus" possible. War is America's central liturgical act necessary to renew our sense that we are a nation unlike other nations.[29]

While he admits that the "sacrificial quality of war" is not unique to the United States, Hauerwas contends that "America is a society and a state that cannot live without war. Though a particular war may be divisive, war is the glue that gives America a common story."[30] World War II and its Greatest Generation provide a story beyond challenge in mainstream discourse, a set of talismans that command loyalty and unquestioned veneration. If the Eucharist makes the Church, World War II has made America, and re-makes it (as in liturgical repetition) in countless commemorations, observances, obeisances, and liturgies.

But can such co-exist in harmony? Here it must be said that, as an area of Catholic social thought, reflection on the claims of nationalism and the catholicity of Christianity is, as I've said elsewhere, a vague and oftentimes incoherent set of ideas and assumptions that fit poorly together, if at all.[31] If the Eucharist creates a new people who themselves are part of the eschatological unity of all humankind, how can nationalism in general and the formation of a political polity built by and for war not be

28. Biesecker, "Remembering World War II," 394.

29. Hauerwas, *War and the American Difference*, 4.

30. Hauerwas, *War and the American Difference*, xvi.

31. Budde, "Political Theology and the Church"; see, generally, Llywelyn, *Toward a Catholic Theology of Nationality*.

anything but inimical to the nature of the Church and the unity created and heralded by the body of Christ?

Such was the embarrassing question asked almost three decades ago by Sister Carol Frances Jegen, who rather delicately noted that although the Church has long struggled with questions of war and peace, "there has been a persistent reluctance to reconcile participation in the eucharist and participation in war."[32] More recently, my colleague Bill Cavanaugh has asked the question in a related context—that is, how do we make sense theologically of a world in which Christians who share Eucharist with one another also torture and kill one another in service to political authority?[33]

One of the more interesting side notes of Jegen's exploration is the extent to which the Christian capitulation to war may have involved (among other things) a disputed interpretation of a third-century Christian leader by post-Constantinian theologians. She references the treatise *On the Goodness of Patience* by Cyprian of Carthage. Calling this "one of the most significant early writings on the incompatibility of eucharistic participation and warmaking," Jegen quotes Cyprian's conclusion that "after the reception of the eucharist the hand is not to be stained with the sword and bloodshed." As Jegen notes,

> At first sight this significant text would clearly outlaw warfare for all Christians, clergy and laity, who gathered for eucharist. Such universal practice forbidding all Christians from engaging in warfare resonated with Cyprian's teaching.[34]

However, Jegen notes, Cyprian's prohibition invited another interpretation, depending in part on what manuscript one uses and on one's translation preference. Two different words can be found in ancient versions of Cyprian's texts—*gustatam*, which means "to taste and enjoy," sometimes was replaced with *gestatam*, "to bear, or carry, or perform functions."[35] If one reads Cyprian as saying *gustatam*, the prohibition would

> more readily be applied to everyone who *received* the eucharist and tasted and enjoyed the Lord. *Gestatam* can be translated

32 Jegen, "The Eucharist and Peacemaking," 202.

33. See Cavanaugh, *Torture and Eucharist*.

34 Jegen, "The Eucharist and Peacemaking," 203; for Cyprian, see "Liber de Bono Patientiae," in Swift, *The Early Fathers on War and Military Service*, 34.

35. For her discussion and citations, see Jegen, "The Eucharist and Peacemaking," 204.

> *celebrate* in the context of performing functions. If so, the translation could imply that only the Eucharistic presider should refrain from warfare, and not necessarily all those who received the eucharist.
>
> Such a translation seems to change the meaning of Cyprian's intent. True to the peacemaking emphasis of the early church, Cyprian was concerned about all Christians who participated in the sacred mysteries. For those earliest Christians, participation in the new covenant in Jesus' blood made the violent shedding of blood in warfare absolutely unthinkable.[36]

Over time, of course, the Eucharistically based prohibition on Christian warfare gave way to the views that while clergy could not shed blood in warfare, lay people were allowed and sometimes required to kill people. Later sacramental theology focused on the sacred nature of priestly consecration and the purity required to confect the sacramental transformation; as well, the direct killing by priests eventually came to be seen as incompatible with the role of clergy as representing and enabling unity, within the Church and among peoples (I welcome further explication from historians and patristic scholars on the so-called Cyprian problem).

This last point—that the eucharist prohibits clergy from shedding blood, but not the laity—strikes me as among the more curious and lamentable byproducts of clericalism, of stark distinctions between clergy and laity in the Catholic world. Consider, for example, the distinction between clergy and lay roles expressed in *Ecclesia in America,* the 1999 post-synodal apostolic exhortation issued by Pope John Paul II after a gathering of North and South American bishops. The document, in line with earlier Vatican documents, prohibits priests from participating in politics because the priestly vocation "requires him to be a sign of unity. Therefore, he must avoid any involvement in party politics, since this would divide the community."[37] The prohibition of clergy as killers in warfare would seem to be covered analogously, given that warfare divides even more fully than does party politics. On the other hand, lay people are instructed to engage in party politics—(and warfare, it seems to me)—because such is their mission to the secular realm. This is the

36. Jegen, "The Eucharist and Peacemaking," 204.

37. John Paul II, *Ecclesia in America,* 126.

same party politics that the document describes as divisive and destructive of the unity of the Church and the larger community. To put it more precisely,

> So what the clergy is to build up—the unity of the church, the church as a communion in a material as well as spiritual sense—the laity is allowed to dismantle via the undeniably divisive operations of party politics and state policymaking. And yet we are told that the unity of the church is the responsible of all baptized Christians, not merely the hierarchy or clergy. One cannot hold these two views simultaneously without doing violence to consistency or hiding behind a sort of double-effect reasoning of the most ignoble sort.[38]

At a minimum, therefore, it seems clear that the sacramental unity presupposed and built in an eschatological fashion by baptism and Eucharist do not fit well with the rival unities and allegiances presupposed by the exaltation of the Greatest Generation and their war. Cyprian's unrestricted condemnation of warfare for Christians understood that; the subsequent legacy of dual ethic thinking, regrettably, does not.

2. Eucharistic Sacrifice and World War II Exaltation as a Sacrificial System

Given the long and tortured history of Christian theological debates on whether and how to understand the sacrificial nature of the Eucharist—in Reformation-era polemics, at a minimum—it is odd that more attention has not been paid to the interactions and tensions between the sacrificial aspects of Christian Eucharist and the sacrificial aspects of war and nationalism. Both have generated an extensive literature, but relatively little that engages them simultaneously.

Amid the varied (and sometimes contentious) Christian reflections on Eucharist and sacrifice, the conviction that Christ's sacrifice brings peace remains undeniable:

> [Y]ou Gentiles by birth . . . remember that you were at that time without Christ, being aliens from the commonwealth of Israel, and strangers to the covenants of promise, having no hope and without God in the world. But now in Christ Jesus you who once were far off have been brought near by the blood of Christ. For

38. Budde, *The Borders of Baptism*, 129.

> he is our peace; in his flesh, he has made both groups into one and has broken down the dividing wall, that is, the hostility between us. He has abolished the law with its commandments and ordinances, that he might create in himself one new humanity in place of the two, thus making peace, and might reconcile both groups to God in one body through the cross, thus putting to death that hostility through it.
>
> So he came and proclaimed peace to you who were far off and peace to those who were near; for through him both of us have access in one Spirit to the Father. So then, you are no longer strangers and aliens, but you are citizens with the saints and also members of the household of God, built upon the foundation of the apostles and prophets, with Christ Jesus himself as the cornerstone. In him the whole structure is joined together and grows into a holy temple in the Lord; in whom you also are built together spiritually into a dwelling place for God. (Eph 2:12–22 NRSV)

The Gospel accounts also present the sacrifice of Jesus as tied to the New Covenant, one in which forgiveness and reconciliation are central. Matthew's account of the Last Supper, for example,

> singles out forgiveness as the main reason why Jesus' blood will establish a covenant. Matthew states explicitly, "for this is my blood, the blood of the covenant, to be poured out on behalf of many for the forgiveness of sins" (Matt 26:28). In this context of Jesus' total gift of himself in forgiving love, can the strong radical passages of Matthew's Sermon on the Mount really be understood . . . In Jesus' way of life, forgiveness is an absolutely necessary part of peacemaking. Forgiveness is truly a sharing in the life of a generous, forgiving God. Forgiveness is a sign of the covenant of peace.[39]

A comparable sense fuels the Eucharistic theology of Schmemann and others, especially as the sacrifice of Christ brings good news to the world—in fact, it is love of enemies that is the "new" aspect of Jesus' proclamation, what He incarnates and recreates among His disciples:

> These words contain nothing less than an unheard-of demand for love toward someone whom we precisely *do not love*. That is why they do not cease to disturb us, to frighten us and, above all, to *judge* us, as long as we have not become thoroughly deaf to the gospel.

39. Jegen, "The Eucharist and Peacemaking," 206.

> Precisely because this commandment is unheard of and new, we for the most part substitute our own cunning human interpretations of it. Already for centuries, and apparently with a pure conscience, not only individual Christians but also whole churches have affirmed that in reality Christian love must be directed toward *one's own*—that to love essentially and self-evidently means to love neighbors and family, one's own people, one's own country—all those persons and things that we would usually love anyway, without Christ and the gospel . . . If coming to Christ signifies the fulfillment of his commandment, then, obviously, Christian love not only is not a simple increase, "crowning," and religious sanction of natural love, but is radically distinguished from it and even contraposed to it. It is really a *new* love, of which our fallen nature and fallen world are incapable and which is therefore impossible in it.[40]

The traditional understanding of Christ as the last sacrifice, completing and sealing the sacrificial system (whatever the contentious history of Christian reflections on the claim), has implications for how the Church should understand all other sacrificial systems and liturgical enactments:

> [I]n the cross of Christ the Father has forever ended our attempts to sacrifice to God in terms set by the city of man. Christians have been incorporated into Christ's sacrifice for the world so that the world no longer needs to make sacrifices for tribe or state, or even humanity. Constituted by the body and blood of Christ, we may participate in God's kingdom so that the world may know that we, the church of Jesus Christ are the end of sacrifice. If Christians leave the Eucharistic table ready to kill one another, we not only eat and drink judgment on ourselves, but we rob the world of the witness it needs in order to know that there is an alternative to the sacrifices of war.[41]

Many have commented on the sacrificial quality of war in general; the idolatry of the Greatest Generation and World War II is a personification and application of the historical interpenetration of warfare and sacrifice. From the US Marine Corp motto (*Semper Fidelis*, always faithful) to aphorisms like those of General Douglas MacArthur ("The soldier, above all other men, is required to practice the greatest act of religious training—sacrifice"),[42] the centrality of sacrifice in war mak-

40. Schmemann, *Church, World, Mission*, 135–36.

41. Hauerwas, *War and the American Difference*, 68.

42. See Iafrate, "Destructive Obedience," 4.

ing is as absolute as forgiveness and reconciliation are to the Eucharistic understanding of Christians (perhaps more absolute, depending on how one assesses conduct formed by these various liturgies). Michael Iafrate provides a useful general summary of the role that sacrifice plays in the formative disciplines and virtues of soldiering in the American context, which he describes as

> the soldier's willingness both to sacrifice himself and to "sacrifice" others—i.e., those he or she will be taught to kill. This willingness is a relatively easy virtue to instill, as it flows from the group camaraderie formed in basic training, building on pre-existing ideals of self-sacrifice learned from American culture and religious traditions. Idealistic images of the soldier dying for his country are presented to Americans from a young age; military training merely taps into and intensifies these ideals. What requires more effort and more intentional practices of discipleship is the willingness to kill other human beings. Despite popular images of virtuous, self-sacrificing soldiers, the ultimate goal of military training is not self-sacrifice and the death of soldiers, but the killing of others on command. Militaries win wars by killing, not by sacrificing themselves.[43]

In his meditation on war, Hedges reminds us that warfare involves a shrunken conception of suffering and sacrifice (unlike that at the heart of the Eucharist, inasmuch as Christ's sacrifice draws in all peoples and all of creation). In the Balkan conflicts, for example, Hedges notes that

> all groups looked upon themselves as victims. . . . They ignored the excesses of their own and highlighted the excesses of the other in gross distortions that fueled the war. The cultivation of victimhood is essential fodder for any conflict. It is studiously crafted by the state. All cultural life is directed to broadcast the injustices carried out against us. Cultural life soon becomes little more than the drivel of agitprop. The message that the nation is good, the cause just, and the war noble is pounded into the heads of citizens in everything from late-night talk shows to morning news programs to films and popular novels. The nation is soon thrown into a trance from which it does not awaken until the conflict ends. In parts of the world where the conflict remains unresolved, this trance can last for generations.[44]

43. Iafrate, "Destructive Obedience," 11.

44. Hedges, *War Is a Force*, 64.

He concludes by noting that "once a group or nation establishes that it alone suffers, then all competing claims to injustice are cancelled out."[45]

One of the most significant features of the sacramental nature of the Greatest Generation as an occasion and object of veneration is the imperative that it be replicated. Many commentators note the extent to which the rhetoric of World War II and its participants—with the presumption of national unity, common purpose, and love of country—works to counter the perceived fissiparous tendencies of multiculturalism, group and individual rights' claims, and insufficient zeal for the common good as defined by mainstream culture and its protectors. Just as Catholic communicants are called to return to the Eucharistic table, the sacramental quality of the Greatest Generation calls on others to gather for worship, transformation, and mission back to the world.

This reiteration of sacrifice, however, joins the past to the present and future in particular ways—more specifically, in how World War II and its worship continues to sanctify those military excursions that followed. Presidents and politicians of both parties make use of the sacrifice in the "Good War" to bless those later wars whose goodness is far less obvious, even to nationalists. If Christians become what they receive in Eucharist—if they become the body of Christ in the world—then those who receive the sacrifice of the Greatest Generation are to become incorporated as warriors in service to the same body politic that sired the winners of World War II.

On one of many occasions, it is George W. Bush using the sixtieth anniversary of V-J Day to build support for his wars in Afghanistan and Iraq, at a key US naval base in San Diego, "surrounded by a sea of sailors in their dress whites and, near the stage, World War II veterans, many of whom were wearing caps and shirts that identified their regiments."[46] As he championed his efforts in the "war on terror," he linked his use of deadly force with the generation of World War II. "I'm *also* proud to stand with those whose achievements we commemorate today, the military veterans of World War II." In all of this,

> [h]is rhetoric drew upon the love for sacrifice that is intertwined with war to cast warriors, both old and new, as exemplars worthy of imitation, while also burnishing his own image by basking in the glow of the heroes he praised. Simultaneously, Bush's

45. Hedges, *War Is a Force*, 67.

46. Bostdorff, "Epideictic Rhetoric in the Service of War," 304.

> words functioned to equate World War II with Iraq, under the guise of paying tribute to particular individuals.[47]

All of this serves an example of the encumbrances that sacrifice imposes. A sort of secular transubstantiation is affected inasmuch as

> [t]o refuse to support the war in Iraq, a conflict [Bush] had consistently depicted as part of the larger war on terror, was not only to disrespect the individuals who had given their lives to that cause, but to show contempt for the veterans who had risked and sacrificed all in World War II. No one wants to think that a soldier died in vain, so the notion of "honoring the sacrifice" can, in the short term at least, provide a compelling reason to continue a war.[48]

This sort of debt, of blood obligation, is a blank check without limit or expiration. Bush made this point a few years earlier when, in dedicating the D-Day Memorial in Virginia, he said:

> all of us incurred a debt that can never be repaid. Today, as America dedicates our D-Day Memorial, we pray that our country will always be worthy of the courage that delivered us from evil, and saved the free world. God bless America. And God bless the World War II generation.[49]

And lest one believe that the liturgical use of World War II is a peculiarity of the Republican Party, one might attend to the example of President Obama's 2009 commemoration of D-Day, where "the selflessness of a few was able to change an entire century." Americans are all called to selfless choices, insofar as "our history has always been the sum total of the choices made and the actions taken by each individual man and woman. It is always up to us."[50]

The sort of liturgical sacrifice demanded by war and the culture it forms admits of no room for exception or conscientious objection—such sacrifices are needed to create, sustain, and strengthen states and the national cultures that sustain them. Hauerwas draws attention to the work of Richard Koenigsberg, author of *Nations Have the Right to Kill: Hitler, Holocaust, and War.* In this study, Koenigsberg argues that Hitler

47. Bostdorff, "Epideictic Rhetoric in the Service of War," 304, 305.

48. Bostdorff, "Epideictic Rhetoric in the Service of War," 313.

49. Luke, "The National D-Day Memorial," 552.

50. Luke, "The National D-Day Memorial," 553.

"understood war as a sacrifice necessary for the renewal of the German people." In this understanding,

> "[t]he Aryan" was therefore understood as someone willing to sacrifice himself or herself for the nation. The Jew, in contrast, was individualistic and selfish. Accordingly, the Jew could be sacrificed for the good of the nation. The destructive character of war is crucial for the moral purposes that war should serve, from Hitler's perspective. For war is a form of sacrifice "whereby human beings give over their bodies and possessions to the objects of worship with names like France, Germany, Japan, America, etc."[51]

One wonders whether the refusal to honor and sustain the "sacrifice" of the Greatest Generation in our time and place, to refuse to "support the troops" (among the most pernicious theological mandates of our cultural ideology), might label persons as similarly outside the pale (pardon the expression) of persons deserving of civil, political, and cultural inclusion.

Conclusion

Sometimes, one finishes a lecture like this with a feeling of having said something new, or in an effective manner, or at least something that might be important in some sense. Finishing this one, I'm convinced I've said nothing new and that others have said it better—more focused, more compelling, more nuanced and enlightening.

I was also wondering about whether all of this is even important, even if I've not done an especially effective job of exploring it. And then I picked up the March 31, 2012, issue of *The Tablet*, the fine liberal-to-progressive Catholic magazine published in the United Kingdom. Its Easter issue combines its usual blend of news, opinion, and theological reflection—high standards across the board and a valuable resource for the Church in Europe and worldwide.

But what stood out for me in this issue were two articles on Britain's war against Argentina over the Falkland/Malvinas Islands, the thirtieth anniversary of which is being celebrated across the UK and is noted in *The Tablet*. One article was by a major general who fought as a lieutenant in the paratrooper corps; the other, by a British war correspondent who

51. Hauerwas, *War and the American Difference*, 21–22, n. 1, referencing Koenigsberg, *Nations Have the Right to Kill*, xv.

wrote on contemporary Argentinian politics and the enduring desire to retake the islands. The latter piece is critical of Argentinian nationalism—citing it five times in a fairly short article—while not at once mentioning the nationalism of Great Britain.[52] The former piece is more disturbing still, presenting itself as a senior military officer's thoughts on what it takes to kill another human being.

Killing another human being, according to the major general, requires good training. The training is made more effective by having been raised in a culture that stresses social conformity, civil obedience, and "a fundamental trust in society and subordination to its practices." Specialized units benefit from training that involves "an attempt to condition officers and soldiers to violence, and to make them comfortable with dealing with it." It is made more powerful and reliable thanks to the deep feelings of family and comradeship constructed among soldiers.[53] And all of this is necessary and all of this works to the good.

The journalist could see the dark nationalism deep in the Argentinian heart but not in that of the British; the community of faith constructed by sharing a common Eucharist seemed not to matter when matters of land and state sovereignty are at stake. The general could talk of obstacles to killing but found the sacrificial love of the Eucharist shared by the British and the Argentinians not to be among them. Those who share the same bread and wine, even though separated by distance, those who are made part of a new people that draws from all cultures and previous ways of life into God's new creation—none of that matters, none of that even draws a mention, in the Easter issue of a Catholic periodical. We don't even need a Eucharistic defense of war, because our Eucharist is so tepid and incoherent.

52. Burns, "Those Who Cannot Learn from History," 10–11.

53. Shaw, "The Soldier in All of Us," 8–9.

CHAPTER 8

Giving Witness, Receiving Testimony

A lecture delivered on November 15, 2012, in Chicago for Witnessing: Prophesy, Politics, and Wisdom—A Conference Commemorating the Twenty-Third Anniversary of the Salvadoran Martyrs, sponsored by DePaul University's Center for World Catholicism and Intercultural Theology (CWCIT) and the Pontifical Catholic University of Rio de Janeiro.

Introduction

One breaks no new ground in observing an exaggerated sense of individualism in many understandings of witness and testimony. Both in formal hagiographies and in popular venerations of prophetic and heroic persons, considerable emphasis rests on the moral courage and determination of individuals and the message they proclaim or affirm.

At another level, of course, there is recognition that witness is fundamentally a communal phenomenon. It is an interplay between giving witness and receiving testimony, an ongoing process in which reception itself defines and constructs testimony; it is a dialectic in which testimony both identifies and challenges the roles of those who testify and those who receive testimony.

We gather today in part to remember the witness of our Salvadoran brothers and sisters whose lives were and are a testimony to the goodness of God and God's hopes for His creation. We gather to reflect on the martyrdom forced upon them, and upon many like them, in a world in which Good News is bad news to be suppressed and silenced. And we gather to ask whether and how those of us still on this part of life's journey can learn from the testimony of others and in the process become more adequate witnesses to the God of the poor who seeks to make all things new and whose Kingdom has already begun for those with eyes to see and ears to hear.

In these remarks, I hope to reflect with you not so much on the giving of witness and testimony—of which we will hear a great deal in our time together—but instead to reflect on the *reception* of this witness and testimony. It is my contention that problems of reception and receptivity draw our attention to certain deficiencies of church life and practice, and invite a rethinking of certain aspects of ecclesiology if the Church is to more adequately be part of the "cloud of witnesses" (Heb 12:1) that express Christ's life in and for the world. Doing so is worthwhile, I hope, not merely to provide a conceptual corrective to excessively individualized notions of witness and testimony, but also to suggest how proclaiming the radical gospel of Christ seems to entail communal practices and dispositions of an everyday, often overlooked sort. Public witness and testimony, I suggest, are built on humble and often unseen practices of the ekklesia seeking to practice discipleship in a world of many messages, countless testimonials, and contradictory witnesses.

I. Witness as Both Pitch and Catch

Scripture scholar Nadine Pence Frantz reminds us of the importance of testimony as a central form in a healthy interpretation of the Bible. She describes testimony as

> a narrative of a people whose self-perception was primarily defined by its interaction with God . . . [T]he intent of the whole [Bible] is testimonial, including a rhetorical function designed to evoke a response of appropriation. In other words, "Scripture is seen as that which was told and recorded with the intent to evoke a similar life and faith in other people. It is intended to evoke an encounter."[1]

1. Frantz, "Biblical Interpretation," 158.

Testimony, witness, martyrdom—all require persons formed by encounter with the Jesus of the Gospels, the Kingdom promises of the Hebrew Bible, and the Holy Spirit as enfleshed in the lives of earlier witnesses and exemplars. Such is more than a simple transmission-belt notion of communication (sender-message-receiver), or some similarly mechanistic notion of information conveyance or data encoding/transmission/decoding; we're not talking about email or texting, in other words. In fact, it is the matter of "formation," no longer the province of religious life, that stands as perhaps the crucial center for thinking theologically and ecclesially about witness and testimony in varied contexts and circumstances.

Put simply, "being a Christian" means among other things that one's imagination, desires, perceptions, standards, and ways of encountering the world are shaped by the stories, images, songs, categories, and norms of Jesus, of His followers, and of antecedents in the Hebrew Bible, and by the elders in the faith who have given it hands and feet and tears and smiles and lessons and laughter and struggle—the grandmothers and aunts, fathers and cousins and those who are the cloud of witnesses in the everyday life of the Christian way.

This is some of what is meant by "being transformed by the renewal of your mind" (Rom 12:2), which too often is reduced to a cognitive or knowledge-based sensibility that focuses too much on propositions, dogma, and intellect. More adequately understood, the formation of Christian communities and members when done well is a holistic process of conversion, a joint venture of the Holy Spirit and the ekklesia through which new Christians are made. To the extent that we Christians engage life with imaginations and minds and habits attuned to the Good News of Christ, to that extent are we the products of processes of craft formation (rather than industrial mass production).

In one sense, the formation of Christians is comparable with the other formative processes by which persons and communities are formed—indeed, rival processes of formation are the rule in most times and places, with different (and sometimes antagonistic) structures and processes seeking to shape human affections, dispositions, and desires. The cultural ecologies of capitalism, the socializing imperatives of nationalism, the identity constructions of white supremacy—these are just a few of the formative rivals to Christianity in our time and place, inasmuch as they cultivate and shape toward ends far from the Kingdom of God as exemplified in the Sermon on the Mount (which John Paul II called the "Magna Carta" of the Christian movement).

It takes a special kind of person and a special kind of community to see "loving one's enemies" as Good News, to understand "repaying evil with good" as how one should act, to encounter the creator of the universe in the person of the destitute, the neglected, or the oppressed. These are not "natural" perceptions, far from where the natural law, however construed, leads, and definitely at odds with the world constructed and maintained by capital, the state, and other formative powers.

Given that the concept of Christian formation extends beyond the realm of the religious and clergy to include all the baptized, and given that the practices of Christianity (worship, prayer, work on behalf of justice, life with and for the poor, study and fellowship) are required for the sustenance and adaptation of Christianity across time and contexts, the processes of testimony and witness presuppose formation done with a minimum degree of adequacy. For ours is a faith handed on from others, a simple-yet-complex bundle that we receive before we change it and hand it on, something that comes first "from hearing" (Rom 10:17) before it can be proclaimed.

If that is true, then being a people formed deeply by the stories of Jubilee and Jeremiah, of Jesus and Mary of Magdala, of the martyrs and the prophets, is necessary if one is to have witnesses, persons whose words and lives give testimony to God's plan for creation. We know this is true, and we hold up those exemplary witnesses who give us a glimpse of who and what God is, of what it means to forgive one's enemies and see God in those the world despises and ridicules. We give them names like Romero and Ellacuría, Daniel Berrigan and Dorothy Day, the martyrs of Uganda and Japan, and many more.

Yet what is no less important but too easily overlooked is that each of these witnesses requires a community not only to form and send them, but one capable of receiving their testimony. This is true of the testimony of word and deed, but especially true of that testimony unto death that the Christian tradition calls martyrdom. And this is where the tendency toward individualism limits our understanding of witness in our day—too much attention to those individuals, famous and unknown, whose life speaks the truth of God, and too little attention to those communities that receive their testimony, who become its caretakers and custodians, in whose hands it has been entrusted.

The stakes in all of this are significant. As Craig Hovey notes, the deaths of martyrs

> are very often not the straightforward witness implied by words that paint an ideal picture.
>
> Martyrs cannot declare their own deaths to be martyr-deaths, and thus their ultimate risk is perhaps dying without any guarantee about how they will be remembered or whether they will be remembered at all. In death, martyrs submit to the collective judgment of the Church and put their own contribution to that judgment on the line. This is because silenced martyrs are not only unable to speak to their killers the testimony for which they died; they also are unable to speak within the Church in ways that would help secure the significance of their own deaths.[2]

Where Christian formation has been done poorly, or in a superficial way, or has been overwritten by the powerful formative dynamics of other claimants on human identity and allegiance, there will witness be inadequately proclaimed, received, sustained, or maintained. There exists an extensive and generally depressing literature on the failures of Christian formation among congregations in advanced industrial countries; historic and contemporary deficiencies among congregations in the global South are also well known among pastors and scholars alike. Indeed, substantial problems in Christian formation seem to be a common dilemma joining Catholic congregations worldwide, communities with otherwise very different contexts and circumstances.

Let us look at a few examples from one particular set of twentieth-century European contexts that I hope will illustrate the matter and allow for conversation across the divergent expressions of Catholic thought and practice in our own time.

II. The Reception of Witness

1. *An Austrian Layman*

On October 26, 2007, the Catholic bishop of Linz (Austria) and the archbishop of Innsbruck announced the formal beatification of Franz Jägerstätter, whom they described as a "martyr" and "a prophet with a global

2. Hovey, *Bearing True Witness*, 5–6.

view and a penetrating insight."[3] Jägerstätter's witness was of a straightforward nature: After returning home from basic military training in 1941, Jägerstätter vowed not to return, refusing to help advance the Nazi cause as a member of the Austrian military (Austria had been annexed by Germany in 1938). He considered Nazi Germany to be an evil regime wholly incompatible with Christianity, describing its wars as unjust plunder and savaging of its neighbors, which his Christian conscience could not allow him to support in any way. Despite repeated efforts on all sides, Jägerstätter refused to change his mind; he was arrested and finally executed by beheading in 1943. In this, we have a classic, almost stereotypical, story of brave Christian witness—a martyr like other shining examples in the twentieth century, held up by the Church for veneration and imitation.

Well, not quite. If Jägerstätter's testimony merited beatification by 2007, the Church that produced him received his witness in an altogether different fashion. What Jägerstätter did, he did in the face of opposition from all sides—from much of his family, his friends and neighbors, his parish priest and bishop, and of course, from his government leaders.

While Jägerstätter's position rested on the duty to follow Christ rather than an evil regime bent on the destruction of the innocent (as well as of the Church), his pastors emphasized that such decisions were not the responsibility of lay persons. Rather, they were to obey civil authority in accord with Romans 13 and similar texts; they also emphasized Jägerstätter's duty to provide for his family, who would be made to suffer if he continued to refuse military service to the Nazis.

In his research on Jägerstätter, including interviews with his family and neighbors, North American sociologist Gordon Zahn described the general sense of the community about Jägerstätter, both during his lifetime and when his witness began gathering international attention after more than a decade of silence:

> [T]he community continues to reject Jagerstatter's stand as a stubborn and pointless display of essentially political imprudence, or even an actual failure to fulfill a legitimate duty. It is to be explained and forgiven in terms of an unfortunate mental aberration brought about, or at least intensified, by religious excess. The question of whether his action was morally right is, for the most part, set aside.
>
> While some of the villagers were quite willing to accept the possibility that he might someday be formally acknowledged as

3. Schwarz and Scheuer, "Foreword," 7.

> a saint, this possibility was not considered at all incompatible with the community's general disapproval of his action.[4]

Zahn notes that, for the most part, Jägerstätter's contemporaries tried to avoid talking or thinking about him—his story was not told to their children, and most seemed to hope the story would go away on its own.[5] When it came to Catholic leaders, Zahn notes that while "they could congratulate him for his unswerving commitment and give him assurances that he would not be committing a sin . . . none had been able or willing to tell him that *he was right*."[6] In fact, many in the Austrian hierarchy after the war had difficulty discussing Jägerstätter's case in ways that didn't reflect poorly on their support for the war effort.[7] Emblematic in this respect, to Zahn, was Bishop Joseph Fleisser of Linz, who after the war could describe Jägerstätter as a "martyr to conscience" but not as an example worthy of imitation:

> I consider the greatest heroes to be those exemplary young Catholic men, seminarians, priests, and heads of families who fought and died in heroic fulfillment of duty and in the firm conviction that they were fulfilling the will of God at their post just as the Christian soldiers in the armies of the heathen emperor had done.[8]

Similarly, the then-cardinal archbishop of Vienna was the influential Cardinal Innitzer, who signed his letters "Heil Hitler."[9] Jägerstätter's witness, in other words, was seed that seemed to land on rocky Catholic soil of a most infertile sort.

2. *Of Catholics and Jews*

By many measures, one of the most dramatic changes in formal Catholic teaching in the past hundred years has been its understanding of and relationship to Judaism and the Jews. Centuries of enmity and competition, persecution and vilification, supersessionism and damnation—all of this

4. Zahn, *In Solitary Witness*, 146.
5. Zahn, *In Solitary Witness*, 146–48, 150.
6. Zahn, *In Solitary Witness*, 162.
7. Zahn, *In Solitary Witness*, 164–65.
8. Zahn, *In Solitary Witness*, 164–65.
9. Connelly, *From Enemy to Brother*, 30–31.

and more typifies Catholicism and its engagement with Judaism. How remarkable—indeed how unbelievable—must have been the pronouncements of *Nostra Aetate,* the Vatican II declaration that marked a new day in Christianity and Judaism. In some respects, this was among the most powerful and perhaps improbable of the fruits of Vatican II, marking as it did a category shift in the Church's theological understanding of Judaism and the role of Judaism in Christian mission, thought, and practice.

But where did this dramatic shift come from? How did the orthodox Catholic rejection of Judaism that lasted until the 1960s undergo such a sea change, to the point where the Jews were no longer the "perfidious Jews" of the Passion liturgy but now our "elder brothers in the faith," according to Pope John Paul II?[10] Jews no longer needed to be converted in order to be saved; God's covenant with the Chosen People remains in force and was not abrogated by the rejection of Jesus by the Jewish leadership of His day. The Jews were not Christ-killers; they did not murder Christian babies for their Passover rituals (the "blood libel" of immense power), and they were not rejected by God.

By itself, the horrors of the Holocaust seem insufficient to explain the change in Catholicism relative to Judaism; by themselves, human atrocities rarely push events in a single, pre-determined direction. From where did the new understanding of the Jews come, and how did it find reception in the formal teaching of the Catholic Church? In the terms we are exploring today, the ecclesial community was distinctly ill-equipped (ill-formed, in fact) to generate and receive a new word—a lifegiving word, for the Jews—from its own resources in the years up to Vatican II. So profoundly had Catholic imaginations, categories, and dispositions been formed by religious and secular notions of Jews as deficient that the prospects for a new witness seemed unpromising in the extreme. If Jägerstätter represented a Church incapable of receiving testimony, Catholic attitudes toward the Jews reflected incapacities on both the sending and receiving ends of witness.

In this, I recommend to you a book by John Connelly, an historian at the University of California at Berkeley. His 2012 book, *From Enemy to Brother: The Revolution in Catholic Teaching on the Jews, 1933–1965*, is an enlightening and persuasive exploration of these and other questions. The first thing one derives from reading Connelly's careful account is how unpromising were the prospects for a reversal of Christian

10. "Pope Praises Jews as 'Our Elder Brothers in the Faith.'"

antipathy—theological and political—toward the Jews. In this, he notes the importance of distinguishing between anti-Semitism (as a modern racial theory, positing a biological inferiority of the Jewish "race") and anti-Judaism (as a Christian theological position "which foments contempt by considering the Jewish people cursed by God and carrying a special burden of suffering through history").[11]

These concepts, while distinct, often overlapped in Christian thought and practice, to the point where anti-Jewish theological thinking limited and sometimes undermined Christian resistance to the "modern" racism of anti-Semitism. Even the most determined Christian opponents of Nazism—including Dietrich Bonhoeffer—shared with the anti-Semites the basic belief that Jews lived under a curse for killing Christ. That robbed them of the language with which to speak unequivocally in favor of Jews during the Holocaust. Nothing in the Christian tradition permitted them to understand Jewish suffering as other than divinely willed.[12]

This interaction of "scientific" racism and theological anti-Judaism created divides that even baptism was unable to erase, erecting barriers that Catholicism had to accept. As Connelly notes:

> In German-speaking Europe . . . Catholicism opened itself to racist theology after World War I, and priests and influential intellectuals told the Catholic faithful that Jews—that region's "racial other" by common consent—bore a second original sin, an *Erbsunde* signaling special propensity to evil, transmitted from generation to generation and not erased by baptism . . . Once Jews entered the Church, they had to be kept from high office and made to "work hard on themselves" over generations to undo the genetic inheritance of a supposed apostasy that took place hundreds of years earlier. In effect, a Jew could not become a full-fledged Christian in his or her lifetime.[13]

While this may sound strange to us today, contradicting the power of baptism to create a new people and erase distinctions between them (neither Gentile nor Jew, slave nor free, as Gal 3:28 reads), Connelly notes that "German theologians of the prewar era believed they faced another "fact": that human races composed part of the natural order and that these races consisted of persons having shared characteristics. Given that

11. Connelly, *From Enemy to Brother*, 6.
12. Connelly, *From Enemy to Brother*, 9.
13. Connelly, *From Enemy to Brother* 12.

the Church derives its ethics from natural law, the question then became how to adapt moral teaching to what seemed to be the realm of nature."[14]

The "best of natural science" proved to be the path of anti-Semitism into Catholic thought in Germany, where it met with the near-universal Catholic anti-Judaism whose reach extended far beyond culturally German lands. The results flowered in the work of the two premier Catholic voices on Catholicism and race in Germany. The first of these was developmental biologist and Jesuit priest Hermann Muckermann, director of the eugenics section at the Kaiser Wilhelm Institute for Anthropology in Berlin and author of more than two hundred and fifty works on eugenics, families, hereditary, and the like (his work on race alone went through thirty editions). In a major work published as the Nazis were entering into power, Muckerman wrote:

> Our first concern is to maintain the untouched, hereditary, elemental nature of the German people . . . The present age, which desires the renewal of the German people from its deepest biological sources, causes us to direct particular attention to this goal. One cause for concern is without doubt the swelling numbers of persons of Jewish origin in essential branches of our cultural life.[15]

In the context of his time in Catholic circles, Connelly notes, "he was not seen as a racist."[16]

The other great Catholic voice on race during this period was Father Wilhelm Schmidt, a Society of the Divine Word priest at the University of Vienna. He so impressed Pius XI that the pope helped finance a museum of ethnology for him at the Vatican. Because of its emphasis on culture and spirituality over physics and materialism, Schmidt was considered a more "moderate" voice on science and Christianity.[17]

Connelly notes that

> Schmidt had all the scientific legitimacy of Muckermann and . . . he and his students controlled appointments in the discipline for decades . . . Like Muckermann, Schmidt proceeded from an a priori belief in a hierarchy of human races. In his view, races had arisen as a result of environmental conditions, and once

14. Connelly, *From Enemy to Brother,* 12.
15. Connelly, *From Enemy to Brother,* 15.
16. Connelly, *From Enemy to Brother,* 15.
17. Connelly, *From Enemy to Brother,* 16.

> they cohered in natural history, they took on a value that was transcendent.[18]

One of the environmental conditions of current interest was the effects that killing Jesus had on the Jews, forever marking them as an alien race in Europe:

> This kind of transgression can by itself distort the being of a people; yet in the case of the Jewish people, the betrayal of its high calling has made this distortion go very deep. In punishment this people, as Christ himself predicted, was driven out of its homeland. Almost two thousand years of distortion and uprooting of its essence has then had a secondary but real effect on its physical race. These racial effects . . . are not neutralized by baptism. For that, Jews will have to work hard on themselves. [Converted Jews] may therefore belong to our number, but not in the same way as our German racial comrades.[19]

The risk one runs in using cases drawing upon German Catholicism at midcentury is that they are too easily written off as abnormal, as outliers and extremes with little relevance for Catholic thought and practice elsewhere. Time constraints forbid a full discussion here, but suffice to say I disagree with this view; German Catholicism continues to be relevant to the Church universal for its strengths as well as its all-too-apparent weaknesses. Connelly is among many who draw attention to the vitality of German Catholicism, calling it "the most cohesive Catholic milieu in Europe," capable of producing "not only uniformed youth legions, but also newspapers and journals, trade unions, and the most powerful Catholic political organization in the world after the Vatican, the German Center Party."[20]

One could go on, and Connelly does, noting the influence of progressive Catholic theologians like Karl Adam, for whom

> discrimination against Jews did not contradict Christ's basic commandment to love one's neighbor as oneself. After all, love of the other assumed love of the self, and the self was German and Christian. He therefore portrayed Nazi-orchestrated boycotts of Jewish businesses as the fulfillment of Christian charity,

18. Connelly, *From Enemy to Brother,* 16–17.
19. Connelly, *From Enemy to Brother,* 17.
20. Connelly, *From Enemy to Brother,* 68.

> acts of Christian-German self-assertion . . . [aimed at stemming the] Jewish deluge.[21]

No fringe voice in the Catholic world, Adam's admirers have included Edward Schillebeeckx, Bernard Haring, Yves Congar, George Orwell, Dorothy Day, Flannery O'Connor, Karl Rahner, Karl Barth, Thomas Merton, Hans Kung, James Carroll, Pope Paul VI, and Pope Benedict XVI.[22] In other words, not even the best and brightest in the German church were of help in getting past Christian racism toward the Jews and theological enmity toward them.

The literature on Catholicism and anti-Semitism (not to mention anti-Judaism) is huge, extensive, and generally depressing. Controversies abound among those who hold up the real but limited efforts of Catholics in the face of racial thinking and policy and those who are more fundamentally convinced of the Church's accommodation and facilitation of such structures and beliefs. Resolving those disputes is not our business here, but even so it remains a puzzle—given the depth and breadth of anti-Jewish theology and pastoral practice, popular beliefs and prejudices, from where could a new testimony come? Who could bear witness to a vision of the Jews as a people to be loved as they are and not as aliens to be subdued, subordinated, or drowned in the distinctly Gentile waters of baptism?

Those who did, inside and outside of Germanic Europe, and those who ultimately played the leading role in the creation of *Nostra Aetate*, all shared a remarkable legacy, according to Connelly. They were converts, not cradle Catholics—not born into the mix of nation and religion that saturated the formation of Catholicism throughout Europe. Some of these witnesses were converts from Protestantism, like Karl Thieme. But the majority, those whose work would change the direction of Catholicism's view of Judaism, were themselves converts from Judaism and Jewish families. For those who know the history of Jewish-Catholic relations in the era before and after Vatican II, the list is a who's who of important theologians, pastors, and scholars: John Oesterreicher, who with fellow converts of Jewish background, Bruno Hussar and Gregory Baum, drafted *Nostra Aetate*.[23] Others playing leading roles included Albert Fuchs, Maximiliam Beck, Hans Zacharias, Walter Berger, Rudolf Lammel, and

21. Connelly, *From Enemy to Brother*, 20.

22. Connelly, *From Enemy to Brother*, 21.

23. Connelly, *From Enemy to Brother*, 7.

Dietrich von Hildebrand; if one goes back just a bit further in time, say to the 1840s, the list of converts, mostly from Jewish backgrounds, would include Leon Bloy, Jacques and Raissa Maritain, Erik Peterson, Waldemar Gurian, Paul Demann, Geza Vermes, and many others.[24]

All of which leads to Connelly's conclusion, relevant to our concern for witness and its reception: "Without converts, the Catholic Church would never have 'thought its way' out of the challenges of racist anti-Judaism."[25] To him, the converts teach a lesson about solidarity, inasmuch as "[i]t turned out [in his study] that virtually all of the Catholics concerned about protecting the 'other' were people Catholics in central Europe considered 'others.'"[26]

As Connelly notes, he started with the

> modest goal of answering the largely unexplored question of how the Holocaust changed the way Catholics thought about Jews. Contrary to widespread assumptions, the revolutionary about-face that took place at Vatican II did not flow "naturally" or "automatically" from reflections about the genocide, but rather resulted from struggle among theologians extending from the 1930s to the 1960s: about how to revise centuries of teaching on the crowd's self-deprecation in Matthew 27 ("let his blood be upon us and our children!"), or the place in the Epistle to the Hebrews declaring God's covenant with the Jews obsolete, or the idea flowing from Matthew 28:19 that Christians had no option but to proselytize Jews. How could a priest who had preached one interpretation of the New Testament for decades suddenly reverse himself and still seem a source of reliable understanding of scripture?[27]

In highlighting the role of converts in breaking through an ecclesial culture too closely tied to its national culture, Connelly describes these voices as "perhaps the least cynical of Catholics, and [their] idealism led them to hone a sense of the practical."[28] We will never fully understand why this motley group converted to Catholicism. The decisions were individual. Like other converts, they felt specially touched by grace: conversion involved embracing a mission from God, and one's life had

24. Connelly, *From Enemy to Brother*, 63–64, 287–88.
25. Connelly, *From Enemy to Brother*, 290.
26. Connelly, *From Enemy to Brother*, 290.
27. Connelly, *From Enemy to Brother*, 10.
28. Connelly, *From Enemy to Brother*, 288.

to be visibly new. We see in John Orseterreicher, but also Dietrich von Hildebrand and Karl Thieme, not only passion but obsessive fervor; not only involvement but extraordinary commitment based not simply in belief but unwavering conviction; not only disinterest in popularity but insistence upon influence. Conversion had involved not just willingness to accept but courage to refuse, and therefore a readiness to defend unpopular positions. Many people are tempted to leave secure communities of origin—religious or otherwise—but converts are those who have summoned the conviction to do so, and it was belief rather than doubt that characterized them.

III. Some Modest Conclusions: Two Lessons on Receiving Testimony

It may seem as though I have wandered from my original intent to focus on how the formation of Christian affections, dispositions, and identities done poorly impedes not only the generation of gospel-centered testimony but also its reception. The cases I have invited you to sit with may seem too particular, too extreme, too parochial to be of much value in thinking more broadly about the imperative of Christian witness from and to the numerous and varied contexts of the contemporary world. After all, what has Berlin to say to Belem, or Germany to Guatemala, or Salzburg to Salvador?

I am not alone in maintaining that testimony in general, and martyrdom in particular, requires the existence of a church or community capable of receiving witness—to name and affirm it, reflect upon and disseminate it, to employ it as a model of Christianity well lived that is taught to others. In the case of Jägerstätter, we have a rather curious martyr, one whose witness was as Zahn notes "a stand *against* his fellow Catholics and their spiritual leaders who were wholeheartedly committed to, or at least willing to acquiesce in, the war effort."[29] This powerful and improbable witness dramatized what one English bishop (during the Vatican II discussion of what would become the Pastoral Constitution on the Church in the Modern World, *Gaudium et Spes*) described as "the major scandal of Christianity," namely that "almost every national hierarchy in almost every war has allowed itself to become the moral arm of its own

29. Zahn, *In Solitary* Witness, 162–63.

government, even in wars later recognized as palpably unjust."[30] How ironic, then, that the successor to Jägerstätter's nationalist bishop would be those describing Jägerstätter as "a prophet with a global view and a penetrating insight . . . an advocate of nonviolence and peace."[31]

It may be fair to say that the Church's about-face on this Austrian farmer testifies to the indispensability of Christian universalism in allowing God to somehow redeem even the most seemingly useless of gospel-based witness. Had Jägerstätter's case not come to the attention of the Church worldwide, thanks in part to the scholarly work of the late Gordon Zahn—had his memory remained within the confines of the Austrian church alone, in other words—it is hard to see this parish sacristan as someone who would later be praised as a martyr and candidate for sainthood. The first lesson to consider might be here: it took the larger Church—transnational, not beholden to a single set of national allegiances or commitments—to recognize and receive this martyr's witness. Such may well be a structural commonplace in the era after modernity, with the worldwide character of the body of Christ sliced into national fragments; tied so closely in many places to nationalist fusions of faith and political identity, such churches may be less capable of receiving witness and recognizing martyrdom in their midst. To counteract the structural shortcomings of national churches requires the entire Church, able and willing even to proclaim some witnesses and martyrs as a means of fraternal correction of local churches.

If Jägerstätter speaks to the need of a wider community of reception, if Christian witness is to be accepted and made part of the life of the Church, those converts to Catholicism who were instrumental in reversing centuries of anti-Jewish hostility speak to another imperative—that of "converting the baptized," in the words of the Jesuit William O'Malley.[32] Oesterreicher, Thieme, Gurian, Baum, von Hildebrand, Fuchs, Zacharias, and more—all of them confronted a church so thoroughly accommodated to its surrounding culture that the Church disappeared itself in crucial ways.

In some respects, this is a more difficult matter than finding ways that Catholic transnational ties might counteract the pathologies of Catholic nationalism as a barrier to witness and prophetic reception. But

30. Cited in Zahn, *In Solitary Witness*, preface.

31. Schwarz and Scheuer, "Foreword," 7.

32. O'Malley, *Converting the Baptized*.

this second lesson is no less crucial: for there to be Christian witness and reception, there has to be—at some significant level of thought and practice—a meaningful distinction between church and world, between the people gathered by God to reflect however imperfectly the dawning Kingdom of God and those parts of reality still tied to other ambitions, other allegiances, and other loyalties.

This is a hard word for many Christians, especially many Catholics, to hear. We are so deeply steeped in those laudable parts of our tradition that stress the continuities between faith and reason, between the work of the Holy Spirit inside and outside the walls of the Church, and the capacity of the gospel to become inculturated in all human communities and traditions. We are so deeply formed by these notions that we too often lose sight of the peculiarity of Christian testimony and the strangeness of Christian witness. If there is no disjunction of any sort between the Church and the world, then there is no Good News to proclaim, there is no need for a people capable of trying to love their enemies, turning the other cheek, or repaying evil with good; the world does not need followers of Jesus if church and world are indistinguishable, saying and wanting the same things just with different terms or jargon.

The Jewish converts to Christianity that are so central to Connelly's account reminded the later Church, at some level, of the irretrievably "other-ness" of the Christian faith—that this received final vindication during the Second Vatican Council, which affirmed the commonalities between church and world in many respects, is no small irony. And yet, perhaps not so surprising: persons witnessing to a new view of Judaism in Catholic circles did so not in response to Kantian ideals or generic ethical systems, but by recourse to resources and readings and spiritual traditions out of step with the modern world of European scholarship. Nouvelle theology, with its return to patristic sources and theological readings of Scripture, was out of touch not only with Catholic Neo-Scholasticism but also with secular modernity and its categories.

What the converts brought to the process, among other things, was a deep and profound encounter with the Jesus of the New Testament—in all His particularity and strangeness. This encounter pushed them beyond the natural law, universal morality, common grace, and secular notions of ethics and equality. In doing so, they sought to revitalize the spiritual taste buds, theological imaginations, and corporate practices of their Catholic brothers and sisters who had previously been more deeply formed by worldly stories and identities in which the distinctions between church and world were obscured, thereby rendering them numb or immune to the call of the gospel as it related to the Jews.

It is this specificity, this insistence that the Church and the world are not yet the same, that makes witness and its reception a radically Christocentric enterprise, and that makes the centrality of the poor in Christian life and reflection something other than nonsensical. Christian formation that loses this part of the dialectic—that stresses the continuities between God's creation and the ubiquity of the Holy Spirit at the expense of the utter otherness of Jesus Christ as the template for Christian discipleship, witness, and reception—finds itself with nothing to say and no ability to hear, rendered mute and deaf in varying measures.

CHAPTER 9

Happy Carnage: Sacrifice and Popular Entertainment

An article published in Concilium: International Journal of Theology, *for a 2013 themed issue on "the ambivalence of sacrifice."*

Catwoman: Come with me. Save yourself. You don't owe these people anymore—you've given them *everything*.

Batman: Not everything. Not yet.[1]

THE HIGHEST-GROSSING FILM OF 2012 (based on worldwide receipts) featured explosions, car crashes, collapsing buildings, helicopter crashes, and multiple killings—all in the first five minutes, all before the opening credits. The second-highest grossing film of 2012 used the most refined tools of cinematic art to present lurid depictions of murder, bone-crunching brutality, torture, and gruesome sadism. The first film, *The Avengers,* drew more than $600 million in worldwide receipts in fewer than seven months; the second, *The Dark Knight Rises,* totaled nearly $500 million in six months. Welcome to the world of Hollywood superhero movies.

1. Nolan, *The Dark Knight Rises.*

In another sector of the for-profit culture industries, video games in all their manifestations—on personal computers, gaming consoles, mobile devices, and more—generate revenues greater than the motion picture industry worldwide. Year in and year out, the list of most popular and commercially successful games are those in which mayhem, mass murder, endless warfare, and destruction rank at or near the top. Successful violent video games, especially those with a "first-person shooter" orientation—in which the player directs gunfire or weaponry at targets of one sort or another—spawn sequels that broaden and deepen the reach of the product. Names like *Halo 4*, *Call of Duty: Black Ops II*, *Assassin's Creed III*, and others dominated the bestseller lists of 2012.

Whereas once the products of Western culture industries might have been viewed worldwide as the province of the privileged—or at least, middle class—the audiences for and users of such leisure products are increasingly available to larger demographic groups worldwide. Illegal downloading, duplicating, piracy, and other extra-market forms of appropriation have eased superhero movies and blood-soaked games into the lifestyle habits of persons previously excluded by cost considerations. The global marketing machine—the billions of dollars spent on advertising each year—ensures that countless more people (especially young people) know about the warfare jamboree that is *Call of Duty: Black Ops II*, for example, than will ever enter its world of "realistic" human suffering and killing.

Sacrifice and Schizophrenia

The postmodern world is one in which "sacrifice" is a term under suspicion. With truth banished and hyperplurality the norm, anyone who sacrifices on behalf of a cause or a conviction is a chump, or at least a naïf. The sort of love that might lead one to take on the suffering of another is seen as bordering on the pathological, except perhaps in the context of intimate family relations (which themselves are often depicted as arenas of pathology and dysfunction). Feminist and other scholars have worked to expose the exploitative qualities infusing much traditional discourse on sacrifice, especially when such constructs an iron cage of patriarchy that imprisons women in crushing levels of self-neglect and abusive obligatory expectations. Anyone asking for sacrifice, or willing to sacrifice, is not someone to be taken seriously.

Cynicism is the default setting of the age. All have fallen short, all have failed, all have sinned, so therefore nobody deserves the benefit of the doubt, nobody deserves a break, nobody deserves anything. Heroes have feet of shit, never mind clay. Sacrificing for somebody else is a suspect move, either proof of a masochistic tendency or a calculated investment aiming to control someone else via expectations of reciprocity, debt, or obligation.

The individualism of the modern era receives an injection of steroids in the postmodern one. The cult of the individual, far from running out of steam, receives new life from technologies, ideologies, capitalist dogma, intellectual fads, and legal doctrines in which the individual comes first, last, and everywhere in between. The cultural ecology of late capitalism rewards the sort of individualized, rational-choice-fixated way of inhabiting the world that makes sacrifice incomprehensible. In this framework, for example, martyrs do not give up their lives in witness to an important value or ideal, but rather they maximize their utility by trading one good for the prospect of a higher one (eternal life, reputation, a lofty sense of self-worth).

But if sacrifice has been repressed or downgraded in some realms of culture, it reappears and thrives in others—in the playground of popular culture, for instance. Yet, this playground is not a free space where noble or humane intuitions roam freely, having slipped the leash of state and market. Contrary to the more naïve celebrations of postmodernity's priests, the precincts of corporate popular culture are places where play and imagination are themselves policed and disciplined, shaped in ways that reinforce notions of identity and community that are more regimented than the hoped-for hyperplurality of the age. Sacrifice is alive and well and in service to the collective violence of states and markets, these days accompanied by a soundtrack, computer-generated images, and cross-promotional tie-ins ranging from dolls and lunchboxes to toys and pajamas.

The same cultures and the same world and the same vectors of discourse that snicker at sacrifice are also those that privilege sacrifice, glorify sacrifice, inspire sacrifice, and demand sacrifice. In schoolbooks, the message is that the world needs more sacrifice, not less. From formal settings to mass advertising campaigns, state leaders call for persons willing to sacrifice for their country. Nonprofit groups urge us to sacrifice on behalf of the environment, on behalf of animals, on behalf of persons we will never meet or ecological indicators we will never ourselves perceive.

War-making regimes have no more potent call to new slaughter than to shame the populace with the claim that aversion to new war discredits the deaths of previous warriors and slaughterers, who "will have sacrificed in vain." The call to "support the troops" is itself a blank check for the next war; questioning the next war threatens to undermine the legitimacy of all wars and the deeds done in war's name.

You can sacrifice for your religion if you want, you can sacrifice for the proletariat if you're nostalgic, and if you want, you can sacrifice your wish to eat meat. You *must* sacrifice to ensure the profitability of the capitalists, you are *required* to sacrifice for the security of the state, you are *compelled* to sacrifice the necessities of the poor to ensure the luxuries of the rich. The line between sacrifice volunteered and sacrifice coerced is thin indeed, and arguably more permeable all the time; the most exquisite form of coercion, after all, is one that comes to be seen as voluntary (see propaganda, advertising, and the manipulation of guilt).

Amidst the confusion surrounding sacrifice, Rene Girard provides a few useful points of anchorage. His assertions are many, the controversies even more numerous; for purposes here, it suffices to concur with his general claim that sacrifice is indispensable to statecraft, ancient and modern. Sovereignty feeds on sacrifice, depends on it like a fire feeds on oxygen. Sovereign entities will do almost anything to avoid their own extinction, thus ensuring that no sacrifice is too great if it maintains the structures and processes necessary for governance and power.

Sustaining the sacrifices necessary to preserve power in the political economy of late capitalism requires more than what the instrumental action of state actors alone can provide. It also requires a hospitable cultural ecology—an aether of stories, songs, symbols, metaphors, images, and experiences—in which people live and move and have their being. The connections between political economy and cultural production are neither straightforward nor simple; nevertheless, even in the postmodern soup one can discern the exercise of cultural power in the service of capital and state.[2]

The Pop Culture of Payback

One of the most powerful tropes in contemporary popular culture, past and present, one that renews and recharges an ethos of sacrifice, is that

2. See Budde, *The (Magic) Kingdom of God*, for one exploration.

of socially approved revenge. Bad guys who escape the long arm of the law; powerful enemies whose carnage can be stopped only by carnage employed by heroes; rogues acting outside the rules of society being put down by more noble rogues acting outside the constrictions of society's rules—with scenarios like these and countless others, popular movies, television programs, and video games set the stage for unbelievable levels of violence, cruelty, and destruction intended to draw cheers and approval from mass audiences worldwide. Graphic depictions of exploding flesh dominate one subset of the genre (think Tarantino), while sterile, antiseptic treatments of killings happen in another subset. What holds it all together is a pandering to, and reinforcing of, a simplistic notion of justice built on payback, revenge, and entitlement. Seeing the designated villains "get what was coming to them" is cathartic, as is the vicarious thrill of being a "rule-breaker" who shoves aside the impotent tools of dialogue, negotiation, and even law (forget about forbearance or forgiveness—such are anathema, beyond the ken of all but the cowardly) in favor of decisive and triumphant action—such are the narrative motors that drive the dioramas of pop-culture killing machines.

These repetitive narratives, joined to ever-more-sophisticated tools of art and presentation, provide simulacra of sacrifice appropriate for a jaded world of the cynical and exhausted. Society has failed—but heroes arise from mediocrity to kill the enemy. Superpowered or superarmed beings threaten the world—so an even more superpowered or superarmed defender arises, often against his/her will, to sacrifice untold numbers of the enemy and bystanders, and perhaps oneself, when the chips are down.

Whether in first-person shooter games or in big-budget superhero movies, the motifs of the Hollywood western movie seem to repeat themselves. Sacrifice and virtue require action, not reflection, patience, or forbearance. One man alone, standing against the chaos of evil and the cowardice of the community, gives up comfort and security to pit himself against evil so unmixed that it evokes neither pity nor sympathy. And if not one man alone, one small group of strong personalities bands together, overcoming their own divisions in service to weak civilians who hardly seem worth the efforts on their behalf (*The Avengers* owing more than a bit to *The Magnificent Seven* or *The Seven Samurai* or even *The A-Team*). Even first-person shooter games build community via multiplayer formats, in which ersatz war generates bonding experiences among the otherwise isolated "combatants."

In *The Avengers*, the political authorities are presented as in over their heads (trying to turn an otherworldly energy source into a weapon), capable of massing destructive technology that nonetheless doesn't save the day (a high-technology flying aircraft carrier), callous regard for the loss of human life (the hidden political leaders order a nuclear strike on Manhattan), and jealous of the powers held by the superheroes who are saving the world. These superheroes face impossible odds, receive incredible punishment, and put their egos aside for the common good—and in the end, it's the most narcissistic member of the team (Iron Man, the billionaire bad boy, Tony Stark) who saves the world by flying away from earth while pushing a nuclear weapon. This is the same Iron Man who, when confronted with defeat earlier, promises that, if he and his friends cannot save the earth, they will avenge it—in case anyone missed the significance of the group's (and movie's) name. Vengeance is mine, says the superhero.

The Dark Knight Rises ends the recent Batman trilogy by focusing on a Batman who has been unjustly labeled a murderous psychotic at the end of the previous film. The audience soon sees that this hero has sacrificed his health, his billion-dollar fortune, and his one chance at true love, all in a futile attempt to protect his city from the ceaseless waves of evil that seem to assail it on a regular basis. Old and weary, Batman is drawn out of retirement to fight a personification of evil named Bane—a brute whose voice is muffled by a metal muzzle. The movie's violence is panoramic and intimate, gruesome and spectacular at the same time; Batman's back breaks with a sickening sound, he is tortured, and other characters suffer and die in ways hard to watch. Mick LaSalle, veteran film critic for the *San Francisco Chronicle*, described the film as "a wallow in nonstop cruelty and destruction, a film that was antilife." This description came not in his review of the film but in a *mea culpa* written about his own self-censorship regarding the pornography of violence that flows freely in so many contemporary films. He came to regret avoiding discussion of the "soul-crushing" quality of the movie only after another classically American mass-murder spree in which life parodied the "art" of cinema.[3]

This Batman rises—from disgrace, from bankruptcy, from a torturer's pit—ultimately with a nuclear weapon that he takes out to sea to spare the city that has only recently branded him a menace and enemy

3. LaSalle, "Violent Media Poisoning the Nation's Soul."

(taking away nuclear weapons seems to be a common thread in self-sacrifice among the superhero set these days). Like Christ, this is a savior rejected by his own people, whose death seems meaningless except to the extent that he inspires others—a coward who discovers his courage, a policeman who steps up to fill the superhero void left by Batman's demise. This self-sacrificing Batman even passes on the chance to redeem his own good name and glory:

> **Commissioner Gordon:** But shouldn't the people know the hero who saved them?
>
> **Batman:** A hero can be anyone. That was always the point.[4]

Happy Carnage and the Kingdom of God

Whatever the strengths and weaknesses of Girard's work on sacrifice, his view on Christian discipleship as the remedy for blood sacrifice is unambiguous. Kingdoms and states, what Paul would call the "principalities and powers"—all of these, Luke asserts, have been given over to Satan, who in turn offers them to Jesus if He will offer worship and sacrifice to the tempter (Luke 4:5–7).

As one interpreter summarizes Girard's view:

> Humans are inhabitants of the kingdom of Satan, captives of violence. Jesus proclaimed another Kingdom, the Kingdom of God, which implies "the complete and definitive elimination of every form of vengeance and every form of reprisal in relations between men." Jesus offered his listeners the chance to escape from the violence of Satan and to enter the Kingdom of God. He invited everybody to renounce violence, to leave it behind, by giving up the idea of retribution. Thus, in Girard's view, the Gospel doctrine is "good news" because it gives us all we need to know in order to escape from violence. The only thing which is needed in order to let the Kingdom of God come is that humankind as a whole, and each individual separately, renounces vengeance.[5]

4. Nolan, *The Dark Knight Rises.*

5. Depoortere, "Gianni Vattimo and Rene Girard," 880–81; referencing Girard, *Things Hidden*, 196–99.

The way out for all humanity is the Sermon on the Mount, which to Girard marks the decisive break with all forms of human sacrifice in the name of order and justice (ancient and modern). Girard aims, especially in his later work, "to portray the renunciation of revenge, violence, and all other forms of rivalrous desire as the intrinsic principle of the Kingdom of God."[6] Far from being a naïve and otherworldly commitment to pacifism detached from the imperatives of a suffering world, Girard points to gospel pacifism as an essential aspect of Christian discipleship that represents the only "realistic" response to a world built upon sacrificing human life.

With popular culture drenched in the thrills and rewards of revenge as entertainment, with vigilante justice as the most satisfying sort of storytelling, the Sermon on the Mount stands as an embarrassing obstacle if taken seriously. In superhero movies, in the wastage of video games, in so much of popular culture, the ancient tropes of "protect your friends/destroy your enemies" are taken to new heights of technological sophistication (and psychological effectiveness, according to some research). Much of popular culture echoes the US war cry of "kill the intolerant," as it justifies its military interventions against regimes that don't share the love of tolerance and pluralism that defines liberalism armed and on the march. It supports the sort of militarized human rights doctrine typified in the real world by the "Responsibility to Protect" doctrine, in which powerful states invade weaker ones in defense of victims of injustice (one will wait a long time before powerful states agree to interventions in their own territory in defense of racial, ethnic, or other minorities, suggesting once again the might-makes-right quality of much of human-rights discourse). And it colludes in the cycle of victimization-revenge-victimization that plays out without end and migrates from the real world back to pop-culture fantasies, back to real-world attitudes and actions.

For-profit culture industries have long worked to undermine the radical demands of the Sermon on the Mount. Christian pacifism is ultimately a selfish indulgence that must be overcome to serve the community—such is the message of *Sargeant York*, the 1941 film about Alvin York, the most decorated US soldier during World War I. The film won numerous Academy Awards, was the highest-grossing film of the year, and set the standard for the sort of Christian "realism" in entertainment

6. Palaver, *Rene Girard's Mimetic Theory*, 220.

products that helped reconcile later Christians with the demands of war in service to the state and its ambitions.

The imperative that belonging requires sacrifice—of one's life, one's convictions, one's revulsion at taking another human life—itself claims victims as a matter of routine. In his book, *Nations Have the Right to Kill: Hitler, Holocaust, and War*, Richard Koenigsberg argues that Hitler saw war as a sacrifice necessary for revitalizing the German people. It followed from this, according to theologian Stanley Hauerwas, that

> "The Aryan" was therefore understood as someone willing to sacrifice himself or herself for the nation. The Jew, in contrast, was individualistic and selfish. Accordingly, the Jew could be sacrificed for the good of the nation. The destructive character of war is crucial for the moral purposes that war should serve, from Hitler's perspective. For war is a form of sacrifice "whereby human beings give over their bodies and possessions to the objects of worship with names like France, Germany, Japan, America, etc."[7]

With every glorification of killing, even (or especially) in its most "justified" forms of justice-seeking and payback, popular-culture industries make a down payment on the next war, the next slaughter in the name of truth or freedom or tolerance or protection. And it underscores even more the need for Christians to act as if Jesus meant what He said when He told His imitators to return evil for good and to love those who hate you. Only in such a fashion will the narratives of heroic revenge and justice be revealed as best suited to the logic of Caiaphas ("it is better for you to have one man die for the people than to have the whole nation destroyed" (John 11:50 NRSV), upon which the entire edifice of politics and sacrifice is built. It is this that the Kingdom of God calls disciples to leave behind, to imitate the Jesus who exposed the human sacrifices at the heart of statecraft by refusing to endorse or participate in them. This is the new exodus for the pilgrim people of God as they follow Jesus as the new Moses from bondage into freedom.

7. Hauerwas, *War and the American Difference*, 21–22 n. 1, referencing Koenigsberg, *Nations Have the Right to Kill*, xv.

CHAPTER 10

Political Theology and the Church

A lecture delivered in Manila on February 24, 2012, to Ateneo de Manila University and Dakateo: Catholic Theological Society of the Philippines.

Introduction

I CONFESS TO BEING behind the times in most things. I don't use the latest social media very much—I've never Twittered or tweeted, at least to my knowledge, and my knowledge of popular music stopped with the arrival of my first child in 1988. I haven't seen any of the most popular current movies, whether made in America or anyplace else.

It seems that this quality carries over a bit into my academic work, as well. When I reflect on what seems to me to be important in thinking about "political theology and the Church"—my assigned topic for today—I'm afraid I continue to concentrate on concerns that many people think are long-settled, resolved, and old news. Nothing to see here. Move along, please.

To be more specific, I continue to believe that being a follower of Jesus Christ means we shouldn't kill people, especially in the organized, structured practices we call politics and war. I don't think Christians should kill anyone, but I think it's especially scandalous that Christians continue to kill other Christians as if the bonds of sacrament and Church mattered not one bit.

I continue to be amazed by the ease with which members of so-called Christian nations slaughtered members of other so-called Christian nations in the twentieth century. As I said, I think Christian nonviolence means that Christians ought not kill anybody, but the wholesale phenomenon of Christians killing one another with impunity remains a huge, perhaps insurmountable, obstacle to any sort of Christian credibility in the world. Why take seriously—whether in interreligious dialogues or anything else—anything coming from a religious movement whose members are willing to kill one another by the millions? And this coming from a movement that invites the world to embrace a Prince of Peace, calling for reconciliation and forgiveness rather than revenge and domination.

There are many ways to get into a topic like this—for example, one could discuss yet again the ethics of warfare, the endless debates on the so-called just war—but today I'd like to raise another set of concerns. More specifically, I'd like to raise anew the question of Christians and lethality as a question of inculturation gone wrong, and of processes of political v. ecclesial formation of human affections, priorities, and dispositions.

To say the least, inculturation remains a major concern in Catholic circles worldwide. One theme highlighted usefully in recent years concerns the recognition that inculturation is an ongoing process rather than a once-and-for-all phenomenon. It is not a finished work but one that requires ongoing renewal, rearticulation, and recommitment as host cultures and the Church both change; in this respect, it remains a constant both for churches in Europe and North America as well as for those in the Philippines and elsewhere.

In all of this, it remains important to recognize that much damage was done to countless human beings, and to the witness of the gospel, by the forcible insertion of Christianity into human cultures during various eras of the past. This sort of inculturation at sword's point, suppressing pre-existing peoples, beliefs, and communities in favor of a Christianity armed and aggressive, created a cultural milieu of a most particular sort. No one, least of all leaders of the Catholic Church, seeks a return to any processes of inculturation that ally themselves with violence and death-dealing.

It is this last point that provides something of a jumping-off point for me today. Much of the past seventy-five years has been spent coming to terms with the legacy of inculturation that comes by way of force, coercion, and power—in missiology, in the anti- and postcolonial movements, in the renewal movements surrounding the Second Vatican Council, and much more. How might the Church be true to its best self, how might it be a herald and foretaste of the Kingdom of God, without tying itself to forms of cultural and political habitation that presuppose the legitimacy of violence and coercively regulated norms of order, belonging, and loyalty? In our time, to repeat, the Church rejects the ambition of being an institution capable of structuring human affections and identities through force or by recourse to violent means. In this, may God be praised as room is made for a vision of religious liberty rooted both in individual conscience and a robust communal sense of discipleship and mission.

And yet, a blind spot of some significance remains, an area of political theology that merits attention and consideration—in some respects, a reconsideration of past accommodations once thought settled but, in my view, in need of revisiting and revision. More specifically, I think the Church worldwide needs to visit anew the conflict between state-based identities (nationalism, citizenship, ethnopolitical movements) and being a member of the Christian Church, that worldwide community of believers joined by baptism and Eucharist and the claim that Jesus is Lord. For much of the so-called modern era, for imperial and colonial/postcolonial regions alike, perhaps the most powerful processes and ideologies of identity and belonging—of culturation and inculturation alike, if you will—have been those that seek to form peoples, nations, states, and homelands. The claims of such, usually and perhaps eventually, tend to become overreaching and thus represent a form of cultural construction incompatible with the radical demands of the gospel and the eschatological nature of discipleship. What makes these overreaching, to be specific, is that they require Christians to kill and die for them as a matter of course.

To the extent that Christianity in general and Catholicism in particular has sought to become "at home" in the various cultures of the world by embracing the norms of nationalism and citizenship that predominate, to that extent has the Church adopted a defective sort of inculturation. In its embrace of nationalism and its claims on identity and allegiance, I suggest, the Church again opts for another sort of inculturation at sword's point, in which Christianity mutes its call for peacemaking and reconciliation as it attempts to gain acceptance and incorporation among the diverse and varied cultures of the world. Such represents another variant on the now-discredited agenda of inculturation by coercion, albeit one in which in most cases the violence is wielded on behalf of a non-Christian ideology to which the Church serves in a subordinate, not defining, role.

Given time constraints, I can only outline the argument I have made in extended form elsewhere and hope to deepen in the future. For now, let me offer a few thoughts on the following:

1. The fundamental violence of national citizenship and the sectarian nature of "nationhood";
2. The limits of Catholic social thought regarding nationalism and citizenship;
3. A brief description of a neglected aspect of Christian theology that might help the Church resituate the relative value of citizenship and national identities with reference to the unity of the Church formed in baptism, Eucharist, and ecclesial practice.

The Violence of Citizenship

The literature on political citizenship, especially in the liberal traditions of the West, is built on the assumption that secular, national citizenship is the solution to the irremediably violent nature of religious (and specifically Christian) notions of identity, allegiance, and belonging. Our colleague Bill Cavanaugh has done path-breaking work on much of this, and I commend his most recent book to you as essential reading. His survey of Western political thought is a helpful overview of the extent to which political, nation-oriented citizenship is largely assumed to be the antidote to sectarian violence and coercion.[1]

Political theology, to the extent that it presumes the normativity of such a view of political citizenship, perpetuates a blind spot with significant consequences for the Church, for human association, and for understanding the trajectory of life in modernity in its many expressions. Indeed, that the churches themselves have subscribed to such a narrative explains in no small degree their own inability to name the violence and coercion built into most notions of citizenship, nationhood, and state sovereignty.

1. Cavanaugh, *The Myth of Religious Violence.*

As a category of membership which ascribes rights and duties, citizenship by necessity is selective and exclusionary. In the modern era, where citizenship came to assume primarily a national character (being "German" was to have the rights associated with German state citizenship; being "Nigerian" was to be recognized as a politically empowered and recognized member of the polity called Nigeria), authentic nationhood found expression in the foundation, governance, or recognition of a sovereign state.

Anthony Marx is one among many scholars to remind us how unnatural and how coercive such notions of nation and citizenship have been. The power to exclude certain groups from national or political recognition should not be seen as an occasional or transitory phenomenon in political history, says Marx; rather, "exclusion is structural rather than fixed or tangential to nation-building."[2] As he notes:

> The term "nation-state" implies some convergence of an institutionalized polity and collective allegiance to it, with "nationalism" defined here as such bounded solidarity and allegiance to a state. The nation is that group viewed as the legitimate owner of the state; the collective sentiment of such ownership (that is, nationalism) is what gives the state legitimacy. This connection can be established in more or less either direction: state first, building national loyalty, or a national community creating a state, though often these processes occur together.[3]

More contemporary scholars are, like Marx, willing to disagree with earlier notions of pre-existing social groups giving rise to state formations; more commonly, it is a project advanced by actors within already-established states, for whom constructing political identities and loyalties requires state action. And this action, as Marx and others notes, is by its nature coercive, exclusionary, and powerful:

> [N]ationalism is often purposefully exclusionary, with such exclusions emerging in fits and starts but encouraged or encoded to serve the explicit requirements for solidifying core loyalty to the nation. Rather than diversity precluding cohesion, diversity and selective allocations of nationalism and related rights may be the tools for building cohesion among the core that is included and demarcated.

2. Marx, "The Nation-State and Its Exclusions," 103–4.
3. Marx, "The Nation-State and Its Exclusions," 104.

> [In addition] . . . much prior analysis has assumed that the imperative for encouraging national unity should be inclusive, but often this is not possible . . . State elites make deals en route to nation building, selecting who to include, reward, and encourage loyalty from as the core constituency. To identify and consolidate the core, elites manipulate established antagonisms against some other group thereby excluded. And the core constituency so demarcated and reinforced may itself change over time according to shifting challenges and allegiances.[4]

The politics of definition looms large in all of this, inasmuch as warring definitions of states, nations, ethnicities, and more show no signs of abating. For many purposes, nationalism may still

> be best understood according to the definition offered by Arthur Stinchcombe nearly forty years ago, as a wish to suppress internal divisions within the nation and to define people outside the group as untrustworthy as allies and implacably evil as enemies . . . It is on the one hand . . . a love of compatriots. But it is on the other hand a spirit of distrust of the potential treason of any opposition within the group and a hatred of strangers.[5]

While it might be comforting to assume that the process of willful exclusion is but a transitory matter, part of the labor pains of state- and nation-building to be superceded by a progressive incorporation of outside groups and former outsiders, such comfort might itself be transitory. Former outcasts may well be incorporated, provided they change themselves in accord with nationalist dictates and narratives, but other groups by necessity often become the objects of exclusion, definition-by-contrast, or similar binary negations. Such may be the fate of immigrants and refugees in our time, as well as other groups who by stipulation can be placed outside the parameters of accepted identity-description (terrorists, extremists, ethnically unassimilable communities, etc.).

Such is emphasized by Adrian Oldfield in his reflections on civic republicanism in the modern world. As he notes,

> [c]itizenship is exclusive: it is not a person's humanity that one is responding to, it is the fact that he or she is a fellow citizen, or a stranger. In choosing an identity for ourselves, we recognize both who our fellow citizens are, and those who are not members of our community, and thus who are potential enemies.

4. Marx, "The Nation-State and Its Exclusions," 259.
5. Stinchcombe, "Social Structure and Politics," 600–601.

> Citizenship cuts across both religious and secular universalism and involves recognizing that one gives priority, when and where required, to one's political community.[6]

While such does not always require unremitting hostility to others, to Oldfield "[i]t simply means that to remain a citizen one cannot always treat everyone as a human being." It means that states must retain the right, according to Peter Schuck and Rogers Smith, "to refuse consent to the membership of those who would disrupt their necessary homogeneity," however defined, in the interest of national unity.[7] As a political phenomenon, citizenship is distinction backed by force.

Rhetorical celebration of multiculturalism and the richness of multinational states notwithstanding, there remains much political energy behind the processes of political homogenization and exclusion in the contemporary world. With reference to the so-called advanced industrial world, Jerry Muller notes that,

> whereas in 1900 there were many states in Europe without a single dominant nationality, by 2007 there were only two, and one of those, Belgium, was close to breaking up. Aside from Switzerland, in other words—where the domestic ethnic balance of power is protected by strict citizenship laws—in Europe the "separatist" project has not so much vanished as triumphed.[8]

He adds that,

> [i]n short, ethnonationalism has played a more profound and lasting role in modern history than is commonly understood, and the processes that led to the dominance of the ethnonational state and the separation of ethnic groups in Europe are likely to reoccur elsewhere.[9]

By most measures, much of the rest of the world is a long way away from the sort of ethnic cleansing/homogenization conducted in contemporary Europe. As one commentator notes, "the overwhelming majority of the world's states have a plurality of ethnes/nations. In many of these multinational or multi-ethnic states one nation or ethne is dominant."[10] The

6. Oldfield, "Citizenship and Community," 81.
7. Shuck and Smith, "Citizenship Without Consent," 28.
8. Muller, "Us and Them."
9. Muller, "Us and Them."
10. Hughes, "Following Jesus as His Community," 331–32.

notion of nation developed, promulgated, and institutionalized in most multi-ethnic states usually reflects the interests and outlook of a dominant group or coalition; alternative pictures of identity and allegiance are neglected, suppressed, co-opted or depoliticized as they are labeled inappropriately sectarian, divisive, tribal, or regressive.

The putative homogeneity of many European states may itself prove to be a transitory phenomenon, in which "globalization" proves to be a disruptive force with many implications. On the one hand, increased migration of various sorts may start to challenge some of the previously constructed notions of national and political identity forged via violence and exclusion in polities around the world. On the other hand, globalization can and often does generate heightened levels of instability and uncertainty as people's sense of who they are comes into question.

As political psychologist Catarina Kinnvall puts it:

> Globalization challenges simple definitions of who we are and where we come from . . . As individuals feel vulnerable and experience existential anxiety, it is not uncommon for them to wish to affirm a threatened self-identity. Any collective identity that can provide such security is a potential pole of attraction. It is a war of emotions, where world leaders and other paramount figures are seeking to rally people around simple rather than complex causes.[11]

She adds later that "[g]lobalization has made it more difficult, but not less desirable, to think in terms of singular, integrated, and harmonious identities as individuals constantly tum their actions to an increasing number of others and issues. The fact that individuals search for one stable identity does not mean, however, that such identities exist."[12] Silvio Ferrari adds that "[g]lobalization, by reducing any particular culture to a regional custom, engenders a sense of alienation and disorientation and fosters the need of a common identity. Today's states, however, are rarely in a position to provide an answer to this need."[13] Taken together, ongoing state interests in creating, re-creating, or reinforcing nationalist loyalties—even as such becomes more difficult or complicated—suggests that the formation of limited, bound-by-exclusion-and-inclusion identities and allegiances will continue unabated into the future.

11. Kinnvall, "Globalization and Religious Nationalism," 742.

12. Kinnvall, "Globalization and Religious Nationalism," 747.

13. Ferrari, "Nationalism, Patriotism, and Religious Belief in Europe," 626.

Some states and political actors continue to build on cultural, racial, or ethnic understandings of nation in building state power. Others, representing another element of the modernist approach to statecraft and statebuilding, have sought to strengthen states and the claims of political citizenship by suppressing ethnic and other differences in favor of a more abstract notion of allegiance to a political project and sovereignty. One variant of this has been the so-called civic republican tradition, which argues for the superiority of allegiances and loyalties built upon shared commitments to ideas like political participation, representation, civil rights, and the like.

In many respects, the ethnic v. civic divide is a largely arbitrary one. First, the difference between them in practice is often hard to discern: states building on an ethno-nationalist base nowadays appeals as well to civic- and rights-based language, and the rationalism of so-called civic approaches is often suffused with notions of peoplehood that are no less emotional or impassioned than those more explicitly rooted in ethnicity. Secondly, both presume the right to build political community and order by way of violence and exclusion, and both elevate the desired end state—a sovereign state, people, or movement—to the highest claimant on human allegiances, identities, and loyalties. To accomplish the superiority of national identity however constructed, thirdly, Christianity in general and Catholicism in particular must be domesticated, fragmented, subordinated, and rendered incapable of providing an alternative or competing sense of belonging, allegiance, or identity.

While all of this plays out differently in postcolonial contexts as well as former or current imperial centers, some of the problems are the same. States continue to construct, by inducement and violence, populations capable of sustaining and perpetuating the states and their ambitions.

While one could draw upon many examples, Uganda stands, in the words of one scholar, as a fairly typical example of a postcolonial state established on the basis of modernist political philosophy under which ethnic identity is considered, at best, a nuisance to be tolerated, and English, the language of the former oppressor, has become the language of the state. This is so because "fifty ethnes or nations in four major divisions are represented in Uganda. The largest division is the Bantu of the southern half of the country who make up over 60 percent of the population and represent almost half the ethnes in the country."[14] Given this,

14. Hughes, "Following Jesus as His Community," 32.

the postcolonial project in Uganda was one in which modernist ideas of nation and state building were dominant in the postcolonial period (at least at the level of theory—practice remained a very different matter). As Hughes writes:

> The elimination of ethnic diversity was believed to be altruistic. Diversity was believed to be a hindrance to the development of a democratized and industrialized society that would lead to greater prosperity and happiness for a greater proportion of citizens. [Behind the move to eliminate ethnic identity or diversity was] the conviction that people's primary needs are physical and that once people receive the material benefits of uniformity they would be more than happy to jettison their ethnic identity. This modernist political creed in its left and right manifestations confidently predicted the demise of ethnic identity in the wake of material prosperity. This was the political creed on which the post-colonial states of the twentieth century were established and that came to dominate the political philosophy of the nineteenth century postcolonial states as well. So, Uganda's independence was premised on the elimination of ethnic diversity and its failures are often blamed on its ethnocentrism or tribalism.[15]

For many postcolonial states, in other words, ethnocentrism and modernist state-building continue to coexist, despite their purported antagonism. As Hughes notes,

> Ethnocentrism is at the root of the modernist nation-states. That is why even in a country like Uganda the state can function only by retaining English as an official language because it finds the residual ethnocentrism of the colonial oppressor more palatable than the ethnocentrism of any one of the Ugandan ethnes.[16]

For some people, the notion that modern citizenship is a coercive and-at least sometimes-violent phenomenon is difficult to accept. Both the imaginative power of social contract theories and the past tense (or off-stage) nature of much of the explicit violence of political formation and reinforcement makes citizenship (especially in its liberal democratic form) seem pacific rather than martial. Max Weber, among others, argues that the West's elevated notions of citizenship and democracy are rooted firmly in the martial nature of the Greek polis. One commentator summarizes Weber's view as follows:

15. Hughes, "Following Jesus as His Community," 332–33.
16. Hughes, "Following Jesus as His Community," 338.

> Weber locates the impetus toward the development of citizenship in the military dimension of the Greek polis. The city-state is based on the association of those who can afford to purchase their own weapons and military equipment first for the protection of the city and later for conquest and the acquisition of land and booty (a venture Weber terms political or military capitalism). Equal access to arms led to the demand for the granting of effective citizenship rights to the armed plebians . . . The identity of soldier and citizen was firmly established in the polis, and participation in the military became the foundation for ancient freedoms.[17]

Weber himself adds that "[c]hronic war was therefore the normal condition of the Greek full citizen."[18] Closer to our own time, and more directly relevant to the project of political theology, stands the work of Harvard political philosopher, Stephen Macedo. In contrast to those of his liberal democratic allies who defend liberalism as a doctrine without social ends—seeing it instead as something of a path of neutral adjudication among competing visions of the good—Macedo is forthright about the aggressive and forceful nature of sovereignty and citizenship in liberal democracy. He speaks primarily in the context of the United States, but some of his ideas may have wider relevance.

Early in his book, *Diversity and Distrust: Civic Education in a Multicultural Democracy*, Macedo notes that "[t]he original problem of normative diversity is the original problem of modern politics."[19] Like other champions of the modern state, he sees that citizenship requires a certain set of beliefs, loyalties, and priorities—namely, to the liberal project of state and nation formation and maintenance. "The project of creating citizens is one that every liberal democratic state must somehow undertake," says Macedo,[20] adding that "[t]he success of our civic project relies upon a transformative project that includes the remaking of moral and religious communities."[21]

What makes Macedo so helpful as a philosopher is his willingness to be forthright in his objectives. While liberal notions of citizenship often wrap themselves in the gauzy language of freedom and diversity, he is

17. Shafir, "The Evolving Tradition of Citizenship," 5.
18. Weber, "Citizenship in Ancient and Medieval Cities," 48.
19. Macedo, *Diversity and Distrust*, 28.
20. Macedo, *Diversity and Distrust*, ix.
21. Macedo, *Diversity and Distrust*, x.

unapologetic in pointing to the restrictive and authoritarian nature of liberal citizenship.

> Not every form of cultural and religious diversity is to be celebrated, and not all forms of what can be called "marginalization" and "exclusion" are to be regretted or apologized for. Profound forms of sameness and convergence should not only be prayed for but planned for without embarrassment.[22]

Much of this important book is a defense of the forced transformation of Catholicism in the United States, especially but not exclusively through compulsory public schooling and civic indoctrination. Throughout, he explains and defends the extent to which Catholic truth claims and practices were forced to accommodate rival understandings of public and private, reason and revelation, ecclesial v. nationalist identity, and more—all in service to a notion of political citizenship that exercised hegemonic power through state coercion and ideological warfare, public and private. At the end of all this, sealed by a particular reading of the Second Vatican Council, Macedo celebrates the complete and total Americanization of Catholicism in the United States—which means, in a quote by Sanford Levinson that Macedo cites with approval, that Catholics "have effectively been forced to proclaim the practical meaninglessness" of their religious convictions as a condition of participation in American life.[23]

The Church and Nationalist Claims

In a comparative context, nationalism often presents itself as a powerful and sometimes hard-to-cage beast—a lubricant to ordinary state operations, with the potential to wreak havoc in ways seen and unseen. The power of a nation's stories and heroes, memorials and commemorations, martyrs and dreamers—such are potent and powerful, especially in a world of uncertainties, suffering, and oppression.

All of this would be challenging enough for an area of Catholic theology that one could consider to be mature, robust, and creative. Such terms, alas, do not describe much Catholic theological reflection on matters of nation and nationalism, patriotism and peoplehood, and what these mean for the life of Christian discipleship. Instead, according

22. Macedo, *Diversity and Distrust*, 2.

23. Macedo, *Diversity and Distrust*, 136–37.

to the Jesuit Dorian Llewelyn, Catholic teaching on nationality, nation, peoplehood, and the like is a confused, vague, underdeveloped, and oftentimes frustrating pile of often disparate and disconnected notions. I recommend to you Llywelyn's *Toward a Catholic Theology of Nationality* for a balanced exploration of the topic even in those areas where I might differ from him.[24]

Llywelyn notes that little exists by way of Catholic reflection on these topics.[25] What does exist frequently confuses or elides distinctions between key terms like states, countries, and nationalities.[26] Further, he notes that Catholic theology provides no crystalline teaching on nationality, and the faith of the Church requires some considerable mining to find relevant material. Biblical teaching on nationality is fraught with the potential for anachronistic eisegesis that reads modern concepts of the nation back into Israelite and early Christian history. It is also rather sparse.[27]

For their part, papal comments and documents have generally failed to make critical analytical distinctions, including that between nations and states, which to Llywelyn reflects a Eurocentric bias that makes the nation-state a presumed universal norm.[28] Or, as he puts it,

> Catholic social teaching accepts the real existence of nationality, even if it does not provide a stable definition of what constitutes a nation . . . [T]he mono-cultural European nation-state is the implicit norm that underpins papal teaching on the nation.[29]

Finally, he notes that the Catechism of the Catholic Church provides no help either—of its 2,857 paragraphs, only two deal with nationality. The upshot of all of this is as follows:

1. Many variants of political theology are silent or complicit in the violent and coercive nature of nationalism, citizenship, and the supremacy such loyalties demand over all others, especially those of religion in general and Catholicism in particular.

24. Llywelyn, *Toward a Catholic Theology of Nationality.*
25. Llywelyn, *Toward a Catholic Theology of Nationality*, 1–2.
26. Llywelyn, *Toward a Catholic Theology of Nationality*, 7.
27. Llywelyn, *Toward a Catholic Theology of Nationality*, 10.
28. Llywelyn, *Toward a Catholic Theology of Nationality*, 11.
29. Llywelyn, *Toward a Catholic Theology of Nationality*, 12.

2. Catholic theological reflection, in some respects, is underequipped in dealing with these sorts of issues. Given that the challenge of ultimate loyalties is not likely to disappear in the future, Catholic reflection on what "being a Christian" can or should mean in a world of jealous political sovereignties might benefit from new or renewed ideas and perspectives.

Time is short, but let me offer a modest proposal, a notion that I suggest should be incorporated into future Catholic reflection on political allegiances, identities, and loyalties. It is something that, for lack of a better term, I call "ecclesial solidarity." In this, I am drawing from a book I published last year entitled, *The Borders of Baptism*.[30] By "ecclesial solidarity," I mean the conviction that "being a Christian" is one's primary and formative loyalty, the one that contextualizes and defines the legitimacy of other claimants on allegiance and conscience—those of class, nationality, and state, for example.

Ecclesial solidarity means that the welfare of one's brothers and sisters in Christ makes special claims on one's affections, resources, and priorities. It means that the unity of the churches in visible and tangible ways is a key expression of Christian conviction and vocation, even in the face of centrifugal pressures and the demands of lesser, more partial communities and ideologies. It means that processes of Christian discernment and worship cross the divides of patriotism and other types of tribalism. It means that Christians look with skepticism on processes and institutions that aim to make sectarian political and cultural identities and affections more determinative than those drawn from the priorities, practices, and commitments of Jesus. It means that one has special bonds of service, love, and mutual support with other members of the Body of Christ, with whom one is called to provide an imperfect foretaste of the Kingdom of God.

Ecclesial solidarity is not in conflict with the love and service that Christians owe their proximate neighbors, those with whom they live and work and interact on a regular basis. Taking care of one's non-local relatives need not, after all, invariably oppress one's next-door neighbors or work colleagues. It does, however, prohibit Christians from harming their non-local relatives on the assumption that one's neighbors always and inevitably present morally determinative claims on Christian allegiance, priorities, and actions.

30. Budde, *The Borders of Baptism*, 3–11.

When Christians take ecclesial solidarity as their starting point for discernment—political, economic, liturgical, and otherwise—it makes them members of a community broader than the largest nation-state, more pluralistic than any culture in the world, more deeply rooted in the lives of the poor and marginalized than any revolutionary movement, more capable of exemplifying the notion of *E pluribus unum* than any empire past, present, or future. Seeing oneself as a member of the world-wide body of Christ invites communities to join their local stories to other stories of sin and redemption, sacrifice and martyrdom, rebellion and forgiveness, unlike any other on offer via allegiance to one's tribe, gendered movements, or class fragment.

That the idea of ecclesial solidarity strikes contemporary Christians and others as an idea both foreign and disturbing testifies to the effectiveness of the modern project to subordinate and domesticate Christianity. For the past five-hundred years, political and economic leaders have worked to undermine Christian unity and fragment the Church in the interests of nationalism, capitalism, and individualism. At the same time, the now-fragmented parts of Christianity—its ideas and institutions, liturgy and laity—have been enlisted as legitimation and cultural cement in service to the radical political, economic, and cultural transformations of modernity. So effective have these processes been that most Christians are frightened by what should have been part of their ecclesial life all along: those large parts of the Christian story (in Scripture, theology, and church history) in which something like ecclesial solidarity has existed but has been ignored, rewritten, or caricatured.

For example, many Scripture scholars in recent decades have reminded us that, just as Israel was created by Yahweh to be a contrast society set apart to instruct and edify the other nations of the world, so did the followers of Jesus see themselves in relation to the rest of the world. The disciples of Jesus, those called out from the nations, leave their old identities and allegiances behind by being baptized into the Way of Christ. The claims of the biological family are qualified by bonds to one's brothers and sisters in Christ; markers of status and hierarchy are set aside in a community in which "there does not exist among you Jew or Greek, slave or free, male or female. All of you are one in Christ Jesus" (Gal 3:28 NRSV). This new type of human community, made possible by the Spirit, creates "a chosen race, a royal priesthood, a holy nation, God's own people, that you may declare the wondrous deeds of him who called you out of darkness into his marvelous light" (1 Pet 2:9 NRSV).

Over and above the picture of a shared purse described in Acts 2 and 4, the New Testament presumes and recommends a high degree of mutuality, intimacy, and bonding among members of the Church. As one example, Gerhard Lohfink offers a brief sampler, which he describes as "far from exhaustive," on the centrality of the reciprocal pronoun "one another" (*allelon*) as a marker for the quality of real-world love and mutuality demanded of believers (I'll spare you the twenty-three verses from the Epistles in which *allelon* features prominently in describing the mutual care and affection believers owe to one another).[31]

Lohfink adds that the early Church, consistent with Jesus' example in the Gospels, never considered capitulating to naive dreams of "all men becoming brothers" or of "millions being embraced." In a very realistic manner, they sought to achieve fraternal love within their own ranks and constantly made simultaneous efforts to transcend their boundaries. In this fashion, an ever-increasing number of people was drawn into the fraternity of the Church, and new neighborly relations became possible.[32]

The earliest Christians would have found nothing exceptional in the idea of ecclesial solidarity. Early Christians saw themselves, and were seen by others, as more than just a new "religious" group, more than a new idea unleashed in the ancient world, and more than a voluntary club like other social groupings or associations. As noted by Denise Kimber Buell, early Christians were more often seen as part of a new ethnic group, even a new race of people, in the Roman world. The focus of their worship was so distinctive, their way of life and priorities were so particular, that they were more properly seen as a *genos*, "a term widely used for Greeks, Egyptians, Romans, and Jews—groups often interpreted as ethnic groups or their ancient equivalents."[33]

Surveying a number of early Christian texts and narratives, as well as the literature of anti-Christian polemicists, Buell explains why early Christians referred to themselves as a distinct ethnic group or people in the world:

> First, race/ethnicity was often deemed to be produced and indicated by religious practices. Early Christians adopted existing understandings of what ethnicity and race are and how they relate to religiosity by reinterpreting the language of peoplehood

31. Lohfink, *Jesus and Community*, 99–100.

32. Lohfink, *Jesus and Community*, 114–15.

33. Buell, *Why This New Race*, 2.

> readily available to them in the biblical texts they shared with . . . Jews, as well as political and civic language used broadly to speak about citizenship and peoplehood in the Roman Empire.[34]

Second, she notes that, although ethnicity and race were often used to indicate a fixity of identity, early Christians and their contemporaries also saw them as fluid and changeable categories. Further, that the concept of ethnicity/race was both fixed and fluid meant that Christians could make universal claims for themselves. By conceptualizing race as both mutable and "real," early Christians could define Christianness both as a distinct category in contrast to other peoples (including Jews, Greeks, Romans, Egyptians, etc.) and also as inclusive, since it is a category formed out of individuals from a range of different races.[35]

The idea that one could "change" one's race or ethnicity seems impossible in a culture in which these are the quintessential ascriptive identities, largely unchangeable or immutable; for us, on the other hand, "religion" is a voluntary, changeable, and fluid part of identity, since one can "change" religions. But for Christianity in the early centuries, becoming part of the Christian "race" or ethnic community was available to all regardless of their communities or identities of origin—"conversion" was the process of changing races, of joining the peoplehood of Christ. In turn, the radical notion of conversion returns to the fore: it is best seen not as "a private matter of individual conscience resulting in an individual's affiliation with a religious movement, but explicitly as becoming a member of a people, with collective and public consequences."[36] And as she notes, "saying that Christianity was open to all was not mutually exclusive with defining Christians as members of an ethnic or racial group. In many early Christian texts, defining Christians as members of a people reinforces rather than conflicts with assertions of Christian universalism."[37]

Seeing oneself as part of a new race or ethnic group had undeniable political implications in the Roman world. Historian Joyce Salisbury, among others, observes that Roman citizens took notice of the distinctiveness of their Christian neighbors, usually with disapproval:

34. Buell, *Why This New Race*, 2–3.
35. Buell, *Why This New Race*, 3.
36. Buell, *Why This New Race*, 46.
37. Buell, *Why This New Race*, 138.

> Christians were perceived by their pagan neighbors to be antisocial in the deepest meaning of the word. They were creating their own society within the Roman one, and their loyalties were to each other rather than to the family structures that formed the backbone of conservative Roman society. Their faith led them to renounce parents, children, and spouses, and Romans believed this actively undermined the fabric of society. In fact, it did.[38]

While terms like "race" and ethnicity mean very different things today, Buell's research reminds us that for Christians to think of themselves as joined first and fundamentally to one another—and only secondarily or derivatively to other corporate claimants on their affections and allegiances—is not a radical novelty in the Christian experience. Ecclesial solidarity is simply a more contemporary term for the same assumptions and aspirations, highlighting the sense in which God creates a new people from all existing nations and races, and the degree to which the worship of God and the practice of discipleship requires and keeps this people distinct and bonded to one another. Talk of the Church as its own "polis," or as a "community" in its own right, may actually understate the extent to which conversion to Christ made for a new people in a strong sense of the term.

The abandonment of the Church as a distinct race, a people drawn out and set apart by baptism, is a story told with various accents, agents, and agendas. For some, the co-optation of Christianity into the Roman Empire marks a decisive dilution of the Church as a community capable of creating and ordering affections, loyalties, and identities. Others draw attention to the fragmentation of transnational Christianity at the hands of entrepreneurial state-builders in the early modern period and the subsequent subordination of the churches (now plural, now competitive) to nationalism and its regimes. Still others point to the role of Christian leaders and thinkers in facilitating these erosions of ecclesial coherence in the name of divine providence (e.g., Eusebius's *Oration in Commemoration of the Thirtieth Anniversary of Constantine)*, theological and intellectual humility,[39] church reform, and/or the progress and emancipations of the Enlightenment.

However the story is told, in many parts of the modern world, the ending is the same. The bonds of baptism are spiritualized and sidelined in favor of the blood-and-iron ties of patriotism and ethnonational

38. Salisbury, "The Blood of Martyrs," 16.

39. See the argument in Milbank, *Theology and Social Theory*.

solidarity, the dollars-and-cents sinews of capitalism, and the idolatry of the modern and postmodern selves. In such a world, it is unremarkable that Christian Hutus can slaughter Christian Tutsis the week after Easter; that Christian interrogators can torture Christian prisoners with impunity; that a Catholic military chaplain can bless the atomic bomb that destroyed the largest concentration of Catholics in Japan, including seven orders of nuns. My argument is that the revitalization and reform of Christianity now and in the future will be both incomplete and doomed to irrelevance until it reclaims the integrity and distinctiveness of the Church. Unless the borders of baptism become capable of defining a people that "seek[s] first the Kingdom of God," that sees itself as God's imperfect prototype for reconciled human unity in diversity, Christianity will become—where it has not already become so—simple window dressing on the more determinative political and cultural formations of violence, division, and domination.

CHAPTER 11

God Bless America—Or Else

An article published in French as "Dieu, bénis l'Amérique—Ou autrement" in En Question *(December 2010), a themed issue on civil religion.*

HAVING WATCHED A NUMBER of major-league baseball games lately—autumn is the season of the playoffs, culminating in the World Series in November—I've been reminded of an American cultural practice I had otherwise forgotten. In playoff games, during the seventh-inning stretch (something of a brief intermission in a baseball game), spectators are treated to a rousing rendition of "God Bless America," written by Irving Berlin in 1918.

Even more than the national anthem ("The Star-Spangled Banner"), "God Bless America" is intended as a hymn, an act of religious worship that begins with a spoken invocation. The invocation calls upon people to "swear allegiance to a land that's free," and "raise our voices in a solemn prayer." It follows with the song's lyrics and melody, culminating in its now-famous refrain:

God bless America,
Land that I love.
Stand beside her, and guide her
Through the night with a light from above.
From the mountains, to the prairies,
To the oceans, white with foam,
God bless America,
My home sweet home
God bless America,
My home sweet home.

No church sponsors or solicits this act of religious devotion; government does not finance or require it. Rather, it is delivered by Major League Baseball, Inc. (MLB), a for-profit corporate monopoly with a worldwide reputation for commercial savvy and success. MLB does nothing without an eye on the bottom line, on its reputation, and on its brand image. "God Bless America" rings out in every playoff game because it is good business and good public relations.

These are strange times to reflect on civil religion and the notion of "American exceptionalism"—the idea that Americans see themselves as being set apart by God to accomplish special purposes in the world, a new Chosen People among the nations. Its imperial ambitions are frustrated at every turn, symbolized by two wars it cannot win and cannot pay for; the future of the world economy may well depend more on voices other than its own; its self-proclaimed ideals languish in secret prisons and explode with the ordnance delivered by drone aircraft and other lethal means.

In its domestic discourse, "God Bless America" seems to mean different things to different people—as it always has, perhaps, but with the contrasts even more evident than in the past. For some, it has a retrospective quality that evokes gratitude—given the liberty and prosperity it has enjoyed over its history, God surely has blessed America. For others, given so many problems without obvious solutions, there is a plaintive quality to it—God bless America, please. And for still others, among the loudest and most insistent, the phrase takes on the form of a demand shouted up to heaven—God, bless America! Or else.

This latter group—for whom "God bless America" becomes an ultimatum delivered to God—crosses partisan divides. While it seems most at home among the "tea party" ideologues of the political right, it has its own version among the center-left epitomized by the Obama apologists. The latter's stridency was most evident in 2008, when they denounced—with much fury—the suggestion by Obama's former pastor that the crimes of the United States in history might well evoke God damning, not merely blessing, America. God wouldn't dare damn America, they thundered; they implied strongly that God had better not damn America if God knows what's good for Him.

Scholars continue to produce books about religiosity in the United States.[1] These note significant generational changes in religious attitudes and practices as many religious communities falter in matters of religious formation and transmission.[2] One finding by Robert Putnam and David Campbell suggests that young people in the United States are even more alienated from institutional religion than earlier generations because they perceive an unbreakable link between religion and the politics of the so-called "Religious Right" and its upsurge since the early 1980s. Over and above the "typical" youth drift from religion, they suggest, young people are leaving and not returning, because they perceive American religion as deeply politicized and opposed to gay rights, sexual expression, and social tolerance.[3]

Beneath these changes, however, one cannot help but be impressed by the durability of the object of worship in American culture—what Will Herberg identified in 1955 as the "American Way of Life," the true object of religious devotion in the United States. While generational cleavages may be deepening between the present generation and its predecessors, considerable unity across age groups seems to exist in matters attendant to civil religion in its varied expressions.

Following baseball in the American secular liturgical calendar is Veterans Day, the successor to Armistice Day and the ending of World War I on November 11. The pleas and demands that God bless America take special form in this swirl of public and private deluge of soldier worship and veneration. Professional athletes, politicians, entertainers, and countless others record messages thanking military personnel for their selflessness, sacrifice for the nation, and protection of freedom, prosperity, and security. Countless local parades and observances abound, and every town seems to lift up select local military personnel—dead,

1. For a useful overview, see Putnam and Campbell, *American Grace*.

2. Catholics in the United States are the poster children among sociologists for formation done ineffectively. See Smith with Dillon, *Soul Searching*.

3. See, for example, Putnam and Campbell, *Amazing Grace*, 130–31.

wounded, or returned from service—to be praised, venerated, and emulated by schoolchildren and the general public.

Glorification of soldiers has long been a part of national mythologies, at least since citizen armies supplanted mercenary forces in many countries. But in the dominant theological self-story of America, soldier worship has become even more potent and central. Soldiers have become martyrs and saints, missionaries for freedom and deacons of democracy; they become more central and beyond reproach in inverse proportion to the dubious morality of the wars they presently fight.

One would be hard pressed to find a heresy worse in American public life than to be opposed to "supporting the troops." No matter what they do, no matter how immoral their mission or conduct may be, the troops must be supported. Even critics of American wars bow in obeisance to the nobility of those who "serve" their country; especially if one opposes a given war, one must be even more vocal in supporting those who carry out the war.

This aspect of American self-worship has built, and built upon, a mythology of the "despised" soldiers who returned from Vietnam only to meet with scorn and rejection. Never again will the United States scorn its suffering servants, goes the renewed orthodoxy of nation worship; having sinned in this way in the 1960s and 1970s, America must atone by venerating its veterans in ever-ascending ways. That these veterans are drawn disproportionately from the lower economic classes and nonwhite communities provides for a ritualistic sort of reversal: the wealthy and powerful, who would never enlist nor push their children to enlist, can sing the praises of their social inferiors in a way that affirms the system that produces and protects such social stratification.

The demand that God must bless America—or else—meets up with the demand that soldiers be glorified—or else. These confluent streams refresh and nurture the insistence that it is the Nation—not the Church, not any real-life religious community or movement—that God chooses to work through in the world. If churches or other religious communities dare to question the salvific role of America, if they demur from the glorification of warrior culture implicit in "supporting the troops," then God will damn them as assuredly as He blesses America.

The last part of the autumnal triduum in American civil religion is the observance of Thanksgiving on the fourth Thursday in November. Unlike a religious observance that has become secularized and pressed into national service (like Christmas), and unlike a secular holiday that has taken on the trappings of religiosity (Veterans Day), Thanksgiving has long inhabited the estuary of civil religion and lived religious communities. Its observance has been more episodic and affected by political decisions than is usually acknowledged in popular renderings of its history. What is beyond dispute is that it has long served American culture as a confirmation for the special status of the American people and the American state in the outworking of salvation history.

On the fourth Thursday of November, the entire country stops working and expresses gratitude for its many blessings; therefore, the United States is a humble power, not an arrogant one. On this day, millions of households enjoy meals whose abundance and variety gives testimony to the wealth and prosperity of America—the fruits of God's blessings apparent to all, available to (almost) all, and proof that God has provisioned America like no other people in history. And on the following day, the Friday after Thanksgiving, the country explodes in a spasm of retail buying (so-called "Black Friday") that marks the ceremonial beginning of the most important month of the capitalist calendar, the Christmas shopping season. Blessings, blessings, and more blessings—what more proof could one want, says the civil religion of America, that God sheds His grace on America in ways unique in the world?

To those with eyes to see, those who believe in America, this autumnal sequence reaffirms that God blesses America. For those who do not see these blessings and who do not believe in America in this fashion, the American faithful pray that the blind may be saved from the error of their ways. For especially in times of war, denying the tenets of national worship is both a treasonous and damnable offense according to the still-vibrant civil religion of America.

CHAPTER 12

After Twenty Years: John Paul II and the Search for Pan-American Catholicism

A lecture delivered on May 1, 2019, for The Twentieth Anniversary of Ecclesia in America*: A North-South Dialogue on Church Reform, Global Politics, and Local Engagement, a conference sponsored by the Office of Latin American-North American Church Concerns and the Kellogg Institute for International Studies at the University of Notre Dame.*

Introduction

Expressions of Pan-American Catholic sensibility exist in many forms, in the cross-training of seminarians, paired parishes, joint statements by groups of bishops on social and political issues, and—perhaps most visibly—Mass and other liturgical gatherings held on both sides of the border, like the US-Mexican border. In one of these, more than three-hundred people gathered with bishops from both countries, including Cardinal Sean O'Malley of Boston; the liturgy was an act of solidarity in opposition to the person the *Los Angeles Times* called the "deporter in chief"—a term used in immigration circles to refer to Barack Obama.[1]

1. Carcamo, "Catholic Leaders Hold Mass at the Border."

More recently, some Catholic bishops have moved beyond joint statements and have experimented with speaking directly to the faithful in another country. In 2018, for example, the Mexican bishops conference released a statement aimed at the Catholic community in the United States—the "brother country" that receives Mexican migrants—reminding them that migrants are not criminals and the border should not be a war zone.[2]

I approached this assignment prepared to find in *Ecclesia in America* at least some seeds for those expressions of Pan-American or transnational Catholic sensibilities that have emerged over the past twenty years. A look backward, I imagined, would be helpful as we broaden and deepen the sense of being one body of Christ across the political, racial, cultural, and other barriers that demarcate the Americas.

What I have found instead is that whatever degree of Pan-American Catholic consciousness that found expression in the past twenty years has occurred outside of, and in some cases in spite of, the influence of *Ecclesia in America*. Those areas in which the notion of membership in the body of Christ has become deeper, bringing Catholics into a more substantive notion of Church that is not strictly national in scope, can be better explained as the results of trends and initiatives largely independent of the apostolic exhortation that gathers us here today.

When looking ahead, while it is my belief that *Ecclesia in America* provides little help in charting a path forward, it does make a contribution to the extent that it models ways not to take. Its weaknesses, some of which are more apparent after twenty years, provide us with cautions and counsels as the Church moves forward in the American hemisphere.

While we lack the time for a complete review of *Ecclesia in America*, I will take a few minutes to highlight what I see as a few major themes in the document. In what remains of my time, I identify a few aspects of the document likely to impede the goal of greater ecclesial solidarity across borders and cultures in the Americas.

As Pope John Paul II's statement following the synod on evangelization, *Ecclesia in America* proclaims that bringing people into relationship with Christ is a call to "conversion, communion, and solidarity."[3] He aimed to

2. See "For the First Time, the Bishops Address the Citizens of Mexico and United States."

3. John Paul II, *Ecclesia in America*, 3.

> reflect on America as a single entity, by reason of all that is common to the peoples of the continent, including their shared Christian identity and their genuine attempt to strengthen the bonds of solidarity and communion between the different forms of the continent's rich cultural heritage. The decision to speak of "America" in the singular was an attempt to express not only the unity which in some way already exists, but also to point to that closer bond which the peoples of the continent seek and which the Church wishes to foster as part of her own mission, as she works to promote the communion of all in the Lord.[4]

Ecclesia in America is meant as another piece in John Paul's "new evangelization" initiative, arguably the defining concern of his pontificate. By engaging with the Americas as a whole, the Pope intended that

> as sisters and neighbors to each other, the particular Churches of the continent will strengthen the bonds of cooperation and solidarity in order that the saving work of Christ may continue in the history of America with ever greater effect. Open to the unity which comes from true communion with the Risen Lord, the particular Churches, and all who belong to them, will discover through their own spiritual experience that "the encounter with the living Jesus Christ" is "the path to conversion, communion and solidarity." To the extent that these goals are reached, there will emerge an ever-increasing dedication to the new evangelization of America.[5]

Given all of this, the exhortation itself ranges widely across a variety of topics and concerns; the connections among them, and with the task of evangelization in the Americas, are not easily discerned in all cases. We learn that the two most important features shaping the new evangelization of the Americas are secularization (in some places and among some groups) and still-existing popular forms of Christian piety and religiosity (in some places and among some groups).[6] Chapter 2 provides a laundry list of situations and qualities that define the encounter of peoples in the Americas with Jesus Christ—these range from the Christian identity of America, the fruits of past evangelization, popular piety and Christian social initiatives, the rise of human rights and globalization, the problems of corruption and drug trafficking, and more. Chapter 3 describes

4. John Paul II, *Ecclesia in America*, 5.
5. John Paul II, *Ecclesia in America*, 7.
6. John Paul II, *Ecclesia in America*, 6.

the nature of conversion as John Paul understands it, while Chapters 4 and 5 outline paths to communion and solidarity in the Americas. These two chapters focus on the roles of bishops, clergy, and lay people in the new evangelization, and why and how the Church must respond to the problems of the day. The final chapter, the part of the exhortation that actually is an exhortation, calls on Catholics to proclaim the gospel anew in a variety of ways and in the face of a variety of obstacles.

I note but will not explore the degree to which *Ecclesia in America* extends some of the defining aspects of John Paul's ministry—for example, protecting the power of the Petrine office from a robust notion of collegiality, the ontologically defined nature of ordination, and his separation of the "sins of Christians" from the "sins of the Church," the same move he employed to exempt the Church from having a share of responsibility in the Rwandan genocide. Instead, I want to draw your attention to a few places where the exhortation is most deficient—places that, if approached differently in the future, might themselves be opportunities for encouraging the sort of transnational Catholic sensibility that John Paul desired as valuable in making Jesus real to the persons of the Americas.

Wrong Moves and Moving Forward

1. Catholic Social Teaching as Ecclesial Penicillin

As it surveys the American landscape—North, Central, and South—the document continues the unfortunate tradition of offering Catholic social teaching (CST) as the cure for all ills. John Paul writes:

> Faced with the grave social problems which, with different characteristics, are present throughout America, Catholics know that they can find in the Church's social doctrine an answer which serves as a starting point in the search for practical solutions. Spreading this doctrine is an authentic pastoral priority.[7]

On one level, it is probably unrealistic to expect the holder of the papacy to ask hard questions about the coherence and adequacy of CST, given the centrality of the category in recent Catholic history and given that it gives the pope a platform and legitimacy to speak to a worldwide audience. On the other hand, the shortcomings of CST have been noted for decades, with some of the most important work being done by

7. John Paul II, *Ecclesia in America*, 54.

theologians committed to the Church and its work for justice and peace. *Ecclesia in America* proceeds with complete disregard for such cautions and concerns and, instead, proffers social analyses of the Americas that are deficient and inhibit worthwhile ecclesial cooperation and mission.

In illustrating this point, one can look at sections 55–65, which identify the barriers impeding "the path to solidarity" and plaguing the world of the peoples of America. In these sections, one can see echoes of the analytical approach of *Centesimus Annus* (1991), for my money among the worst of the major twentieth-century encyclicals, based on the incoherence of its social analysis. *Ecclesia in America*, like *Centesimus*, offers a laundry list of social problems—the drug trade, public corruption, racial discrimination, destruction of the environment, and more—without any sense that there are structures and processes that hold these together in ways that makes "solving" them an altogether different matter than simply saying "you politicians should stop taking bribes" or "you drug dealers should stop selling drugs." *Centesimus Annus* had no coherent theory of capitalism; in John Paul's hands, social analysis consisted of creating two lists—a list of good things to advance and a list of bad things to avoid. Leaders were to choose the good things and not choose the bad things—with no sense that such may well be impossible given the transnational nature of capital and its disciplining of political and other decision-makers. John Paul reflects a world of unlimited powers of agency in a world in which structures and constraints on agency get a hand wave and not much more. In *Ecclesia in America*, for example, the pope makes mention of something he calls neoliberalism, but he doesn't mention capitalism; following CST means saying no to some parts of "neoliberalism" while leaving capitalism unexplored. It's not clear that one builds Pan-American Catholic solidarity by affirming both the preferential love for the poor[8] and the need to show love and pastoral affection for the elites that run the world.[9] But since individual actors have near-limitless agency in the social and religious spheres, one can comfort the elites (and ask them to evangelize other elites) without compromising the Church's mandate to liberate, assist, and uplift the poor and anyone who has been marginalized.[10]

8. John Paul II, *Ecclesia in America*, 58.

9. John Paul II, *Ecclesia in America*, 67.

10. John Paul II, *Ecclesia in America*, 58.

Similarly, it is odd that, in a document calling for a shared sense of church that joins believers across the Americas, there is virtually no mention of nationalism. None. It is as if nations do not engage in their own formative processes by which people are molded into loyal citizens whose primary allegiance is to one's country or national grouping. The almost willful naivete about the Church's ability to "form Christians" comes through in this gaping omission, even as the document as a whole can be read as a lament regarding the inability of the Church to form people into any sort of discipleship worthy of the name (e.g., problems regarding youth, the bugaboo of "cults and sects," and the cancer of secularization). Both nationalism and capitalism are formative enterprises (shaping the affections, dispositions, desires, and actions of people), and if the Church is going to evangelize or form anybody in the years ahead, it will need to come to terms with the extent to which formation is always a contested process, in which Christian proclamation and nurture walk into the teeth of structures of formation and socialization that are in many ways inimical to the gospel.

2. *"The Greatest Gift Which America Has Received"*

While rereading *Ecclesia in America* in advance of our gathering, I was reminded—brutally, I must confess—by the triumphalism that infuses this document. From the opening section to the end, the evangelization of the Americas is presented in a way that would embarrass anyone not named Steve Bannon.

Section 1 rejoices in the "immense gift" that was the first preaching of the gospel on American soil five-hundred-plus years ago. Section 14 sees the gospel brought by the Europeans as "the greatest gift" ever given to the New World by the Lord; this immense gift has given rise to countless martyrs and witnesses to the faith and saints who "are the true expression and the finest fruits of American Christian identity."[11] It declares that gratitude for this gift should motivate people in the Americas to strive for a deeper personal conversion and fidelity to the gospel (section 26); and in its conclusion, section 75 calls for people in America to renew their thanks for having received the gospel in 1492, "when America welcomed the faith."

11. John Paul II, *Ecclesia in America*, sec. 15.

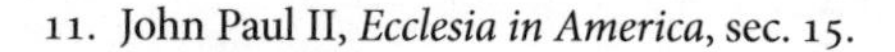

All of this is remarkable inasmuch as John Paul and the rest of the Euro-American Church passed through the intense controversy over the quincentennial "celebration" of Columbus's 1492 arrival in the Americas. Charges of genocide, of ethnic cleansing, of conquest at swords' point, and so much more—all of this filled the air, inspiring protests, counterprogramming, public statements, and more—much of this from Catholics in the Americas, not from enemies of the faith. Yet apart from a throwaway line or two about being respectful of the popular pieties of indigenous peoples and persons of African descent (section 16), and a few short paragraphs opposing discrimination against indigenous and African-descended persons (section 64), the re-evangelization of the continent appears as a process building upon an originating blessing to the Americas rather than a curse brought upon the people already here. The way the gospel was inserted into the New World, and the depth to which it depended on conquest and slavery, puts one into the realm of originating sin rather than foundational blessing.

So, how might this major shortcoming in the document point toward another, potentially more faithful and valuable, path forward for the Church in the Americas? Let me make one suggestion. One path forward in re-presenting the gospel in the Americas, in showing how it can be good news to a world bathed in pain and oppression, is for the Church to lead the region in an intensive—and extensive—exploration of the creation of white supremacy in the settlement of the Americas. There is not a country in the Americas that does not bear the scars of indigenous extermination/expropriation, that does not live with the legacy of racialized African slavery—these are not matters of the past better left to slumber but, in fact, are powerful and ongoing monsters that plague our lands. Some people argue that the deepest commonalities across the Americas is not Christianity but white supremacy—even further, that the commonality of white supremacy has remade Christianity in its image much more than Christianity has purged the continent of racial, economic, and cultural domination.

The academic framework called settler colonialism is not without its problems, but it has emerged in the past thirty years as a way to think systemically about some of the deepest and most intractable problems of modernity. We lack the time to explore it fully here, but a brief description may be useful. According to one overview,

Settler colonialism is a distinct type of colonialism that functions through the replacement of indigenous populations with an invasive settler society that, over time, develops a distinctive identity and sovereignty . . .

Settler colonialism can be distinguished from other forms of colonialism—including classical or metropole colonialism, and neocolonialism—by a number of key features. First, settler colonisers "come to stay": unlike colonial agents such as traders, soldiers, or governors, settler collectives intend to permanently occupy and assert sovereignty over indigenous lands. Second, settler colonial invasion is a structure, not an event: settler colonialism persists in the ongoing elimination of indigenous populations, and the assertion of state sovereignty and juridical control over their lands. Despite notions of postcoloniality, settler colonial societies do not stop being colonial when political allegiance to the founding metropole is severed. Third, settler colonialism seeks its own end: unlike other types of colonialism in which the goal is to maintain colonial structures and imbalances in power between colonizer and colonized, settler colonization trends towards the ending of colonial difference in the form of a supreme and unchallenged settler state and people. However, this is not a drive to decolonize but rather an attempt to eliminate the challenges posed to settler sovereignty by indigenous peoples' claims to land by eliminating indigenous peoples themselves and asserting false narratives and structures of settler belonging . . .

Settler colonial societies around the globe tend to rely on remarkably similar spatial constructs, power structures, and social narratives. Beginning with *terra nullius*—the perception that lands in long-term use by indigenous peoples are empty or unused—settler colonization proceeds to carve up indigenous-held lands into discrete packets of private property. As settler collectives invest their identity and material belonging in these properties, they simultaneously create or empower a state to "defend" these properties from indigenous peoples and nations who are seen as inherently threatening . . . The narrative dehumanization of indigenous peoples supports parallel narratives of peaceful, adventurous, and virtuous settlement and expansion, as "brave pioneers" are held up as paragons of new settler nations carved out of frontier spaces.[12]

12. Barker and Lowman, "Settler Colonialism."

Intrinsic to the creation and maintenance of settler societies in the Americas was the Atlantic slave trade, in which captured Africans were tortured and brutalized to provide the labor necessary to build wealth on the land taken from indigenous groups. Holding it all together—the justification for expropriation, the justification for slavery, the justification for evangelization fastened to civilizing and modernizing projects—was a complex of political economy, anthropology, and philosophical theology that we now call white supremacy.

There is no country in the Americas not affected by racialized hierarchies that shape who rules and who does not, who prospers and who does not, who lives a long life and who dies too soon.[13] The countries of the Americas—North, Central, and South, islands and mainlands—live in a present shaped by immigration policies driven by considerations of race and vulnerability, and with legal and land-tenure systems built upon early modern Catholic edicts deserving of explicit repudiation in the present.

We are also living in an era of worldwide indigenous resurgence and activism—reaching from rural zones targeted by mining and mineral conglomerates through pipeline activism and water protectors in places like Standing Rock and into the halls of the United Nations. I can think of no better way to relaunch a "new" evangelization of the Americas—as a joint venture of Catholics and other Christians across the hemisphere—than to engage in a long-term, multilevel exploration and dialogue on the legacy of the initial evangelization. Pick your issue—the predations of capitalism, state and private violence targeting non-whites, the final exploitation of the ecosystem, the malleability of patriarchy—all of them, and more, have roots in the original sins of the Americas. And for the Americas to have the sort of metanoia that John Paul called for in *Ecclesia in America*—for Christians to embody news that is both good and new in a world grown cynical of the Christian movement—a communal exercise in discernment, confession, and amendment of life would be a religious pilgrimage that could usefully cross borders and barriers en route to becoming a foretaste of the promised Kingdom of God. One could do worse than start with what Pope Francis said to and about indigenous groups in 2015:

13. For an introduction on Latin America as the product of white settler colonialism, see Gott, "Latin America as a White Settler Society," a 2006 keynote lecture to the Society of Latin American Studies.

Here I wish to bring up an important issue. Some may rightly say, "When the pope speaks of colonialism, he overlooks certain actions of the Church." I say this to you with regret: many grave sins were committed against the native peoples of America in the name of God. My predecessors acknowledged this, CELAM, the Council of Latin American Bishops, has said it, and I too wish to say it. Like Saint John Paul II, I ask that the Church—I repeat what he said—"kneel before God and implore forgiveness for the past and present sins of her sons and daughters." I would also say, and here I wish to be quite clear . . . I humbly ask forgiveness, not only for the offenses of the Church herself, but also for crimes committed against the native peoples during the so-called conquest of America.[14]

14. Francis, "Participation at the Second World Meeting of Popular Movements."

Bibliography

Anderson, Benedict. *Imagined Communities: Reflections on the Origin and Spread of Nationalism*. London: Verso, 1998.

Aristotle. *Politics*. Translated by Ernest Barker. Rev. ed. Oxford: Oxford University Press, 2009.

Augustine. *Confessions*. Translated and edited by Carolyn J. B. Hammond. Cambridge: Harvard University Press, 2014.

———. *Contra Faustum Manichaeum*. Translated by Roland Teske. Hyde Park, NY: New City, 2007.

Aquinas, Thomas. *Summa Theologica*. Translated by Fathers of the English Dominican Province. Westminster, MD: Christian Classics, 1981.

Barker, Adam, and Emma Battell Lowman. "Settler Colonialism." *Global Social Theory*. https://globalsocialtheory.org/concepts/settler-colonialism.

Barsamian, David. "Tariq Ali Interview." *The Progressive*, February 1, 2002. https://progressive.org/magazine/tariq-ali-interview-barsamian/.

Benedict XVI. *Africae Munus: In Service to Reconciliation, Justice, and Peace*. Abuja: Catholic Secretariat of Nigeria, 2011.

Berger, Peter. *Pyramids of Sacrifice*. New York: Basic, 1974.

Berrigan, Daniel. *The Nightmare of God*. Portland, OR: Sunburst, 1983.

Biesecker, Barbara A. "Remembering World War II: The Rhetoric and Politics of National Commemoration at the Turn of the Twenty-First Century." *Quarterly Journal of Speech* 88:4 (2002) 393–409.

Biggar, Nigel. *In Defence of War*. Oxford: Oxford University Press, 2013.

Bostdorff, Denise M. "Epideictic Rhetoric in the Service of War: George W. Bush on Iraq and the Sixtieth Anniversary of the Victory over Japan." *Communication Monographs* 78:3 (2011) 296–323.

Boyd, Greg. *Crucifixion of the Warrior God*. 2 vols. Minneapolis: Fortress, 2017.

Brokaw, Tom. *The Greatest Generation*. New York: Random House, 1998.

Budde, Michael L. *The Borders of Baptism: Identities, Allegiances and the Church*. Eugene, OR: Wipf and Stock, 2011.

———. "Collecting Praise: Global Culture Industries." In *The Blackwell Companion to Christian Ethics*, edited by Stanley Hauerwas and Samuel Wells, 123–38. London: Blackwell, 2011.

———. *The (Magic) Kingdom of God: Christianity and Global Culture Industries*. Boulder, CO: Westview, 1997.

———. "Political Theology and the Church." Paper presented at International Theological Conversations Conference, Ateneo de Manila University, Manila, February 24, 2012.

———. "Real Presence and False Gods: The Eucharist as Discernment and Formation." *Modern Theology* 30:2 (2014) 282–99.

———. *The Two Churches: Catholicism and Capitalism in the World System*. Durham, NC: Duke University Press, 1992.

Budde, Michael, and Robert Brimlow. *Christianity Incorporated: How Big Business Is Buying the Church*. Grand Rapids: Brazos, 2002.

Buell, Denise K. *Why This New Race: Ethnic Reasoning in Early Christianity*. New York: Columbia University Press, 2005.

Burns, Jimmy. "Those Who Cannot Learn from History." *Tablet*, March 31, 2012, 10–11.

Büscher, Bram. "From Biopower to Ontopower? Violent Responses to Wildlife Crime and the New Geographies of Conservation." *Conservation and Society* 16:2 (2018) 157–69.

Büscher, Bram, and Maano Ramutsindela. "Green Violence: Rhino Poaching and the War to Save Southern Africa's Peace Parks." *African Affairs* 115:458 (2016) 1–22.

Büscher, Bram, and Robert Fletcher. "Under Pressure: Conceptualising Political Ecologies of Green Wars." *Conservation and Society* 16:2 (2018) 105–13.

Capizzi, Joseph E. "For What Shall We Repent? Reflections on the American Bishops, Their Teaching, and Slavery in the United States, 1839–1861." *Theological Studies* 65:4 (2004) 767–91.

Carcamo, Cindy. "Catholic Leaders Hold Mass at the Border to Urge Immigration Overhaul." *Los Angeles Times*, April 1, 2014. https://www.latimes.com/nation/la-na-bishops-immigration-20140402-story.html.

Carr, E. H. *Michael Bakunin*. New York: Vintage, 1961.

Carter, Stephen. "Laws Come with Deadly Consequences." *Baltimore Sun*, December 6, 2014. https://www.baltimoresun.com/maryland/carroll/opinion/ph-cc-carter-1206-20141206-story.html.

Cavanaugh, William T. *The Myth of Religious Violence: Secular Ideology and the Roots of Modern Conflict*. Oxford: Oxford University Press, 2009.

———. *Torture and Eucharist: Theology, Politics, and the Body of Christ*. Malden, MA: Blackwell, 1998.

Christie, Ryerson. "The Pacification of Soldiering and the Militarization of Development: Contradictions Inherent in Provincial Reconstruction in Afghanistan." *Globalizations* 9:1 (2012) 53–71.

Clough, David. "On the Relevance of Jesus Christ for Christian Judgments about the Legitimacy of Violence: A Modest Proposal." *Studies in Christian Ethics* 22:2 (2009) 196–207.

Cohen, Dara Kay. "The Ties That Bind: How Armed Groups Use Violence to Socialize Fighters." *Journal of Peace Studies* 54:5 (2017) 701–14.

Connelly, John. *From Enemy to Brother: The Revolution in Catholic Teaching on the Jews, 1933–1965*. Cambridge: Harvard University Press, 2012.

Cornwall, Andrea, and Karen Brock, "What Do Buzzwords Do for Development Policy? A Critical Look at 'Participation.'" *Third World Quarterly* 26:7 (2005) 1043–60.

Cutler, Robert. *From Out of the Dustbin: Bakunin's Basic Writings*. Ann Arbor, MI: Ardis, 1985.

Daly, Herman. *Steady State Economics*. San Francisco: Freeman and Company, 1977.

Davies, Nicolas J. S. "Calculating the Millions-High Death Toll of America's Post-9/11 Wars." *MPN News*, April 26, 2018. https://www.mintpressnews.com/how-many-millions-have-been-killed-in-americas-post-9-11-wars/241144/.

Davis, Darren, and Don Pope-Davis. *Perseverance in the Parish? Religious Attitudes from a Black Catholic Perspective*. New York: Cambridge University Press, 2017.

Davis, Mike. *Planet of Slums*. London: Verso, 2006.

Day, Dorothy. "About Cuba." *Catholic Worker,* July/August 1961. https://www.catholicworker.org/dorothyday/articles/246.html.

———. "More about Cuba." *Catholic Worker*, February 1963. https://www.catholicworker.org/dorothyday/articles/800.html.

———. "On Pilgrimage." *Catholic Worker*, April 1948. https://www.catholicworker.org/dorothyday/articles/467.html.

———. "On Pilgrimage in Cuba—Part II." *Catholic Worker*, October 1962. https://www.catholicworker.org/dorothyday/articles/795.html.

———. "On Pilgrimage in Cuba—Part III." *Catholic Worker*, November 1962. https://www.catholicworker.org/dorothyday/articles/796.html.

———. "Peter the Materialist." *Catholic Worker,* September 1945. https://www.catholicworker.org/dorothyday/articles/152.html.

———. "Pilgrimage to Cuba—Part I." *Catholic Worker*, September 1962. https://www.catholicworker.org/dorothyday/articles/793.html.

———. "Reflections on Work." *Catholic Worker*, December 1946. https://www.catholicworker.org/dorothyday/articles/229.html.

———. "We Are Un-American: We Are Catholics." *Catholic Worker*, April 1948. https://www.catholicworker.org/dorothyday/articles/466.html.

———. "We Go on Record: CW Refuses Tax Exemption." *The Catholic Worker*, May 1972. https://www.catholicworker.org/dorothyday/articles/191.html.

Depoortere, Frederiek. "Gianni Vattimo and Rene Girard on the Uniqueness of Christianity." *Heythrop Journal* 50:5 (2009) 877–89.

Dowie, Mark. *Conservation Refugees: The Hundred-Year Conflict between Global Conservation and Native People*. Cambridge: Massachusetts Institute of Technology Press, 2011.

Duffy, Rosaleen, et al. "The Militarization of Anti-Poaching: Undermining Long Term Goals." *Environmental Conservation* 42:4 (2015) 345–48.

Duke, Paul. "The Greatest Generation?" *Virginia Quarterly Review* 96:3 (2002) 19–25.

Dunbar-Ortiz, Roxanne. *Loaded: A Disarming History of the Second Amendment*. San Francisco, CA: City Lights Open Media, 2018.

"Editorial." *Christian Century,* September 21, 1949.

Endō, Shūsaku. *Silence*. New York: Taplinger, 1969.

Estes, Nick. *Our Past Is the Future: Standing Rock Versus the Dakota Access Pipeline, and the Long Tradition of Indigenous Resistance*. New York: Penguin, 2019.

Ferrari, Silvio. "Nationalism, Patriotism, and Religious Belief in Europe." *University of Detroit Mercy Law Review* 83:5 (2006) 625–39.

Field, David N. "The Gospel, the Church, and the Earth: Reflections on an Ecological Ecclesiology." *Journal of Theology for Southern Africa* 22:111 (2001) 67–79.

Finnegan, Ellen. "Was Dorothy Day a Libertarian?" *LewRockwell.com*, January 30, 2009. http://archive.lewrockwell.com/orig9/finnigan3.html.

"For the First Time, the Bishops Address the Citizens of Mexico and United States 'for the Dignity of Migrants.'" *Agenzia Fides*, April 9, 2018. http://www.fides.org/en/news/64004-AMERICA_MEXICO.

"Fortieth Anniversary: Berrigan Debates." *National Catholic Reporter*, October 22, 2004.

Francis. "Address at the Participation at the Second World Meeting of Popular Movements." *Vatican.va*, July 9, 2015. http://www.vatican.va/content/francesco/en/speeches/2015/july/documents/papa-francesco_20150709_bolivia-movimenti-popolari.html.

Frankopan, Peter. *The First Crusades: The Call from the East.* Cambridge: Belknap, 2012.

Frantz, Nadine Pence. "Biblical Interpretation in a 'Non-Sense' World: Text, Revelation, and Interpretive Community." *Brethren Life and Thought* 39:3 (1994).

French, Shannon E., and Anthony I. Jack. "Dehumanizing the Enemy: The Intersection of Neuroethics and Military Ethics." In *Responsibilities to Protect: Perspectives in Theory and Practice,* edited by David Whetham and Bradley Jay Strawser, 169–95. Boston, MA: Brill, 2015.

Friberg-Fernros, Henrik. "Allies in Tension: Identifying and Bridging the Rift between R2P and Just War." *Journal of Military Ethics* 10:3 (2011) 160–73.

Gates, Henry Louis, Jr. *Blacks in Latin America.* New York: New York University Press, 2012.

Georgescu-Roegen, Nicholas. *The Entropy Law and the Economic Process.* Cambridge: Harvard University Press, 1971.

Gibson, David. "St. Dorothy Day? Controversial, Yes, But Bishops Push for Canonization." *National Catholic Reporter,* November 15, 2012. https://www.ncronline.org/news/spirituality/st-dorothy-day-controversial-yes-bishops-push-canonization.

Girard, Rene. *Things Hidden Since the Foundation of the World.* London: Athlone, 1987.

Goode, Richard. "The Calling of Crappy Citizenship: A Plea for Christian Anarchy." *Other Journal* 30 (2018). https://theotherjournal.com/2018/11/01/the-calling-of-crappy-citizenship-a-plea-for-christian-anarchy.

Goodman, Amy. "Counter-Revolution of 1776: Was US Independence War a Conservative Revolt in Favor of Slavery?" *Democracy Now*, June 27, 2017. Video, 58:56. https://www.democracynow.org/2014/6/27/counter_revolution_of_1776_was_us.

Gott, Richard. "Latin America as a White Settler Society." *Bulletin of Latin American Research* 26:2 (2007) 269–89.

"A Greener Bush." *The Economist,* February 13, 2003. https://www.economist.com/leaders/2003/02/13/a-greener-bush.

Greenstein, Fred I., and Nelson W. Polsby, eds. *Macropolitical Theory*. Vol. 3, *Handbook of Political Science.* Reading, MA: Addison-Wesley, 1975.

Grimes, Katie Walker. *Christ Divided: Anti-Blackness as Corporate Vice.* Minneapolis: Fortress, 2017.

Gueilich, Robert A. "Interpreting the Sermon on the Mount." *Interpretation* 41:2 (1987) 117–30.

Guorian, Vigen. "Liturgy and the Lost Eschatological Vision of Christian Ethics." *Annals of the Society of Christian Ethics* 20 (2000) 227–38.

Hall, Gary. "Jeremiah 29: A Theological Foundation for Urban Mission? A Case Study in Old Testament Hermeneutics." *Stone-Campbell Journal* 20:1 (2017) 53–62.

Hauerwas, Stanley. *War and the American Difference: Theological Reflections on Violence and National Identity*. Grand Rapids: Baker Academic, 2011.

Haworth, Alida R., et al. "What Do Americans Really Think about Conflict with Nuclear North Korea? The Answer is Both Reassuring and Disturbing." *Bulletin of the Atomic Scientists* 75:4 (2019) 179–86.

Hedges, Chris. *War Is a Force That Gives Us Meaning*. New York: Anchor, 2003.

Himes, Kenneth. "Just War, Pacifism, and Humanitarian Intervention." *America* 169 (August 14, 1993) 10–15; 28–30.

Hoppe, Thomas. "Just Peace as a Leading Perspective: Towards the Concept and Task Profile of an Ethics of International Politics." *Studies in Christian Ethics* 20:1 (2007) 68–76.

Horne, Gerald. *The Counter-Revolution of 1776: Slave Resistance and the Origins of the United States of America*. New York: New York University Press, 2014.

Hovey, Craig. *Bearing True Witness: Truthfulness in Christian Practice*. Grand Rapids: Eerdmans, 2011.

———. *To Share in the Body: A Theology of Martyrdom for Today's Church*. Grand Rapids: Eerdmans, 2008.

Hughes, Dewi. "Following Jesus as His Community in the Broken World of Ethnic Identity." *Evangelical Review of Theology* 31:4 (2007) 331–41.

Iafrate, Michael. "Destructive Obedience: US Military Training and Culture as a Parody of Christian Discipleship." *Conrad Grebel Review* 29:2 (2011) 4–30.

"Indigenous Peoples Control One Quarter of World's Land Surface, Two-Thirds of that Land is 'Essentially Natural.'" *Mongabay.com,* July 17, 2018. https://news.mongabay.com/2018/07/indigenous-peoples-control-one-quarter-of-worlds-land-surface-two-thirds-of-that-land-is-essentially-natural.

Jegen, Carol Frances. "The Eucharist and Peacemaking: Sign of Contradiction?" *Worship* 59:3 (1985) 202–10.

John Paul II. "Address at Seventeenth World Youth Day, Papal Welcoming Celebration." *Vatican.va*, July 25, 2002. http://www.vatican.va/content/john-paul-ii/en/speeches/2002/july/documents/hf_jp-ii_spe_20020725_wyd-address-youth.html.

———. *Ecclesia in Africa: The Church in Africa*. Washington, DC: US Catholic Conference, 1995. http://www.vatican.va/content/john-paul-ii/en/apost_exhortations/documents/hf_jp-ii_exh_14091995_ecclesia-in-africa.html.

———. *Ecclesia in America: The Way to Conversion, Communion, and Solidarity in America*. Washington, DC: US Catholic Conference, 1999. http://www.vatican.va/content/john-paul-ii/en/apost_exhortations/documents/hf_jp-ii_exh_22011999_ecclesia-in-america.html.

———. *Mane Nobiscum Domine: Stay with Us, Lord*. Vatican City: Libreria Editrice Vaticana, 2004.

———. "Message of His Holiness John Paul II For World Mission Day 1979." *Vatican.va*, June 14, 1979. https://www.vatican.va/content/john-paul-ii/en/messages/missions/documents/hf_jp-ii_mes_14061979_world-day-for-missions-1979.html.

Kauffman, Bill. "Flashback: Saint Dorothy." *American Enterprise* (December 1995).

Kennedy, Paul. *The Rise and Fall of Great Powers: Economic Change and Military Conflict from 1500 to 2000*. New York: Vintage, 1989.

Kilcullen, David. *Out of the Mountains: The Coming Age of the Urban Guerrilla*. London: Oxford University Press, 2013.

Kinnvall, Catarina. "Globalization and Religious Nationalism: Self, Identity, and the Search for Ontological Certainty." *Political Psychology* 25:5 (2004) 741–67.

Kissinger, W. S. *The Sermon on the Mount: A History of Interpretation and Bibliography*. ATLA Bibliography Series. Meteuchen, NJ: Scarecrow, 1975.

Koenigsberg, Richard. *Nations Have the Right to Kill: Hitler, Holocaust, and War*. New York: Library of Social Science, 2009.

Kuokkanen, Rauna. "Indigenous Economies, Theories of Subsistence, and Women: Exploring the Social Economy Model for Indigenous Governance." *American Indian Quarterly* 35:2 (2011) 215–40.

LaSalle, Mick. "Violent Media Poisoning the Nation's Soul." *San Francisco Chronicle*, January 1, 2013.

Lehning, Arthur, ed. *Michael Bakunin: Selected Writings*. London: Jonathan Cape, 1973.

Liberti, Stefano. *Land Grabbing: Journeys in the New Colonialism*. London: Verso, 2013.

Llywelyn, Dorian. *Toward a Catholic Theology of Nationality*. Lanham, MD: Lexington, 2010.

Locke, John, and Thomas P. Peardon, ed. *Second Treatise of Government*. New York: Liberal Arts, 1952.

Lohfink, Gerhard. *Does God Need the Church?* Wilmington, DE: Michael Glazier, 1999.

———. *Jesus and Community*. Philadelphia: Fortress, 1984.

Luther, Martin. *Luther's Works*. Vol. 21. Edited by Jaroslav Pelikan. St. Louis, MO: Concordia, 1956.

Luke, Timothy W. "The National D-Day Memorial: Art, Empire, and Nationalism at an American Military Monument." *New Political Science* 32:4 (2010) 547–59.

Macedo, Stephen. *Diversity and Distrust: Civic Education in a Multicultural Democracy*. Cambridge: Harvard University Press, 2000.

MacPherson, C. B. *The Life and Times of Liberal Democracy*. Oxford: Oxford University Press, 1977.

Manoussakis, John P. "The Anarchic Principle of Christian Eschatology in the Eucharistic Tradition of the Eastern Church." *Harvard Theological Review* 100:1 (2007) 29–46.

Martin, James. "Don't Call Me A Saint?" *America*, November 14, 2012. https://www.americamagazine.org/content/all-things/dont-call-me-saint.

Marx, Anthony. *Faith in Nation: Exclusionary Origins of Nationalism*. Oxford: Oxford University Press, 2003.

———. "The Nation-State and Its Exclusions." *Political Science Quarter* 117:1 (2002) 103–26.

Marvin, Carolyn, and David Ingle. *Blood Sacrifice and the Nation: Totem Rituals and the American Flag*. Cambridge: Cambridge University Press, 1999.

Massa, James. "The Priority of Unity in the Mystery of the Church." *Journal of Ecumenical Studies* 42:2 (2007) 589–607.

McCarthy, Colman. "Cardinal an Unlikely Champion of 'St. Dorothy.'" *National Catholic Reporter*, December 5, 1997.

McLaughlin, Kelly. "One of America's Most Popular Police Trainers is Teaching Officers How to Kill." *Insider*, June 2, 2020. https://www.insider.com/bulletproof-dave-grossman-police-trainer-teaching-officers-how-to-kill-2020-6.

Middleton, J. Richard. *A New Heaven and a New Earth: Reclaiming Biblical Eschatology.* Grand Rapids: Baker Academic, 2014.

Milbank, John. *Theology and Social Theory.* London: Blackwell, 1991.

Moltmann, Jurgen. *The Church in the Power of the Spirit.* London: SCM, 1977.

Moncrief, Stephen. "Military Socialization, Disciplinary Culture, and Sexual Violence in UN Peacekeeping Operations." *Journal of Peace Research* 54:5 (2017) 592–605.

Mostert, Christiaan. "The Kingdom Anticipated: The Church and Eschatology." *International Journal of Systematic Theology* 13:1 (2010) 25–37.

"Mr. Truman's Spiritual Blindness." *Christian Century,* June 28, 1950.

Muller, Jerry Z. "Us and Them: The Enduring Power of Ethnic Nationalism." *Foreign Affairs* 87:2 (March/April 2008) 18–35.

Myers, Ched. "From 'Creation Care' to 'Watershed Discipleship': Re-Placing Ecological Theory and Practice." *Conrad Grebel Review* 32:3 (2014) 250–75.

Nolan, Christopher, dir. *The Dark Knight Rises.* 2012; Burbank, CA: Warner Home Video. DVD.

Nzwili, Fredrick. "Kenya's Catholic Church to fight hunger by farming its vast land reserves." *The Washington Post,* March 10, 2015.

O'Connor, Cardinal John. "Dorothy Day's Sainthood Cause Begins." *Catholic New York,* March 16, 2000. https://www.cny.org/stories/dorothy-days-sainthood-cause-begins,1784.

O'Driscoll, Cian. "The Heart of the Matter? The Callousness of Just War." *Studies in Christian Ethics* 28:3 (2005) 273–80.

Okonkwo, Izunna. "The Sacrament of the Eucharist (as Koinonia) and African Sense of Communalism: Toward a Synthesis." *Journal of Theology for Southern Africa* 137 (2010) 88–103.

O'Leary, Cecelia. *To Die For: The Paradox of American Patriotism.* Princeton: Princeton University Press, 2000.

O'Malley, William. *Converting the Baptized.* Allen, TX: Tabor, 1990.

Oldfield, Adrian. *Citizenship and Community: Civic Republicanism and the Modern World.* London: Routledge, 1990.

Ophuls, William. *Ecology and the Politics of Scarcity.* San Francisco: Freeman, 1977.

Orwell, George, et al. "Pacifism and the War: A Controversy." *Partisan Review* 9:5 (August/September 1942) 414–21.

Palaver, Wolfgang. *Rene Girard's Mimetic Theory.* East Lansing, MI: Michigan State University Press, 2013.

Pandolfi, Mariella. "From Paradox to Paradigm: The Permanent State of Emergency in the Balkans." In *Contemporary States of Emergency: The Politics of Military and Humanitarian Interventions,* edited by Didier Fassin and Mariella Pandolfi, 104–17. Cambridge: Zone, 2010.

Pannenberg, Wolfhart. *Systematic Theology.* Vol. 3. Translated by G. W. Bromiley. Grand Rapids: Eerdmans, 1998.

Paul VI. *Progressio Popolorum: On the Development of Peoples.* Washington, DC: US Catholic Conference, 1967.

Pearce, Fred. *The Land Grabbers: The New Fight over Who Owns the Earth.* Boston: Beacon, 2013.

Perelman, Michael. *The Invention of Capitalism: Classical Political Economy and the Secret History of Primitive Accumulation.* Durham: Duke University Press, 2000.

Pfeil, Margaret. "Whose Justice? Which Relationality?" In *Just Policing, Not War: An Alternative Response to World Violence*, edited by Gerald W. Schlabach. Collegeville, 111–129. MN: Liturgical, 2007.

Plekon, Michael. "The Church, the Eucharist, and the Kingdom: Towards an Assessment of Alexander Schmemann's Theological Legacy." *St. Vladimir's Theological Quarterly* 40:3 (1996) 119–43.

Pontificium Consilium de Iustitia et Pace. *Compendium of the Social Doctrine of the Church*. Vatican City: Libreria Editrice Vaticana, 2004.

"Pope Praises Jews as 'Our Elder Brothers in the Faith.'" *Los Angeles Times,* August 20, 1987. https://www.latimes.com/archives/la-xpm-1987-08-20-mn-3718-story.html.

Prill, Thorsten. "Martin Luther, the Two Kingdoms, and the Church." *Evangel* 23:1 (2005) 17–21.

Putnam, Robert, and David Campbell. *American Grace: How Religion Divides and Unites Us*. New York: Simon and Schuster, 2010.

Riederer, Rachel. "The Other Kind of Climate Denialism." *New Yorker,* March 6, 2019. https://www.newyorker.com/science/elements/the-other-kind-of-climate-denialism.

Roediger, David. *Working Toward Whiteness: How America's Immigrants Became White*. New York: Basic, 2005.

Roosevelt, Theodore. *Roosevelt: His Life, Meaning, and Messages*. Vol. 3. Edited by William Griffith. New York: Current Literature, 1919.

Russell, F. H. "Love and Hate in Medieval Warfare: The Contribution of Saint Augustine." *Nottingham Medieval Studies* 31 (1987) 108–24.

Sachs, Jeffrey. *The Age of Sustainable Development*. New York: Columbia University Press, 2015.

Said, Edward. "Orientalism Once More." Lecture delivered at the 50th Anniversary of the Institute of Social Studies, the Hague, Netherlands, May 21, 2003. https://www.iss.nl/en/media/saidlecture.

Salisbury, Joyce. *The Blood of Martyrs: Unintended Consequences of Ancient Violence*. New York: Routledge, 2004.

Schaab, Gloria L. "'As Christ, So We': Eucharist as Liturgy." *Liturgical Ministry* 18 (2009) 171–81.

Schlabach, Gerald. "Just the Police Function, Then." *Conrad Grebel Review* 26:2 (Spring 2008) 50–60.

———. *Just Policing, Not War: An Alternative Response to World Violence*. Collegeville, MN: Liturgical, 2007.

———. "Just Policing, Responsibility to Protect, and Anabaptist Two-Kingdom Theology." *Conrad Grebel Review* 28:3 (Fall 2010) 73–88.

Schmemann, Alexander. *Church, World, Mission: Reflections on Orthodoxy and the* West. New York: St. Vladimir, 1979.

———. *Liturgy and Tradition*. Crestwood, NY: St. Vladimir, 1990.

Schwarz, Ludwig, and Manfred Scheuer. "Foreword." In *Franz Jägerstätter, Martyr: A Shining Example in Dark Times*, by Erna Putz, 7–8. Grünbach: Franz Steinmassl, 2007.

Scott, Peter Manley. "The Future as God's Amnesty? A Public Theology of Resistance for a Changing Climate." *International Journal of Public Theology* 4:3 (2010) 314–31.

Shafir, Gershon. *The Citizenship Debates*. Minneapolis: University of Minnesota Press, 1998.

Shannon, Noah Gallagher. "Climate Chaos is Coming—and the Pinkertons are Ready." *New York Times,* April 10, 2019. https://www.nytimes.com/interactive/2019/04/10/magazine/climate-change-pinkertons.html.

Shaw, Jonathan. "The Soldier in All of Us." *Tablet,* March 31, 2012.

Shuck, Peter, and Smith, Rogers. *Citizenship without Consent: Illegal Aliens in the American Polity*. New Haven: Yale University Press, 1985.

Sirvent, Robert, and Danny Haiphong. *American Exceptionalism and American Innocence*. New York: Skyhorse, 2019.

Smith, Christian, and Melinda Lindquist Dillon. *Soul Searching: The Spiritual Lives of American Teenagers*. Oxford: Oxford University Press, 2005.

Smith, David. *Less Than Human: Why We Demean, Enslave, and Eliminate Others*. New York: St. Martin's, 2012.

Smith, Rogers. *Stories of Peoplehood: The Politics and Morals of Political Membership*. Cambridge: Cambridge University Press, 2003.

Staples, Brent. "How Italians Became White." *New York Times,* October 12, 2019. https://www.nytimes.com/interactive/2019/10/12/opinion/columbus-day-italian-american-racism.html.

Stassen, Glen H. "Healing the Rift between the Sermon on the Mount and Christian Ethics." *Studies in Christian Ethics* 18:3 (2005) 89–105.

Stinchcombe, Arthur. "Social Structure and Politics." In Vol. 3, *Handbook of Political Science,* edited by Fred I. Greenstein and Nelson W. Polsby, 557–620. Reading, MA: Addison-Wesley, 1975.

Stringfellow, William. *My People Is the Enemy: An Autobiographical Polemic*. Eugene, OR: Wipf and Stock, 2005.

Swift, Louis J. *The Early Fathers on War and Military Service*. Wilmington, DE: Geoffrey Chapman, 1985.

Terkel, Studs. *The Good War: An Oral History of World War II*. New York: New Press, 1984.

Turkson, Cardinal Peter. "Integral Ecology and the Horizon of Hope: Concern for the Poor and for Creation in the Ministry of Pope Francis." Trócaire Lenten Lecture at St. Patrick's Pontifical University, Maynooth, Ireland, March 5, 2015. https://www.icatholic.ie/2015-trocaire-lecture-turkson.

Turse, Nick. *Kill Anything That Moves: The Real American War in Vietnam*. New York: Picador, 2013.

"US Defense Spending Compared to Other Countries." *Peter G. Peterson Foundation,* May 13, 2020. https://www.pgpf.org/chart-archive/0053_defense-comparison.

Waldron, Stephen. "Hans Urs von Balthasar's Theological Critique of Nationalism." *Political Theology* 15:5 (2014) 406–20.

Wallace-Wells, David. *The Uninhabitable Earth: Life after Warming*. New York: Tim Duggan, 2019.

Wallerstein, Immanuel. "The Three Instances of Hegemony in the History of the Capitalist World-Economy." *Social Forces* 64:3 (March 1986) 810–813.

Warmback, Andrew. "'Bread and Butter' Issues: Some Resources from the Work of Steve DeGruchy for the Church's Response to Climate Change." *Journal of Theology for Southern Africa* 142 (March 2012) 21–36.

Watts, Craig. "Just War, Pacifism, and the Ethics of Protection." *Encounter* 71:1 (2010) 35–62.

Weber, Max. "Citizenship in Ancient and Medieval Cities." In *The Citizenship Debates*, edited by Gershon Shafir, 43–52. Minneapolis: University of Minnesota Press, 1998.

Weinandy, Thomas. "Henri de Lubac: The Church as the Body of Christ and the Challenge of Ethnic Nationalism." *Nova et Vetera* 8:1 (2010) 161–83.

Whitehead, Alfred N., and Lucien Price. *Dialogues of Alfred North Whitehead*. Boston: David Godine, 2001.

Winright, Tobias. "Community Policing as a Paradigm for International Order." In *Just Policing, Not War: An Alternative Approach to World Violence*, edited by Gerald Schlabach, 130–52. Collegeville, MN: Michael Glazier, 2007.

———. "Just Policing and the Responsibility to Protect." *Ecumenical Review* 63:1 (2011) 84–95.

Winright, Tobias, and Laurie Johnston. *Can War Be Just in the Twenty-First Century? Ethicists Engage the Tradition*. Maryknoll: Orbis, 2015.

Wolfe, Alan. *America's Impasse: The Rise and Fall of the Politics of Growth*. New York: Pantheon, 1981.

Wood, Elizabeth Jean. *Rape as a Practice of War: Toward a Typology of Political Violence*. New Haven: Yale University Press, 2018.

Young, Matt. "I Hope the Military Doesn't Change My Brother Like It Did Me." *Time*, March 13, 2018. https://time.com/5193840/military-afghanistan-service-marine-corps.

Zahn, Gordon. *In Solitary Witness: The Life and Death of Franz Jägerstätter*. Springfield, IL: Templegate, 1964.

Zizoulas, John. *Lectures in Christian Dogmatics*. New York: T&T Clark, 2009.

Index